INVISIBLE HOUSEMATES

INVISIBLE HOUSEMATES

The secret lives of monkeys, geckos, pigeons and other creatures we live with...

DEEPA PADMANABAN

HARPER

NON-FICTION

An Imprint of HarperCollins Publishers

First published in India by Harper Non-fiction 2025
An imprint of HarperCollins *Publishers*
HarperCollins *Publishers* India, Cyber City,
Building 10-A, Gurugram, Haryana – 122002, India
www.harpercollins.co.in

2 4 6 8 10 9 7 5 3 1

P-ISBN: 978-93-6989-646-2
E-ISBN: 978-93-6989-157-3

Typeset in 11 pt/15.2 Minion Pro
by HarperCollins *Publishers* India Pvt. Ltd

Printed and bound at
Replika Press Pvt. Ltd.

This book is produced from independently certified FSC® paper to ensure responsible
forest management.

HarperCollins *Publishers*, Macken House, 39/40 Mayor Street Upper, Dublin 1,
D01 C9W8, Ireland

*To the extraordinary creatures who share our spaces—
the ones who annoy and intrigue us, and yet are
always intertwined with our lives.*

CONTENTS

CHAPTER 1

THE GECKO

ALL it took was three notes to disturb the silence of the night. The rhythmic 'chuck-chuck-chuck' jolted me from the depths of slumber. As I lay awake, wide-eyed, my mind conjured images of the reptilian intruder, stealthily scaling the ceiling. The very thought of its potential descent onto my bed was enough to keep me awake for hours.

With age, I learnt to ignore the wall-crawling acrobat, acknowledging its role as my unofficial insect-patrol officer. This composure, however, didn't come easy. As a kid, I would freeze in fear at the sight of a lizard and avoid the space at all costs. Once I tried to shoo one that was climbing up the bathroom wall by spraying water on it. Later I was told that this act could turn me into a lizard in my next life. Not wanting to take such chances, I resorted to other means— using a broom or banging on the wall, to coax the creature out. After hundreds of encounters, doing the anxious-avoidance dance, I learnt that these are harmless creatures and pose no real danger.

But for some, the mere sight of these small reptiles can send shivers down the spine. These tiny creatures, with their agile movements and suction-cup feet, have sparked curiosity, fear, and a whole lot of whimsy in the minds of people across the globe. The fear of lizards, or herpetophobia, is a common phobia that many people experience. While house lizards are generally harmless to humans, their appearance and unexpected presence can trigger irrational fears.

The humble house lizard, also known as a gecko, has long been a silent observer of human life, taking up residence in the nooks and crannies of our homes. In its book, the house gecko probably considers himself a mini superhero—guzzling unwanted flies and mosquitoes, providing humankind a service by keeping insect populations in check. These tiny reptiles, often no bigger than your palm, have a knack for blending into their surroundings and creeping up on us unsuspecting humans. They are masters of camouflage and can seemingly materialize out of thin air, reducing even grown adults to fits of screams. Their quick movements, darting between walls and ceilings, add an unexpected element to daily life.

For some reason, house geckos seem to have a deep appreciation for the bathroom. One could mistakenly think that they come as an optional feature in this important real-estate space. You could be reaching for a towel or singing a ballad in the shower, when the sudden appearance of a gecko makes you perform an impromptu dance, which involves a frenetic leap away from the wall followed by a graceful pirouette as you attempt to regain your composure.

Perhaps the gecko sings its own ballad, unknown to us humans. After all, they're the only reptiles known to possess a real voice. Their distinctive shrill sound 'chuck, chuck, chuck', has led to onomatopoeic names in Southeast Asian languages, such as 'toki' and 'chichak'. In Hindi, they go by 'chipkali', 'tiktiki', and 'chikchiki', while their association with leprosy (korha in Punjabi) has given rise to the name 'korkhili'.

They have a penchant for drama, and their performances are nothing short of spectacular. Watch a gecko stalk and capture a wayward fly or playfully chase its own reflection on a glass surface, and you will know what I mean. Their pursuit of small insects, locked in epic battles with mosquitoes, flies, and moths is like watching a David Attenborough documentary, complete with the suspenseful chase scenes and the inevitable 'gotcha!' moment.

If you want to up the ante on drama and entertainment, get a dog and you'll have a ringside seat to a Nat Geo show. My dog thinks that geckos are her best friends. Every time she sees one, she wants to play 'doctor-doctor' with the reptile. She tries to do a physical investigation of its health, first with her paw, and then sniffs it to check its vitals before scooping it up in her mouth to give it a full body scan. Unfortunately, the gecko doesn't quite get the game, and its weak heart traumatized by the ordeal of being in a dog's mouth, goes into cardiac arrest. I have had to discard many unsuspecting geckos that found themselves a drooly grave.

While I believe in sharing space with these creatures, I expect them to respect boundaries and not push my hospitality. One day, I walked into my bedroom to find a baby lizard luxuriously resting on my bed. I froze mid-step, then darted with a newspaper and picked up the opportunistic guest and threw it into the garden. Years of composure was lost and for days, I had nightmares of lizards crawling up my bed and on my hand.

Despite their repulsiveness, lizards have found a special place in the hearts of reptile enthusiasts as pets, particularly in the United States. They are often less demanding and less expensive than traditional pets like dogs or cats, and have become beloved members of many households. Yet, even these low-maintenance companions require a bit of care, from providing food, water, and scheduling regular check-ups to getting the right enclosure with enough room for them to climb and hide and a substrate to maintain humidity. The bearded dragon, a lizard that looks like a miniature dragon, is a popular pet due to its gentle and curious nature. Named for the tiny spines on its chin and neck that look like a beard, this lizard, as long as your forearm, can be easily tamed and loves to be taken for a walk or to play with other animals.

Lizards have also found their way into pop culture. The Star Trek universe features many lizard men, such as Jem'Hadar, Reptilian Xindi, and the Gorn. The Gorn were a high-tech race. Equipped with starships and advanced knowledge, they viewed other species with contempt and aggression. In stark contrast, the Jem'Hadar were mindless and fuelled by drug addiction. Sharing the Gorn's hostile nature, the Reptilian Xindi were territorial predators, driven by instinct and a thirst for domination.

Fans of *Doctor Who* and its eponymous, eccentric but lovable time traveller would be familiar with the Silurians, a subterranean race of lizard men. These prehistoric but scientifically advanced reptile humanoids went into self-induced hibernation to survive a catastrophic Earth event. There is even a Silurian hypothesis written in 2018 by two American scientists suggesting the presence of an ancient species more advanced than humans. Perhaps this hypothesis and *Dr Who*'s Silurian were inspired by the 7,000-year-old figurines with lizard-like faces supposedly worshipped by the Ubaids in Mesopotamia[1].

Then there's Rango, a flamboyant chameleon with delusions of grandeur. Voiced by the inimitable Johnny Depp, Rango is a quintessential anti-hero. Thrown into the dusty, lawless town of Dirt, this accidental sheriff becomes an unlikely saviour. With a flair for the dramatic and a penchant for improvisation, Rango's journey from pampered house pet to fearless lawman is a comical yet captivating ride.

No lizard, real or fictional, has quite managed to eclipse the towering, terrifying shadow of Godzilla. Since his incendiary debut in 1954, this behemoth has reigned supreme as the undisputed king of monsters. Six decades later, Godzilla's roar still echoes through the hearts of fans worldwide, a testament to his enduring power and cultural impact.

All said and done, lizards have long been an intriguing part of human cohabitation. These small creatures are found in many homes around the world, but they are also shrouded in numerous myths. In the world of gecko superstitions, even the minutiae hold significance, and these charming reptiles have carved out a unique place in our collective imagination.

In many parts of Southeast Asia, house geckos are also thought to protect homes from evil spirits and malevolent forces. It is said that they act as sentinels, warding off negative energy and deterring evil entities. Some people even welcome house lizards into their homes, viewing them as benevolent spirits in reptilian form.

As Chithra Madhavan noted in a *New Indian Express* article on 26 June 2023, Shiva is supposed to have appeared as a monitor lizard in Magaral, Tamil Nadu. The temple has a sculpture of the monitor lizard on the gopuram, the conical roof, and the deity is referred to as Udumbeshwarar (after the Tamil word 'udumbu' for monitor lizard).

In the Varadharaja Perumal temple at Kanchipuram in Tamil Nadu, silver and gold lizards are embedded on the ceiling of a small chamber in this temple. Thousands of devotees flock to touch these metallic lizards as it is believed that doing so will remove all sins and cure illnesses. While it's one thing to touch metallic lizards and wipe your life slate clean, it's completely different if a lizard touches you, or heavens forbid, one falls on you. Some Hindus believe that if a gecko falls on a person, illness is sure to follow unless they cleanse themselves in the sacred waters of the Ganges. In Uttar Pradesh, the omen can mean good or bad depending on which shoulder the gecko lands.

In a journal article, 'The Folklore of Geckos: Ethnographic Data from South and West Asia', the author Jurgen W. Frembgen documents several tales intertwined with these creatures. In Uttar

Pradesh, there is a saying, 'he can keep secrets like a gecko' (*chipkali ki tarah muh band rakta hai*). On the other hand, Bengalis believe that when a gecko calls while someone is speaking, their words are true, or the events described are bound to happen. In parts of north India, the sound of a gecko's call can herald evil unless it's mimicked. In the region between north India and Afghanistan, contact with a gecko or its excreta is thought to cause the skin disease, leukoderma. Hindu mythology even weaves a tale where Lord Shiva prepared a unique poison for the gecko, as the gecko was the last to arrive and he ran out of poison while dispensing it to all living creatures[2]. Of course, house geckos have been proven to be non-poisonous and harmless to humans. That said, they carry various types of pathogens in their bodies, which can cause food poisoning if one consumes food contaminated with a gecko or its excreta.

Despite these tales and superstitions, the belief that geckos should not be killed is widespread. In north India, it is said that a housewife's meal might lose its taste if she kills one. In Punjab, geckos should not be killed, but taken out of the house with a stick tied with a cloth, to prevent the house from being cursed. In UP, a house with many geckos is seen as prosperous, and harming a gecko may hinder fertility for the women in the house. In fact, across cultures, geckos symbolize fertility[2]. This makes one wonder if there's a story somewhere which foretells that if a baby lizard falls on someone, a baby will be born in that house in the next nine months!

The Tamil Panchangam (traditional calendars with Hindu festival days) has even got a page devoted to lizard predictions, divided into two parts. The first part predicts events based on the number of calls, and the direction from which the lizard calls. The second part of the Tamil Panchangam portends good or evil based on which part of the body the lizard falls. If it falls on one's head it portends sorrow or loss. If it falls on the forehead or the right arm, it means wealth[2]. All this calling and falling though brings to mind a Bollywood film hero who, after falling for a girl, has a calling to break into song and dance.

We Indians are not the only ones to have omens and folklore about geckos. For Native American tribes, lizards are said to symbolize survival and healing. In some tribes, children are given amulets (good luck charms) in the shape of lizards for protection and strength. As for Arab countries, their beliefs take an even more unexpected turn, with gecko parts being used for unconventional purposes. Gecko blood and urine are believed to be effective when applied for certain medical conditions[2].

In Christianity, lizards are generally looked upon as evil due to the story of Adam and Eve, where a snake (related to lizards) convinced Eve to eat the forbidden fruit. However, lizards are mentioned in the Bible as one of four things that are wise despite their small size. The passage states that lizards are wise because they can get into the king's palace undetected [2]. So the next time you are overcome with a feeling to shoo away these humble creatures, remember that they have the blessings of the Lord himself and perhaps would be the first to be welcomed on the next Noah's ark, whenever that may be. The same cannot be said of us humans.

Abhijeet Christopher Loreng writes in a *Times Now* article on 25 April 2023, that in Celtic culture, there's a story of a night goddess called Evaki who stole sleep from the lizard's eyes and gifted this sleep to all other creatures in the land. Therefore, the lizard is thought of as a creature that symbolizes restlessness. On the other hand, newly married Celts listen for a gecko's call on their wedding night to solidify their new relationship and to bring them luck.

Whether they are heralded as protectors of the home, or feared as omens of bad luck, or even mystical beings, house lizards have woven their way into the cultural fabric of many societies. They are creatures that embody the complex interplay between culture, mythology, and the natural world, revealing the intricate web of human-animal relationships. In fact, lizards have fascinated humans to the extent that they have spurred world-wide quests to reveal their secrets. Many scientists have taken up the study of lizards, called saurology, from the Greek word, 'sauros' meaning lizards.

Dr Aaron Bauer, an American scientist, has made the study of lizards both his passion and profession. He has trekked across continents in search of lizards and has identified more than 230 reptile species, the most any living scientist has discovered. Among his many discoveries is a new and extinct species of lizard, trapped in amber 110 million years ago[3]. Conferred with the moniker, 'lizard king', he even has a lizard species named after him, the Gekko aaronbaueri[4].

James Stroud at the Georgia Institute of Technology, conducted a fascinating long-term study of lizards to examine how evolution unfolds in a community. His research was so elegantly simple, even a curious school kid could replicate it in their backyard. He collected four different species of Anolis lizards (anoles) on a small island in Florida, measured each lizard's head, legs, feet, weight, and even the stickiness of their toes. Each one was tagged and released in the same area. He collected groups of lizards over ten years, with each group spanning two-and-a-half years, representing approximately two to three generations. Every six months, he caught the same lizards and measured them again. Some years, lizards with longer legs would survive better, and other years, lizards with shorter legs fared better. Other times, there was no clear pattern at all. His research showed that contrary to conventional knowledge of constant change, species can appear static while still undergoing intricate evolutionary adjustments beneath the surface[5].

Maria Thaker, a scientist at the Indian Institute of Science, Bengaluru, studies how lizards communicate with each other, and learn to adapt to fast-changing urban environments. Her lizard of interest is the Indian rock agama, a lizard commonly found basking on rocky hills in south India, and on stony compound walls of yesteryear Bengaluru homes. Maria's research found that the males are a living canvas, changing hues across their bodies in the blink of an eye, differently during courtship and during aggressive interactions. Most lizards get their grey or brown colours soon after they hatch. However, the vibrant yellow and red of rock agamas develop as they grow, extracting the colours from their diet of caterpillars, wasps and bees. Like most males of the animal kingdom, only the adult male rock agamas are flamboyant. The reason: to attract a mate. When courting a female, the male's dorsal stripe shifts from sunny yellow to fiery orange or red, but turns an even brighter yellow when confronted by a rival male. Meanwhile, their lateral stripes dramatically darken to black for potential mates, a colour that is particularly attractive to females. On encountering a rival male, the black changes to yellow or red—a warning sign. The colour change is more intense and rapid in male-male encounters[6]. Sadly, with Bengaluru's changing landscape as individual houses gave way to high-rise buildings, these lizards have all but vanished from the city.

Other scientists like Neil Losin and Nate Dappen believe that lizards, with their versatility and ability to occupy every possible habitat, are the key to understanding the past, present and future of life on Earth. In their 2017 documentary, *Laws of Lizards*, the two scientists embark on a year-long journey chasing lizards to understand their history and that of life itself.

The history of lizards, in fact, starts from the time dinosaurs walked the earth. The very name 'Dinosauria' means 'terrible lizards'. But as we dig deeper into the evolutionary archives, a fascinating truth begins to emerge. While lizards and dinosaurs share an ancestry that stretches back millions of years, and have common genetic traits, they are only distantly related[7].

Dinosaurs, the colossal creatures, once roamed the Earth between 250 to sixty-five million years ago during the Mesozoic era, aptly known as the age of reptiles. At the end of the Mesozoic era, all of the dinosaurs went extinct. Other reptiles survived, however, and they eventually gave rise to modern reptiles. The saga of reptilian evolution has many chapters. Long before lizards scampered into existence, the stage was set by their predecessors. The first modern reptiles to chart their own course in the evolutionary journey were Lepidosauria, the forerunners of lizards and snakes (belonging to the order Squamata) and tuatara, the only surviving member of the order Rhynchocephalia[8].

Squamata came into existence approximately 250 million years ago[9]. Within the Squamata order, an astounding diversity of life has flourished. According to the reptile-database.org website, as of September 2024, there are around 4,000 species of snakes and 7,000 species of lizards, with more species being discovered every year. The lizard species commonly known include geckos, iguanas, worm lizards, monitor lizards, skinks and Komodo dragons.

Most lizards are small creatures, measuring a few inches in length, except for the Komodo dragon, that stands the largest with a length of three meters. Two lizard species, *Sphaerodactylus ariasae*, discovered in Beata in the West Indies, and *Sphaerodactylus parthenopion*, found in the British Virgin Islands, hold the record for being the smallest of all known species of reptiles, birds and mammals. With a mere length of 1.6 centimetres, they are smaller than a cockroach[10].

Apart from geckos, India is home to a fascinating array of lizard species, each with unique adaptations and behaviours. India is home to four monitor lizards: the Bengal monitor, the Asian water monitor, the yellow monitor, and the desert monitor[11]. These solitary lizards, that look like miniature dragons, are unfortunately hunted and trafficked for their meat and body parts, including their genitals, which are sold as the Hatha Jodi plant, which is falsely believed to bring good luck.

The Indian spiny-tailed lizard is India's only herbivorous lizard found in the arid and semi-arid regions of western India. This solitary lizard burrows underground, coming out only to forage for food or occasionally to sun-bask. Locally known as sanda, the fat in their broad tails is believed to be a cure for male impotence and hence they are frequently hunted. The extracted sanda oil is sold not only in India but also exported to countries in the Middle East. As a result, their populations have dwindled drastically, and these reptiles are now listed as 'vulnerable' on the International Union for Conservation of Nature (IUCN) red list[17].

Flying lizards, found mainly in the hilly forests of India, are nature's gliders, using flaps of skin to glide between trees. Fan-throated lizards are known for their vibrant throat fans, which they use to attract females during mating season. There are fifteen species found primarily in dry shrublands and coastal areas. Chameleons are renowned for their colour-changing abilities and lightning-fast tongues, which can shoot out to capture prey in the blink of an eye. Garden lizards, or calotes, are adept at blending into their surroundings. Males, in particular, sport a striking red head and crest during mating season. Rock agamas are well-adapted to life in rocky habitats, where they blend seamlessly with their surroundings. Skinks, with their sleek, shiny scales, are commonly found in gardens and open fields.

Lizards boast of a unique chemosensory system that lets them smell by tasting the air around them. The chemosensory organ, called Jacobson's organ, which normally resides in the nose in most other reptiles and mammals, including us humans, is nestled within the mouths of lizards and snakes. Smells and chemicals picked up by the tongue are transferred into the Jacobson's organ in the roof of the mouth, where the signal is processed[13]. This evolutionary adaptation has enabled them to detect and discriminate prey chemically, giving them an uncanny advantage. But that's not all—lizards, in their quest for survival, have perfected the art of self-renewal. Every year, without fail, they shed their skins. This process, a kind of natural rebirth, ensures their vitality in a world filled with ever-changing challenges.

Just like humans, most lizards possess eyelids to keep their eyes clean and safe. But some, such as geckos, are unique. They can't blink, relying instead on a transparent membrane to protect their eyes from dust and intense sunlight. To maintain their vision, geckos employ their tongues to gently wipe away any debris. Many lizards, like iguanas, are blessed with colour vision. Their colourful bodies serve as a visual language, allowing them to communicate with one another and distinguish between males and females.

The common house gecko (*Hemidactylus frenatus*) belongs to the lizard family Gekkonidae, which has around 2,000 species[14]. The house gecko was originally a tree-dweller and has now successfully adapted to buildings and urban environments. These little reptiles boast a colour palette that spans from beige and grey to light brown and even iridescent greenish hues. Measuring in at around 11 to 15 centimetres in length, these geckos are covered in protective scales. Males often outweigh their female counterparts, flaunting wider jaws.

The house gecko's love story knows no bounds. They reproduce sexually, with breeding occurring year-round in tropical climates and seasonally in cooler regions. A unique ability of the female gecko is to store sperm for up to a year post-mating. This helps increase their reproductive success, especially when it comes to embarking on journeys to new habitats or when suitable males are scarce[15].

Their mating season typically occurs between March and July, and the female lays a clutch of two eggs between April and August.

The female's translucent belly unveils the magic happening inside. The eggs are hard-shelled, unlike those of other reptiles which are soft and can dehydrate under dry conditions. The house gecko lays its eggs in crevices or other hard-to-reach places to protect against predators. As these eggs incubate over a period of forty-five days to two months, the female's body heat serves as a nurturing cradle[15].

And let's not forget their young, for they are as self-reliant as their parents. With caruncle-shaped teeth, they skilfully crack their way out of the egg and into the world. After a brief period of absorbing the yolk's goodness, the hatchlings, not much bigger than a fingertip, attain maturity within a short period of six months, and are ready to embark on their own journeys.

The house gecko is ectothermic, which means that they can regulate their body temperature based on the environment. They seek out warm places when it's cold and hide in crevices when it's warm. They regulate their body temperature during the day and forage for food at night. The gecko will eat any insect they can catch and swallow with their prehensile tongue. They are most active around midnight, so if you are heading to the kitchen for a midnight snack, make sure you don't intrude upon the gecko savouring their meal.

House geckos are native to Asia and Southeast Asia, and ideally prefer tropical and sub-tropical environments. But they can endure any environment, even harsh climates and deep waters. They also have a high tolerance to light. House geckos are quite territorial. When confronting other members of the same species, they can become violent and are known to be more aggressive than other gecko species. Their aggressive nature and ability to adapt has led to their widespread distribution across the globe and caused the decline of native species of geckos in America and the Pacific[15].

But what truly sets geckos apart is their remarkable resilience in the face of adversity. Most possess fracture planes in the bones of their tail, enabling them to shed their tails when cornered by predators. Some can even cast off their tails voluntarily, demonstrating the incredible ways nature has equipped them to escape danger. This ability of the lizard to shed its tail in danger has inspired scientists to design a building resistant to collapse. With extreme weather events such as floods, landslides, earthquakes, or even design errors, buildings can collapse causing loss of property and lives. The new design arrests the collapse from spreading and prevents the building from collapsing[16].

After the lizard loses its tail, it can regenerate another one rapidly, although the regrown tail does not have the usual bony vertebrae but rather a cartilaginous rod. Scientists at the University of Southern California are studying the science behind this process where lizards regenerate cartilage as a possible therapeutic treatment for millions of people suffering from osteoarthritis[17].

Lizards also use their tails to control the orientation of their bodies when leaping through the air. By deftly adjusting their tail's angle mid-leap, these agile reptiles can effortlessly correct their body orientation and land gracefully on their feet. Inspired by this natural marvel, scientists have engineered Tailbot, a tiny robotic marvel equipped with a motorized tail and advanced sensors. By mimicking the lizard's tail movements, Tailbot achieves astonishingly precise landings, transforming a simple leap into a feat of robotic engineering[18].

Despite their adaptations and resilience, a house gecko's lifespan is generally no longer than three to five years. But they can live anywhere up to twenty years in captivity or while being kept as pets. Climate change and global warming is expected to hit these reptiles pretty hard as they are not equipped to regulate their body temperatures to high heat. It is estimated that one-fifth of lizard species globally will go extinct by 2080 due to global warming. Lizards are also impacted by the illegal wildlife trade. The flying gecko, Gekko kuhli, is targeted both for the illegal pet trade and consumption. The monitor lizard, Indian spiny-tailed lizard and many other species are illegally traded for traditional medicinal purposes. Tokay geckos, one of the largest living gecko species, are in demand for consumption in wine or whisky to increase strength and vigour[19].

The gecko's tale is one of survival and adaptability. They remind us that even in the face of immense change, life finds a way to endure and thrive. No wonder Dominique Lapierre in his book on Calcutta, *City of Joy*, wrote that the cry of a gecko is regarded an omen for long life. These creatures are living relics, survivors of a bygone era, and their ongoing journey through time is a testament to the wonders of evolution. They keep us on our toes, reminding us that, in the grand scheme of things, we're just guests in their world.

CHAPTER 2

THE PIGEON

THE magnificent banyan tree outside my Mumbai apartment was a haven for birds for years. Crows, mynas, pigeons and sparrows nested and crooned as they sat on its motherly branches. Imagine my surprise when, one morning I discovered two delicate beige eggs nestled in a pot of our cramped Mumbai balcony. Like a curious kid, I was instantly hooked. Who could have chosen my humble home instead of the magnanimous tree to lay these tiny treasures? My heart skipped a beat when a graceful pigeon claimed her spot as the proud parent.

For the next few weeks, I turned into a balcony-bound birdwatcher, peeking through the mesh door, careful not to disturb the mother proudly protecting her eggs. Then came the day when two fluffy, pink bundles of joy hatched—two tiny squabs, blinking at the world. It was like witnessing a miracle unfold. Like a proud parent, I watched them grow, their little bodies getting plumper and their feathers filling out, as they fed on 'crop milk', a special milk packed with nutrition produced by the pigeon parents in their intestines.

But just as quickly as the little ones arrived, they were gone, spreading their wings to explore the big city. A pang of sadness hit me, mixed with an overwhelming sense of pride. I had witnessed the circle of life, right there on my tiny city balcony. Today, about thirty years later, a pigeon sits on the ledge of my house every day, regaling and sometimes annoying us with its throaty cooing.

The common pigeon (*Columba livia*), an unassuming urban companion, has woven itself into the tapestry of our lives. Everyone, it seems, has a pigeon tale. One of over 350 species of pigeons belonging to the family Columbidae[1], these feathered creatures have a knack for making themselves at home, from bustling metropolises to quaint villages. This unassuming bird has captured the human imagination in ways that belie its ordinary appearance. From being revered as symbols of peace and love to being reviled as pests, pigeons have occupied a complex and contradictory place in human culture. Who can forget the iconic scene in the film *Dilwale Dulhaniya Le Jayenge*? Shah Rukh Khan, the quintessential Bollywood lover, transformed into a charming dhoti-wearing pigeon-feeder in a desperate attempt to win over his sweetheart's father, Amrish Puri. Or the ethereal beauty of Bhagyashree in the 1989 Bollywood film, *Maine Pyaar Kiya*, as she sang her heart out with a pigeon in her arms, '*Kabootar Ja Ja Ja*' to send a message to her beloved. Shakespeare's Hamlet famously lamented his cowardice, describing himself as 'pigeon-livered'. This gentle bird has since left its mark on the English language, with terms like 'pigeon-toed' and 'pigeonholed' becoming commonplace.

Pigeons come in an astounding variety of colour palettes, from classic neutrals like grey, white and black to vibrant hues of blue, green and brown. Some fancy pigeons bred for certain traits are extraordinarily beautiful with unusual forms and colours. Jonas Grinevičius and Beverly Noronha in an article on *Bored Panda* on 21 October 2023 describe these fancy pigeons. The Victoria crowned pigeon has stunning blue plumage and an elegant crest, and the Jacobin pigeon has a tuft of feathers around its head resembling a fur coat with a high collar, and can give any fashion model a run for their money. The Victoria crowned pigeon, a New Guinea native, is also the world's largest pigeon, weighing over two-and-a-half kilograms. The Maltese pigeon captivates with its upright stance and long slender form, a prized attribute in pigeon shows, and is considered the sexiest of all pigeons. Roller pigeons are another standout breed, meticulously bred to perform breathtaking aerial acrobatics.

These elegant birds can offer you dating tips and set relationship goals. When a pigeon reaches sexual maturity around six months, to win his mate's heart, a male pigeon engages in an elaborate courtship display. He bows deeply, coos softly, puffs out his chest, and circles the female gracefully. As their bond deepens, they may lovingly preen each other, and he might offer her regurgitated food as a tender gesture. He also helps build a nest one twig at a time. When the nest is ready, female pigeons typically lay two eggs per clutch. After an incubation period of approximately seventeen days, the hatchlings fledge a few weeks later. Renowned for their fidelity, pigeons often form lifelong monogamous bonds, and both parents equally care for the young, feeding them with crop milk[2].

Like us humans, pigeons are inherently social creatures. They gather in various formations— flocks, colonies, and aggregations— for a variety of reasons. Flocks, for example, often form for communal feeding or enhanced protection against predators. Intriguingly, these groups can display complex social structures, with certain individuals, like the kingpins of an organization, consistently claiming prime positions within the feeding hierarchy. By flocking together, they create a living shield against predators. When danger looms, they can execute intricate aerial manoeuvres to evade attack. Hawks, falcons, eagles and owls are relentless hunters, always on the lookout for a vulnerable target. To survive, these birds must be lightning-fast, ready to soar to safety at the first sign of danger[3].

Whoever came up with the term 'birdbrain' probably had not met a pigeon. These intelligent birds can recognize themselves in mirrors, learn complex tasks, and remember long-range routes. Recent experiments with the pigeon in Ohio State University showed that pigeons can be trained to categorize tasks, like AI machines. They were showed a series of geometric figures such as lines and concentric rings, and over a period of time learnt to categorize them correctly, with accuracy levels going up from 55 per cent to 95 per cent for simple tasks[4].

Before the advent of telegrams and mail, they were the original, feathered couriers, carrying important messages across vast distances. These avian messengers of the eighteenth and nineteenth centuries, are descendants of wild rock doves, rugged residents of coastal cliffs, today only found on the coasts of Scotland and Northern Ireland[5]. Wild rock doves were first domesticated for their meat and later bred as homing pigeons, which transformed into the feral birds we know today.

Homing pigeons, also called carrier pigeons, born with an innate ability to find their way home from any direction or distance, were carefully bred over centuries to hone their incredible homing instincts. Some scientists believe that homing pigeons use the position of the sun, and visual landmarks, while others believe they use magnetoreception, the ability to detect and use the Earth's magnetic field to orient themselves and locate their homes[6].

One of the earliest tales of using pigeons to carry messages comes from the Bible. Genesis 8:6-12 says that Noah sent a pigeon from the ark as a messenger to see if the deluge was over. It came back with a branch of an olive tree in its beak, which proved to Noah that the waters had begun to subside. Dr Elizabeth Bruton, in an article published on 21 February 2020 for the *Science Museum* blog, UK, writes that in documented history, homing pigeons were used over 3,000 years ago, dating back to 1150 BCE in Baghdad. The Sultan of Baghdad tied tiny containers carrying papyrus sheets to the legs of pigeons and used them as messengers. This system lasted until 1258, when the Mongols conquered Baghdad and destroyed the system.

Anthropologists believe that pigeons were probably the first animals to be domesticated. The earliest record of pigeons being kept under domestication occurs in the fifth Egyptian dynasty. An Egyptian bas-relief from around 1350 BCE depicts a flock of pigeons being released from their cages to fly and then return. In the Negev desert during the Byzantine period (fourth to seventh centuries CE) pigeon poop was used extensively as fertilizer[7].

Dovecotes—earthen towers built to house domestic pigeons—were used to breed them, particularly in Egypt and Israel, beginning around 2,000 years ago, writes Shoshi Parks in an Atlas Obscura article published on 25 January 2023. As the demand for pigeons grew, they were bred in structures called columbarium, large circular towers capped with conical roofs. Inside, nests were arranged in rows, opening to the outside. Just beneath the roof, branches were strategically placed to allow the pigeons to perch before entering the nests.

Ancient columbaria have been found in Israel, England, Scotland, Wales, France, Central Europe and Italy. The breeding and trade of pigeons once constituted a lucrative enterprise, a fact underscored by the prevalence of dovecotes on medieval castles. These structures were often a symbol of nobility, reflecting the high esteem in which pigeons were held. Homing pigeons also had the honour of participating in the first Olympic Games held in 776 BCE in the city of Olympia in Greece. Many people believed that Nathan Rothschild, who helped finance Britain's war efforts against Napoleon, received news of Napoleon's defeat at Waterloo via a carrier pigeon, a full three days before the official word reached London through a human messenger[8].

The pigeon's homing instincts have been cultivated since at least the twelfth century. However, training them was not easy. Initially, pigeons were capable of carrying messages only one way, towards their home. This meant they required physical transport for each new message. Through clever training techniques, they were transformed into reliable two-way carriers. By strategically placing food and shelter, pigeons were conditioned to fly between two locations up to twice daily, covering distances of up to 160 kilometres.

Recent research on pigeons' navigation abilities show that they can refine and improve their skills through a process known as Cumulative Cultural Evolution. This is the accumulation of knowledge and skills learnt through collaboration with others, and passed down generations. In an experiment by Oxford scientists, when a solo homing pigeon was released, it found its way back home through a roundabout path. But when teamed up with a more experienced bird, the pair developed slightly more efficient flight paths. To study this further, scientists continually introduced new, untrained birds to replace the most experienced member of each pair. The efficiency of pairs continued to improve over generations. At the end of the fifth generation, they were using routes 1.2 kilometres shorter than those of the first generation[9].

Their unparalleled navigational abilities and extraordinary resilience made them invaluable assets for military purposes. These silent, swift flyers could traverse long distances, unaffected by the horrors of warfare, outpacing the fastest human runner or horse rider. As a result, they were employed as both spies and soldiers.

Pigeons played an important role in World War I in August 1914, carrying messages. One of the most decorated and heroic pigeons, Cher Ami, ('dear friend' in French), was one of 600 Army Signal Corps pigeons who undertook a dangerous mission in 1918. Cher Ami was part of an American troop, the 77th Division stationed in the Argonne Forest in NE France. The battalion was trapped behind German lines and could not make their position known to their American counterparts, from whom they were cut off. To make matters worse, the American army started bombing them. They tried to use homing pigeons to communicate their position, however, all but one of their pigeons were shot down by the Germans. The 77th Division's hope now lay on the lone surviving pigeon, Cher Ami[10].

The American soldiers sent Cher Ami with a note attached to the pigeon's leg, 'We are along the road parallel to 276.4. Our own artillery is dropping a barrage directly on us. For heaven's sake, stop it.' However, soon after she took flight, the Germans shot Cher Ami through the chest, and she fell to the ground. Miraculously, she recovered and flew determinedly at a record speed of fifty miles per hour. She arrived at the American base with the message, but wounded with severe injuries. Though she was treated, the injuries ultimately led to the loss of a leg and blindness. But thanks to Cher Ami's heroism, the bombardment of the Lost Battalion was halted and 194 soldiers were rescued. In recognition of her extraordinary courage, the French government bestowed upon Cher Ami the prestigious Croix de Guerre, a medal honouring bravery in battle. Her bravery inspired a novel, *Cher Ami and Major Whittlesey* authored by Kathleen Rooney, that won rave reviews for its heartwarming fictionalized retelling of the story.

The German army too employed pigeons in World War I, albeit as spies, thanks to a very novel invention. Andrea DenHoed in a *The New Yorker* article dated 14 April 2018, notes that in 1907, an apothecary named Julius Neubronner developed a small camera with a timer, which could be strapped to a pigeon. These feathered photographers carrying his patented invention—the pigeon camera—soared above Earth, clicking away, producing images with a raw, unfiltered quality reminiscent of today's GoPro footage.

The use of pigeons as spies continued in World War II. Between 1941 and 1944, British intelligence unleashed 16,000 homing pigeons into Nazi-occupied Europe as part of the clandestine operation, Columba. These winged couriers carried tiny, rice paper messages back to MI14, offering a unique window into life under the German yoke. From humorous anecdotes to harrowing accounts of occupation, the pigeon post provided invaluable intelligence. Military movements, weapon development, and the deployment of terrifying V-rockets were all exposed through these feathered spies[11].

As recently as 2023, pigeons have been suspected of being spies. On 24 February 2024, *The Guardian* reported that the Mumbai police captured a pigeon with two rings tied to its legs, carrying a note resembling the Chinese script. The pigeon was held for eight months, suspected of being part of an espionage plan. Eventually, it was released when it became known that the pigeon was a racing bird from Taiwan that had escaped and made its way to India.

From carrying messages to performing entertaining acts, pigeons have done it all. Ursula Sims-Williams in a blogpost for the British library in February 2013 notes that King Akbar had more than 20,000 pigeons in his court, of which 500 were 'khaas' (select), trained to perform special acts. Abul Fazl, author of the Akbarnama, the official record of Akbar's reign, also wrote the *Ain-i-Akbari* ('Akbar's regulations'), which had an entire section devoted to pigeon training, flying and breeding. Select pigeons were trained to perform intricate aerial manoeuvres. A particularly challenging feat was the 'wheel', a dynamic sequence culminating in a complete aerial somersault. Some exceptionally skilled pigeons could execute fifteen of these wheels and an astonishing seventy somersaults in a single flight, showcasing the pinnacle of avian acrobatics. During the Mughal era, a poet, Sayyid Muhammad Mūsavī, known as Vālih wrote The *Kabūtarnāmah,* an illustrated pigeon manual, with a poem of 163 couplets, followed by a short prose treatise explaining the different types of pigeons, their colours and characteristics, and the art of pigeon-flying.

Darwin himself referred to the translation of Sayyid Muhammad Mūsavī's treatise, which he mentions twice in his book *The Variation of Animals and Plants Under Domestication'*. Darwin's theory of evolution was profoundly shaped not only by the iconic finches of the Galapagos but also by the humble pigeon. Embarking on a study of pigeon breeding in 1856, Darwin found himself captivated by the astonishing diversity within this single species.

He obtained various birds including pigeons from India and Burma in 1856. Through meticulous observation, he delved into the intricacies of pigeon breeds, measuring skeletons, and studying the astonishing diversity in behaviour, colour and body structure. His keen eye for detail also allowed him to identify patterns of inheritance across various traits. He documented these in *The Variation of Animals and Plants Under Domestication*. The book's extensive and visually stunning exploration of pigeons remains a valuable resource for both scientists and pigeon enthusiasts alike.

In India, the eighteenth-century ruler Tipu Sultan relied on pigeons for rapid communication. These birds carried messages to and from his headquarters, the Jama Masjid mosque in Srirangapatna. Evidence of this system remains visible today in the form of pigeonholes embedded in the mosque's minarets. The 2020 news article, 'The Long History of Speed at Reuters' notes that in 1850, Paul Reuter, the founder of Reuters, employed a fleet of over forty-five pigeons to transmit news and financial data between Brussels and Aachen, bridging the gap in the early telegraph network.

Until the early twenty-first century, the remote regions of Odisha, India, relied on homing pigeons for communication. This avian postal service, a legacy from the British era, had served the state's police force since 1946. Particularly invaluable during natural disasters like floods and cyclones, when modern communication systems faltered, these feathered messengers proved their worth. However, the march of technology eventually caught up, and with the widespread adoption of the internet, the Odisha Police Pigeon Service was retired in 2002, marking the end of an era[12].

Homing pigeons also have been used in competitive racing due to their flying speeds. Flights as long as 1,800 kilometres (1,100 miles) have been recorded by birds in competitive homing pigeon racing. Colloquially called racing homers, their average flying speed over moderate distances (600 miles) is around sixty miles per hour[13].

In his book, *Pigeons: The Fascinating Saga of the World's Most Revered and Reviled Bird,* Andrew Blechman writes about pigeon racers in the New York metropolis, who train their birds for competitive racing. These racers dedicate up to thirty hours weekly to prepare for the lucrative competitions of the forthcoming season. Trained pigeons are sold in auctions and can command prices up to $100,000. In May of 2013, Bolt, the world's fastest racing pigeon at the time, was sold to a Chinese businessman by a Belgium breeder for $453,000. Flying in long-distance pigeon races, pigeons can reach speeds of up to 100 mph[14].

Pigeon racing is a popular sport in South Asia in the countries of India, Pakistan and Bangladesh. In India, Chennai is the sport's capital with nearly half of India's 7,000-strong fanciers (a person who keeps and breeds pigeon) residing there. The sport even has an official body, The Indian Racing Pigeon Association (IRPA) that conducts races. While pigeon racing was previously associated with daily wage workers, it has now gained popularity with elite professionals such as doctors and engineers[15].

Pigeon racing isn't just a hobby; it's a passion project that demands both time and money. While the thrill of the race and the camaraderie of fellow enthusiasts are priceless, the financial investment can be significant. Cash prizes, often modest, rarely exceed Rs 5,000, while the monthly expenses for a flock of 100 birds can easily surpass that figure. These feathered athletes require meticulous care, from a balanced diet of corn, groundnut, wheat, horse gram, finger millet, and oilseeds to regular flight training. Their homes, or lofts, are more than just shelters. Equipped with perches, nests and feeders, these lofts are where the birds are nurtured and conditioned for the rigorous challenges of the race.

A favourite pastime of Queen Elizabeth II, one of the world's most famous fanciers, was pigeon racing. The royal family's connection to pigeons dates back to 1886 when King Leopold II of Belgium bestowed them a gift of racing pigeons. The royal lofts are still being maintained today and participate in the Royal Pigeon One Loft Race, held every year, where pigeon breeders from all over UK vie to win the £35,000 cash prize[16].

Mike Tyson, another pigeon fancier, once famously said, 'The pigeon was the first thing I ever loved in my life … My love for pigeons kept me from killing someone.' The king of rock-and-roll, Elvis Presley, the champion quarterback Terry Bradshaw, and the godfather himself, Marlon Brando, are also known for being pigeon fanciers.

Across diverse cultures and religions, the pigeon/dove is imbued with profound symbolism. Often considered a messenger of peace, it has also been linked to concepts of the soul, love, divine grace, motherhood and femininity. The book, *Feral Pigeons* by Richard Johnston and Marian Janiga lists many of the mythologies linked with pigeons[3]. In Mesopotamia, the mother goddess Ishtar is depicted cradling a dove, signifying fertility and nurturing. Clay shrines of the goddess, dated as being 6,500 years old, have been found with pigeons placed on perches. The Phoenicians associated Astarte, their goddess of love and fertility, with the dove as well. This association continued with the Greek goddess Aphrodite and the Roman Venus, both linked to doves. Pigeons are the only birds that breed through the year, even in the cold of winter. It is possible that these ancient civilizations observed this capability and considered them to be sacred for fertility.

Judaism, too, holds the dove in reverence, depicting it as a symbol of God's love, salvation, and eternal life in many paintings and motifs.

Its appearance in biblical texts, like King Solomon's Song of Songs, further solidifies its status as an allegory for love and beauty. The Bible has several references to the pigeon. In the Genesis 15:6 verse, God says to Abram, 'Take me an heifer of three years old, and a she goat of three years old, and a ram of three years old, and a turtledove, and a young pigeon.' The verse is considered to be one of the key verses in the Old Testament where Abram doubts God's promise to him, and yet keeps his faith. Christianity embraced the dove as the Holy Spirit descending upon Christ during his baptism, further solidifying its association with the divine[3].

In China, the dove transcends love, becoming a symbol of enduring loyalty and a long life. Meanwhile, medieval Europe held a fascinating superstition: devils and witches could morph into birds, except the dove, which remained an untouchable symbol of purity. King Ramesses II of Egypt is said to have made a religious offering of over 50,000 pigeons to the God Amon, about 3,000 years ago. This could mean that the Egyptians were possibly breeding or holding pigeon colonies[3].

In a journal article, 'Pigeon in the Vedic Mythology and Ritual', Hukam Chand Patyal writes about how these birds were perceived in ancient India. The birds were referred to as pārāvata, kalarava, kapota. The pigeon and dove were sometimes used interchangeably, and it wasn't easy to make a sharp distinction between them. The pigeon was considered to be an ominous bird, as it was said to be the messenger of Yama, the god of death. The pigeon was also believed to be the messenger of Niryti (the goddess of destruction), and considered to bring misfortune. There are several verses found in the Rigveda and also in the Atharva Veda to appease the bird or make an atonement so that it may bring well-being to humans and animals. 'O gods, let us worship for that, desiring which the pigeon sent as Niryti's messenger, has come to this[ceremony]; let us make atonement, may prosperity be given to our bipeds and quadrupeds…'[17].

Ancient beliefs attributed significant meaning to the behaviour of pigeons. A bird flying towards or striking a house was considered an omen requiring ritual purification. Similarly, a dove perching on the hearth was deemed inauspicious. To rectify these events, specific rituals were prescribed, including bathing, wearing clean clothes, performing certain rites, and chanting hymns. If a frightened or lost dove sought refuge within a home and left traces of its presence, such as footprints in food, elaborate purification ceremonies were necessary. These involved chanting specific hymns and making offerings to ward off potential misfortune.

The sound of a departing pigeon was generally considered auspicious, but if its cries were particularly loud and came from the south, it was interpreted as a portent of negative events. The dove or pigeon is associated with some rites connected with deceased ancestors. The heap of ashes are to be prepared in a way such that a dove may not sit on its shade in order to ward off evil effects. It is one of five birds forbidden for eating. These birds (the partridge, the pigeon, the francoline partridge, the crane, peacock) feed by scratching with their feet, and were perhaps considered impure. These practices reveal the intricate relationship between humans and nature in ancient times, where the actions of animals were imbued with profound spiritual significance.

Hindu mythology has a tale linking pigeons to Lord Shiva. According to the story, one day the goddess Parvati asked Lord Shiva about the secret of immortality. Shiva said that the secret was known only to the Trimurtis—Shiva, Vishnu and Brahma. But Parvati was insistent on learning the secret, so Shiva decided that he would tell her the secret in a remote place where nobody else could hear. He took her to into the heart of the Amarnath cave in the Himalayas to reveal the long-awaited secret. As Shiva started narrating the secret, Parvati fell asleep. Unknown to Lord Shiva, two pigeons dwelling in the cave were listening to his narration. When Lord Shiva realized that instead of Parvati, it was the pigeons who had heard the secret, he was enraged. Lord Shiva attempted to kill the pigeons. However, they beseeched him saying that if he killed them, the story of immortality would then be proved false. Lord Shiva spared their lives, blessed them with a boon that they would reside at the Amarnath caves for eternity. These immortal Amarnath pigeons were forever enshrined as symbols of Shiva and Parvati within the Amarnath cave. Even today, some devotees feed the birds as a mark of devotion to the gods[18].

Feeding pigeons is a common practice across India, seen as a pious act in many communities. Some believe it's akin to paying homage to one's deceased ancestors and some believe pigeons symbolize Goddess Lakshmi and wealth. The Dadar kabootarkhaana in Mumbai is a famous landmark and tourist attraction for locals as well as tourists. The kabootarkhaana, a Grade II heritage structure, was built as a water fountain in the early nineteenth century[19]. In the 1989 gangster Hindi film *Parinda*, a poignant scene shot here that sent the pigeons fluttering away, is still remembered decades later. Maintaining these pigeons is no mean task. The pigeons need about 500 kgs of grain such as jowari, channa, moong, bajra and makali, every day. The Dadar Kabootarkhaana Trust raises the funds for feeding these pigeons. Apart from feeding, these pigeons are also nursed back to health when they fall sick[20].

The Trafalgar Square pigeons in London make for another iconic sight. According to travel writer Tim Moore's book *Do Not Pass Go*, pigeons made the building their home in 1844. As pigeon-feed sellers settled there, making a quick business selling grain on the square, the place attracted more pigeons. Celebrities such as Elizabeth Taylor have been seen surrounded by pigeons while feeding them on Trafalgar Square[21].

However, in 2020, the London mayor prohibited the feeding of pigeons at Trafalgar Square. There were concerns that the birds' acidic poop was damaging heritage structures such as Nelson's Column, built to commemorate Horatio Nelson, a famous British vice admiral who was killed in the Battle of Trafalgar, where Britain triumphed over France. But in 2002, the Save the Trafalgar Square Pigeons group (STTSP) intervened and negotiated a managed feeding programme to feed the birds small amounts of seed[22].

Many Indian households continue to feed these birds in their homes. My gardener, for instance, is tasked with a Sunday feeding ritual. He visits a household where a flock of pigeons await their weekly feast. The birds, with their bobbing heads and eager eyes, create a charming spectacle as they descend upon the terrace.

This easy availability of food, and their ability to adapt to urban environments, has allowed them to thrive in cities worldwide. It is estimated that there are 130 to 330 million feral pigeons globally[23]. The population of pigeons in New York City alone is estimated to be more than one million. Cities, with their high-rise buildings and elevated ledges, also provide ideal nest sites for feral pigeons, and create an environment reminiscent of their ancestral rocky homes.

But even these adaptable birds are not immune to extinction. The passenger pigeon, once numbering in the billions in the 1800s, met a tragic end. In less than a century, unchecked hunting for its meat and the relentless destruction of its habitat drove this magnificent bird to extinction. Martha, the last known passenger pigeon, died in captivity in Cincinnati Zoo in 1914. The book *A Message from Martha: The Extinction of the Passenger Pigeon and Its Relevance Today* documents the demise of the bird and serves as a poignant reminder of our power to irrevocably harm the natural world and the importance of cherishing the biodiversity that remains[24].

With their bobbing head, relentless cooing, and an uncanny knack for turning statues into avian art galleries, they have garnered a reputation as less than desirable neighbours. In pop culture, they are depicted as birds of destitution. The pigeon ladies in the films, *Home Alone* and *Mary Poppins* represent the poor and homeless. But admittedly, they are also compassionate women who help both pigeons and people in need. Disney's heartwarming tale, *The Pigeon That Worked a Miracle*, portrays the birds in a positive light. The film follows young Chad, a wheelchair user, who raises pigeons. His bond with his birds becomes a powerful force, inspiring him to defy his physical challenges and walk again.

Once prized possessions, signifying wealth and power, today they are often vilified and called 'rats of the sky'. The notion that pigeons are dirty does not have much truth to the matter, they take great pains to preen themselves and keep clean. Their droppings, though, contain ectoparasites which can cause diseases such as hypersensitivity pneumonitis, cryptococcal meningitis (a fungal infection that spreads from the lungs to the brain with symptoms that include confusion or changes in behaviour) and psittacosis (a bacterial infection with pneumonia-like symptoms). Because of these health risks, many cities have implemented plans to curtail their population. In March 2023, following an order by the High Court of Bombay, the Pune Municipal Corporation has started imposing a fine of Rs 500 on citizens feeding pigeons in public places[25].

Cities in the developed world have taken to deterring pigeons from roosting or nesting in apartments, houses and high-rises by setting up nets or spikes. Basel, Switzerland, a city once home to an estimated 20,000 pigeons, implemented a drastic population control measure. Between 1961 and 1985, a staggering 100,000 pigeons were removed through shooting and trapping. Despite these aggressive efforts, the pigeon population persisted at a steady level. In response to the escalating pigeon population, the organization Pigeon Action was established in Basel in 1988. Their approach focused on public awareness and habitat management. By discouraging public feeding and providing alternative roosting sites, they implemented a humane population control strategy. A key component of their program involved removing and destroying pigeon eggs, effectively reducing the population by half within four years[26].

Although many regard pigeons as pests, there are some who believe they are unfairly reviled and rescue them as pets. They are both low-maintenance and high on personality, but do require a large aviary or cage to allow them to fly. Those worried about their poop can adorn their pigeons in the latest in avian apparel: pigeon pants. These tiny harnesses lined with a diaper keep things tidy, making your feathered friend the most stylish bird on the block.

Pigeons are emotionally intelligent creatures, able to differentiate between friendly gestures and potential threats. They can spot a kind soul from a mile away and will reward you with a pigeon kiss—a gentle peck, their way of saying 'thanks for the treats, human'. It's undeniable that these birds are clever—they've managed to outsmart countless attempts at pigeon control. They may not take over the world yet, but the pigeon pose, kapotasana, has certainly made its mark around the world as millions sweat it out in their yoga pants mimicking the humble pigeon.

Humans and pigeons live very different lives, but they can sometimes understand each other, according to Catherine Legg from Deakin University[27]. This 'shared understanding', called pragmatic agreement, happens when we all expect others to act the same way in the same situations. For example, a soldier in World War I and a pigeon would both know that someone shooting at them is dangerous and would try to get to safety. Just like the famous pigeon Cher Ami, who knew to fly back to its 'home base', both humans and pigeons can understand the idea of a safe place. This shared understanding, even between different species, shows how important it is for shaping how we all experience the world.

From their early domestication to their current ubiquitousness in bustling cities, pigeons have been intertwined with humanity's journey toward civilization. Whether admired or reviled, they are an integral part of our city's biodiversity. While I'm more wary today of the presence of the pigeon in my home, acutely aware of the potential health risks posed by their droppings, I would still welcome a nesting mother pigeon—a small price to pay for the miracle of new life.

CHAPTER 3

THE COCKROACH

THE large Bournvita tin rustled and creaked ominously. Inside, packed like sardines, were dozens of cockroaches ready to be sacrificed at the altar of science. Dissecting one with a pair of forceps, teasing apart the tracheae, thorax and abdomen, was a rite of passage for high school biology students in India till the late 2000s. Those who came through unscathed went on to become doctors, zoologists or veterinarians. Others, like me, chose less adventurous paths, being marred by the sight of live writhing cockroaches being plucked from the tin. The vision remained etched in my memory for many moons and manifested in many nightmares.

Beyond school, roaches continued to haunt my summer vacations, which were otherwise delightful, in my grandmother's house in Bengaluru. The holidays were filled with get-togethers with cousins, parties with extended family and the sweet fragrance of the magnolia (champaca) trees that lined the street. Just one image tarnished these memories. The bathrooms at the end of the house were a no-man's land, a territory claimed by some of the most colossal cockroaches I'd ever encountered. Bath time became a high-speed event, my eyes darting around for the inevitable ambush. These creatures, with their uncanny ability to blend into the tiles, would launch surprise attacks with an enthusiasm that could put a seasoned fighter pilot to shame. And then there was the nightly spectacle at the dustbin. It was no less than a war zone that drew in hordes of these armoured invaders.

I'm probably not alone in my aversion to cockroaches. Humans may be evolutionarily primed to fear them due to their slimy look, and the health risks they pose. Cockroaches eat almost anything, including human food, garbage, and even sewage. They carry germs on their bodies and spread them through their saliva, poop, and the tiny hairs on their legs. These germs can cause food poisoning, infections, and other diseases. Perhaps these reasons have led to a deep-rooted fear of roaches, katsaridaphobia.

Some people are so terrified that they are unable to get out of bed at night to go to the bathroom out of fear of seeing a roach. The sight of a cockroach can cause people with intense phobia to be paralysed with fear. Rachel Nuwer in an article for BBC Future dated 18 September 2014 writes about Emily Driscoll, a New York-based documentary producer, who once became trapped in a hotel room in India because a roach was sitting on the door handle. 'I couldn't move, I was paralysed,' she said. 'I needed to keep it in my sight.' Scientists think that the cockroach is the most feared insect of all, although they believe there is no logic or rationale to it.

The truth is that, once you get to know these critters a bit better, you would appreciate how similar they are to us. Cockroaches, at least the ones found in our homes, are social creatures, just like humans. When forced to live a solitary life, they start to show signs of stress and even 'depression'. Their development slows down, and they lose interest in the finer things in life, like courtship or foraging for food[1]. Like most teenagers, social interaction is crucial for them to learn the ropes of adulthood, assessing potential partners and recognizing their own kind. Loneliness, it turns out, isn't just a human problem.

Cockroaches belong to the order Blattodea (Blattaria) that also includes termites. The scientific name derives from the Latin *blatta*, 'an insect that shuns the light'. Recent genetic studies strongly indicate that termites share a common ancestor with cockroaches, and are closely related to the wood-eating cockroach. This suggests they evolved directly from this group. Interestingly, the term 'cockroach' itself is a linguistic twist. Originating from the Spanish 'cucaracha', it underwent a transformation in seventeenth-century English into the now familiar 'cockroach'.

India has about 170 diverse species of cockroaches. North America is home to fifty species, while Australia has a staggering 450 varieties[2]. Cockroaches vary greatly in their size, colour and lifestyle. Some are about the size of a thumbnail, and some are as large as a human palm. The species familiar to most of us, found in our homes and categorized as pests are the German cockroach (*Blattella germanica*), the Oriental cockroach (*Blatta orientalis*), and the American cockroach (*Periplaneta americana*). The tiny North American Attaphila fungicola, measuring less than 3 millimetres, is the world's smallest cockroach and makes its home in the bustling nests of leafcutter ants[3]. At the opposite end of the scale, the wingless Australian rhinoceros cockroach is the heaviest. Also known as the giant burrowing cockroach, this behemoth can grow as large as your palm, weighing up to 33.5 grams and stretching 80 millimetres long[4]. Renowned for its complex lifestyle and extraordinary longevity, exceeding ten years, this insect is a true marvel. Rather than laying eggs, females give birth to live young, with up to thirty offspring in a single brood.

The Madagascar hissing cockroach, one of the largest species, lives for two to five years. When agitated, the Madagascar hissing cockroach emits a loud hissing sound. Males, often reaching lengths of up to 4 inches, possess a distinctive pair of prominent horns near their heads. Males engage in territorial encounters, with rivals locking horns, ramming into each other and hissing intensely in a display of dominance[5]. Finally, taking the crown for wingspan is the Central and South American Megaloblatta longipennis, with an impressive wingspread of 20 centimetres[6].

Cockroaches use a secret language of chemical signals to communicate. They secrete powerful perfumes, or pheromones, to attract potential mates, and release alarm signals that trigger hasty retreats when they sense a predator. German and American cockroaches can even distinguish their full siblings from other relatives and strangers through odours. They have a particularly sophisticated chemical, cuticular hydrocarbons, whose scent signature varies among individuals—somewhat like a chemical ID card. In fact, German cockroaches rely on this to recognize their own kin and to adjust their behaviour towards other members of their group. These smart cockroaches abstain from mating with their siblings to avoid the perils of inbreeding[1]. If only humans such as King Commodus from *The Gladiator*, who wanted an heir from his sister, Lucilla, had such wisdom.

Male cockroaches are quite the romantics, performing elaborate displays to win over their mates. They raise their wings and groom their antennae to court females[7]. While most species require a partner, some females can reproduce solo, a feat known as parthenogenesis. A few species directly give birth to their young, but most carry their eggs in a protective case, called ootheca, within or outside their bodies. The German cockroach carries thirty to forty eggs in the ootheca, outside her body, until it's time to hatch[8].

The hatching begins with the combined power of the ootheca's tiny inhabitants as they inflate their bodies together and emerge as pale nymphs, quickly hardening into their brown form. The progression of nymphs to adults takes place swiftly, within four to five months. Although the lifespan of a German cockroach is just one year, a female can produce eight egg cases in her lifetime—that's about 300 offspring in a year! Other species can produce a far greater number of eggs. In some cases, a single fertilization event is enough to fuel a lifetime of egg production.

World leaders could learn a thing or two from German and American cockroaches, who function quite democratically. When faced with choosing a new home, these insects engage in a collective decision-making process. Rather than acting alone, they consider factors like overcrowding, food scarcity, and shelter quality before reaching a group consensus. A cockroach's choice is influenced by factors like darkness, space, temperature, and humidity, but the presence of other cockroaches is a powerful draw. The more cockroaches settled in a spot, the likelier it is that newcomers will join them[1].

Scientists demonstrated this decision-making of the group in house selection using robotic cockroaches. With the help of engineers, they built wheeled robots shaped like matchboxes to infiltrate a group of lab cockroaches. Remember that cockroaches distinguish each other through specialized chemicals? So, the robots were sprayed with cockroach perfume and programmed to prefer crowds and darkness, just like roaches. The scientists created two shelters, one dark and one lightly tinted. When the robots were introduced to the group, all the roaches scrambled around at first and eventually both real and robot roaches chose the dark shelter. Then, the scientists reprogrammed the robots to prefer lighter spots. This time, after scurrying around, the robots chose the lighter shelter and the real cockroaches followed. This showed that once cockroach numbers hit a critical point, they exhibit a preference for locations already inhabited by their kin[9].

These critters can find homes in the most unexpected places. Cockroaches can thrive in the damp, decaying embrace of leaf litter to the heart of rotting wood, and in cavities under tree bark. Some are even desert dwellers, having evolved incredible survival tactics to combat the arid conditions. Others have taken to water, developing ingenious breathing techniques to explore the underwater world. These aquatic cockroaches carry a bubble of water under the thorax when they submerge, others use the tip of their abdomen as a snorkel to breathe. Some roaches have reached the lofty heights of the forest canopy, where they hide among dead leaves, and in bird and insect nests during the day, and emerge under the cover of darkness to feed[10].

These unassuming creatures are the ultimate survivors. From the sweltering tropics to the icy fringes of the world, cockroaches have conquered almost every corner of the planet. Some even boast a superpower: the ability to produce their own antifreeze out of glycerol, allowing them to endure temperatures colder than dry ice![11] They can even hold their breath for up to seven minutes to conserve moisture[12].

Their resilience is so well-known that they are the only creatures considered to possibly survive a nuclear war. Some can even live for weeks without their heads, and since they do not have blood, they don't bleed out. Cockroaches don't rely on lungs or blood to get oxygen. They have tiny breathing holes, spiracles, on every body segment that pipe air directly to their tissues through a network of tubes called tracheae. Even their brains don't control their breathing. In fact, cockroaches have mini-brains, nerve tissues, scattered throughout their body, each capable of handling basic tasks for reflexes. So if their heads are cut off, roaches can still survive. Bizarrely, the head can also survive for hours without the body, fluttering its antennae around. If the head is refrigerated or fed, it can survive longer[13].

Even without its brain, the insect can learn with the right motivation. Professor G.A. Horridge from St Andrews University devised a method to stimulate a headless cockroach to move its legs. By subjecting the insect's limbs to electric shocks whenever they dropped below a specific point, he observed a remarkable behavioural adaptation. Within approximately thirty minutes, the cockroach instinctively adjusted its leg positioning to minimize the electrical stimuli[13].

If you are wondering why anyone would conduct such peculiar experiments, I would put it down to scientific curiosity and the ubiquitous nature of these insects. In fact, roaches lend themselves well to a suite of laboratory research, and the insects have been subject to many behaviour experiments. The world's leading authority on cockroaches, Louis Roth, studied the critter in great detail at the US Army's research laboratory in Massachusetts. He published over forty papers during a period of over thirty years, covering a range of topics including behaviour, anatomy, physiology, and new species descriptions. His obsession with cockroaches was so profound, he would often conceal them in his pockets during social gatherings, startling unsuspecting companions[14].

C.H. Turner of Sumner Teachers College in Saint Louis trained cockroaches to navigate complex mazes, a feat rarely achieved by insects. He constructed intricate pathways using copper strips elevated above a water-filled pan. At the maze's end, an inclined plane led to the cockroach's designated 'home'. Remarkably, after only a few practice sessions, within a day, most roaches reached their homes faster, swiftly traversing the maze with increasing accuracy[15].

While many of us humans are still dreaming of travelling through space, a humble cockroach has already beaten us to it. Not only did it conquer space, but it even managed to start a family up there! In fact, a cockroach has the honour of being the first creature to give birth in space. In September 2007, an unmanned Russian spacecraft, Foton-M bio-satellite was launched with the creatures sealed in special containers. A cockroach called Nadezhda (Hope) conceived in space and gave birth to thirty-three baby roaches on the flight[16].

Cockroaches can even be a valuable part of a police detective's toolkit in solving murders. Wendy Ruderman in an article in

The New York Times on 1 June 1997 noted that at a forensic science conference in Manhattan, entomologists demonstrated how police teams can utilize cockroaches in criminal investigations, and track murderers. They've discovered that these insects can inadvertently become carriers of crucial evidence, such as human blood. By collecting and analysing cockroaches from crime scenes, investigators can potentially extract and test DNA. If the blood type found is different from the victim's, it can provide valuable clues to solve cases. There are even documented cases of medico-criminal entomology dating back to thirteenth-century China.

Cockroaches are also providing ideas for ingenious designs for the betterment of human lives and society. Robert D. Howe, head of Harvard's Biorobotics Laboratory, is studying cockroach legs to design the next generation of prosthetic legs and mechanical hands for humans. The mechanical hand could be capable of smoothly glide along objects and grasping them, such as picking up a coffee cup[17].

The spring action of cockroach legs has been the subject of fascination for many scientists. Prof. Robert Full at the University of California, Berkeley, explained in a 2014 Ted Talk how the design of insect's legs and exoskeleton allowed for unlimited manoeuvrability and stability over different terrain such as grass, rods, walls, etc. This inspired him to build a six-legged robot that is robust, damage resistant and can move through tiny gaps and climb walls like a cockroach.

Roach inspired robots might well be part of search and rescue missions in disaster zones. University of Colorado Boulder researchers built a roach-inspired robot that is lighter than a ping-pong ball. The roach-bot named CLARI (Compliant Legged Articulated Robotic Insect), is extremely malleable and with some advancements could be deployed to search for missing people in disaster zones[18].

These often-reviled creatures could be our unsung heroes in environmental monitoring. Cockroaches, with their resilient nature and physiological similarities to humans, have emerged as valuable tools in scientific research. Their hearts, brains, muscles and digestive systems function in ways remarkably similar to our own. This shared biological blueprint makes them ideal models for studying the effects of various toxins on human health. Cockroaches have been instrumental in unravelling the effects of various toxins, including scorpion venoms, bacterial toxins such as staphylococcus aureus, also known as staph that cause a variety of infections in humans, and the algal toxin, saxitoxin, a potent neurotoxin. Cockroaches have been employed to assess the toxicity of chemical warfare agents like sarin, cyclosarin, and tabun, providing valuable information for developing protective measures and medical countermeasures[19].

Given their surprising role in scientific research, perhaps it's time to reconsider our fear of cockroaches. While maintaining a clean environment is crucial, an irrational phobia of these creatures may not be warranted. To treat cockroach phobia, some scientists are exploring the potential of augmented reality. A group of Spanish researchers recruited six women with severe, clinically diagnosed cockroach phobias. Their fear was so debilitating that one woman considered selling her home after seeing a cockroach. As a therapy to their cockroach phobia, a headset and motion-tracking system were used to project virtual cockroaches crawling on the participants' hand. The six women initially refused to enter a room containing a live cockroach. However, after undergoing multiple one- to three-hour augmented reality therapy sessions, the women's anxiety gradually decreased. Remarkably, at the end of the treatment, they could approach and even touch a live cockroach. The effects of the therapy lasted for at least a year[20].

With edible insects emerging as a sustainable and nutritious food source, cockroach farming is not far behind. In Thailand and Mexico, the body of a cockroach (without the head and legs) is cooked in various ways including boiling, sautéing, grilling, or drying. Frying transforms the insect into a crispy exterior with a soft, cottage cheese-like interior. Adventurous eaters can find inspiration in cookbooks like *Entertaining with Insects* and *The Eat-a-Bug Cookbook*, which delve into the world of cockroach cuisine. Phillip Charlier in an article in *Taiwan English News* dated 23 June 2023 wrote about a Taiwanese man's recipe for cockroach omelette made out of dubia cockroaches that he bred at home for his pet reptiles, which went viral on social media.

In China, cockroach farming is all the rage for its use in medicine. The largest cockroach farm in the world is perhaps the one in the city of Xichang, in the Sichuan province. Six billion adult cockroaches are bred in a highly controlled environment every year. This isn't your typical insect farm. Here, artificial intelligence oversees every aspect of the operation. It's like a bug's version of the Big Brother house, but without the drama. The system continuously monitors over eighty data points, from environmental conditions like humidity and temperature to the specific dietary needs of each cockroach. It even tracks individual insects, noting genetic variations and their impact on growth rates. It's like a personal trainer, nutritionist, and genetic counsellor, all rolled into one. Once these insects reach optimal size and weight, they are processed into a medicinal potion. According to the Chinese provincial government, the potion that has a subtle sweet taste and fishy odour has cured more than forty million patients of stomach pain, respiratory disease and other conditions[21].

Since ancient times, cockroaches have been used to treat a variety of ailments in Chinese traditional medicine. In some rural parts of southern China, even today, infants are sometimes given a concoction of cockroaches and garlic to alleviate fever or digestion problems. Scientists in Yunnan Dali Medical Academy are studying the use of cockroaches in making drugs—and for a possible AIDS cure[22].

Fried cockroaches were used, as per African American folklore, to treat indigestion. Jamaicans drank the ashes of cockroach as a tonic and mixed bruised roaches with sugar to get ulcers and tumours to burst[23]. In the nineteenth century, Lafcadio Hearn, a journalist and writer who travelled through the southern states of the US, observed that many Americans in New Orleans believed in cockroach tea as a remedy for tetanus[24].

If the idea of eating insects doesn't quite tickle your fancy, perhaps you'd be interested in a different kind of bug-related activity: cockroach racing. This peculiar sport is gaining popularity, with enthusiasts gathering to watch these speedy critters compete for the ultimate prize. Cockroach racing originated in Australia's Story Bridge Hotel, Brisbane, in 1982. A friendly dispute between two patrons over which suburb boasted the swiftest cockroaches escalated into the first-ever cockroach race. This unusual competition has since become an annual tradition, held on Australia Day, 26 January, and fittingly named the 'Australia Day Cockroach Races'[25]. The cockroach athletes are given unique names like Cupcake 'Speedster' Carnegie, Franklin 'Supersonic' Carnegie and Franklin 'The Flash' Carnegie and even have web pages dedicated to them with their hobbies, favourite food and secret techniques listed[26].

The cockroach race itself takes place within a circular arena measuring 6 metres in diameter. Competitors are housed in glass bottles until they are released into the centre of the ring. The first cockroach to cross the arena's boundary is crowned the victor. In the past years, The Hall of Fame has had winners named Osama Bin Liner and Alfred Hitcocky, and Kim Roach-Dashian.

In some places, big bucks are up for grabs. In the annual Cockroach Cup, held in Karratha, Western Australia's Pilbara region, the owner of the fastest cockroach takes home a $1,500 prize. These high-speed racers are sourced directly from the local sewers, ensuring a truly authentic competition. To add to the excitement, a cockroach auction precedes the races, with sixty insects fetching prices between $5 and $500[27].

Cockroach racing has gained popularity in the United States too. Every four years, the New Jersey Pest Management Association hosts a presidential race unlike any other, pitting two Madagascar hissing cockroaches against each other. These six-legged contenders, adorned with miniature caricatures of the presidential candidates, sprint down a three-foot track in a battle for White House glory. This unusual contest boasts an impressive 84 per cent accuracy rate in predicting election outcomes. History bears this out, with Obama's cockroach outpacing McCain's in 2008 and Gore's insect edging out Bush's by a whisker in a previous election[28]. Unfortunately, this year though the roach representing Kamala Harris won the race, the prediction failed for the real election outcome[29].

Cockroach racing even inspired a scene in the 1995 film, *Race the Sun*. The movie, based on a real-life international competition of a solar-powered race car event, had an entry from Hawaii, named 'Cockroach'. The design of the race car was inspired by the cockroach running across the room. In the American television series *CSI*, in the episode 'Ellie', the lead investigator has a fascination with cockroach racing. The investigator and entomologist Gil Grissom packs a jar of Madagascar hissing cockroaches for an upcoming conference, rather than focusing on the intricacies of the murder case at hand[23].

Cockroaches have long served as literary symbols of squalor, degeneration, and the hidden, often sinister aspects of human existence. Frank Kafka's best known story *The Metamorphosis*, is about a salesman Gregor Samsa who transforms into a giant insect. Although Kafka does not name the insect, most readers imagine it to be a cockroach. The novella has triggered many psychological, religious and sociological interpretations, including one that suggests Samsa's rejection and alienation from society is similar to that of a cockroach. Don Marquis, an American columnist, and poet's best-known work is a series of books about Archy and Mehitabel. Archy is a philosopher-poet cockroach who uses satire and humour to comment on the everyday travails of life.

Howard E. Evans, curator of insects at the Museum of Comparative Zoology at Harvard referred to Archy while elucidating the fine points of roaches. In a 1966 issue of *Harper's Magazine*, he writes in an essay titled 'The Intellectual and Emotional World of the Cockroach', '…I heartily recommend cockroaches. Unlike Archy, the average roach has little or no poetry in his soul. But he is a marvellous beast nonetheless. A few years ago, a cockroach was served to me in an order of beefsteak and onions in Texas (I believe it was American, but accurate identification of fried specimens is difficult). I was ravenously hungry after a day in the desert, so I ate everything except the cockroach, which I spread out neatly in the centre of the empty plate, arranging his antennae and legs as best I could. The expression on the waiter's face when he cleared the table was ample compensation for the health risk I took.'

Travel literature is replete with cockroach encounter stories. As a correspondent for the Sacramento Union in March 1866, Mark Twain set off to Hawaii on a ship. He wasn't happy about his accommodation and wrote in a letter to the Sacramento Union, 'first glance at the pillow showed me a repulsive sentinel perched upon it, cockroaches as large as peach leaves—fellows with long quivering antennae and fiery malignant eyes. They were grating their teeth like tobacco worms and appeared to be dissatisfied about something.' His experiences inspired him to write, 'Results of Kindness to a Cockroach' published in 1872[23].

Artists have used roaches as symbols for resilience or survival in the face of adversity. Dalí's 'The Metamorphosis of Narcissus' is a surrealist masterpiece that incorporates a cockroach crawling across a fractured eggshell. This seemingly incongruous element serves as a potent symbol, introducing a sense of unease and representing the darker, more corrupt aspects of narcissism. Pop queen Madonna has been famously quoted as saying, 'I am a survivor. I am like a cockroach, you just can't get rid of me'.

The Cockroach, a 2019 novella by Ian McEwan, explores the transformation of Jim Sams, an unremarkable individual, into the most powerful person in Britain. As Prime Minister, Sams is willing to sacrifice anything and anyone to achieve his goals. Describing his novel, the author said, '*The Cockroach* is a political satire in an old tradition. Mockery might be a therapeutic response, though it's hardly a solution. But a reckless, self-harming, ugly and alien spirit has entered the minds of certain politicians and newspaper proprietors. They lie to their supporters. They express contempt for judges and the rule and norms of law. They seem to want to achieve their ends by means of chaos. What's got into them? A cockroach or two, I suspect.'[30]

Martin Scorsese's 2002 epic, *Gangs of New York*, introduced audiences to the infamous 'Roach Gang' from Mulberry Street. This criminal outfit, notorious for its brutality and territoriality, may have inadvertently popularized the abbreviated term 'roach' as a slang reference to cockroaches. This word trend is speculated to have originated in the gritty underworld depicted in the film[23]. And then there's the iconic scene in *Men in Black*, where Tommy Lee Jones and Will Smith fight a giant slimy alien cockroach to protect the galaxy.

National Geographic Explorer documentary *Doctor Cockroach* is based on the life of Dr Austin Frishman, popularly known as 'the doc', an expert in the pest control industry for over sixty years. One of his pioneering contributions was the development of cockroach bait in the early 1980s[31]. This groundbreaking bait led to the elimination of many cockroaches by successfully enticing them to consume a sweet but lethal substance. The documentary film was the first to use a roach wrangler, a person who collects and manages cockroaches for films and ensures they are safe. Roach wranglers were later used in movies like *Race the Sun*, *Joe's Apartment* and *Mimic*.

The cockroach has been imbued with a range of symbolic meanings across different cultures. Khnum is one of the earliest Egyptian deities, originally the god of the source of the Nile River. A lesser-known facet of the deity involves his role as a protector against cockroaches. Ancient texts, such as *The Book of the Dead*, reveal incantations invoking Khnum's aid in repelling these creatures. As the soul navigated the perilous underworld after death, it would recite a plea to Khnum for protection, 'Be far from me, O vile cockroach, for I am the god Khnum.'[32]

In certain affluent households of Russia and Finland, a peculiar superstition once held that cockroaches were harbingers of good fortune. Newlyweds were said to invite prosperity by introducing cockroaches into their homes. To kill such an insect, especially by fire, was deemed a grave misfortune[33].

A lesser-known Aesop's fable spins a tale of unlikely retribution. A cockroach, grieving the loss of its hare companion at the talons of an eagle, devises a cunning plan for revenge. The cockroach targets its nest, destroying it completely. The eagle seeks refuge with the gods, placing its eggs in the lap of Zeus, the king of the gods. By depositing dung on the god's lap, the cockroach forces Zeus to jump up in disgust, causing the eggs to shatter. This fable underscores the potent message that even the most insignificant creature can topple the mighty, demonstrating that power and strength are not invincible[23].

When a creature has lived in such close proximity to humans as the cockroach, perhaps it is natural for some humans to keep them as pets; though many would question this proclivity. The most common cockroach species that are kept as pets are the Madagascar hissing cockroach, the giant burrowing cockroach, the death's head roach and the Indian domino cockroach. According to the entomology department at the University of Kentucky, Madagascar hissing cockroaches are the best insects to keep as pets. They are low maintenance, can adapt to home environments and they are not dangerous to humans or other pets in a household. Some US states, including Florida, require individuals or institutions who want to keep Madagascar hissing cockroaches to have a special permit, whether for captive breeding colonies or as pets. The Blattodea Culture Group, an organization active for fifteen years till 2009, provided a dedicated platform for cockroach rearing enthusiasts. One of its members even published a book, *Introduction to Rearing Cockroaches,* a comprehensive guide to the subject[34].

The three pest species have received the most attention due to the trouble they cause to people. Swedish biologist Carl Linnaeus was the first scientist to describe these cockroach species. When he received a roach from America he called it *americana*, while a roach from Asia he called *orientalis*. According to James A.G. Rehn of the Academy of Natural Sciences in Philadelphia, the American cockroach and its Australian counterpart both originate from a species group predominantly found in tropical Africa. Similarly, the Oriental cockroach shares ancestral ties to Africa, but it arrived in Europe very long ago[15].

In 1776, Linnaeus named another specimen he collected in Germany as the German cockroach, which now dominates the entire world except Antarctica. Although thought to have originated in Europe, recent research suggests that this species originated in South Asia. A group of scientists analysed the genomes of 281 German cockroaches collected from seventeen countries, including Australia, Ethiopia, Indonesia, Ukraine and the United States. They used a method called 'DNA barcoding' comparing the DNA sequences for one particular genetic region, called CO1. They found a match with a cockroach species *blattella asahinai* from the Bay of Bengal. They further analysed the DNA sequences to calculate when and where different populations might have been established[35]. They suggest that around 1,200 years ago, the German cockroach travelled from Bay of Bengal westwards into the Middle East hitchhiking with the traders and armies. Then, around 390 years ago, they spread to Indonesia, and further to Europe in the seventeenth century through ships of the Dutch and British East India Companies. From Europe, the German cockroaches spread around the world more rapidly through modern modes of transportation.

As these pest species proliferated globally, spreading disease and fear, a booming industry developed dedicated to its eradication. Ever the survivor, the insect has managed to overcome all such efforts. Cockroach baits, once a cheap and highly effective solution introduced in the 1980s, have lost their potency against the German cockroach. The baits used sugary products that cockroaches are extremely fond of, laced with poison to kill them. However, in order to survive, some cockroaches have evolved to taking a dislike to sugar, rendering this bait ineffective. Incidentally, this has disrupted their mating style. During courtship, the male offers a mix of sugars and fats as a gift to the female. Scientists have found that the new sugar-averse females are rejecting these gifts. But before you think that this might be a good thing, the males have found a way around this and may be changing the chemistry of their offering to attract the females[36].

If the Indian ethos of 'jugaad' could be applied to any creature, perhaps it would have to be the cockroach. As pesticide manufacturers moved away from using glucose baits to insecticide sprays, the cockroach evolved further, developing resistance with Olympic-like agility and disappearing into the abyss of the kitchen cabinet like a six-legged Houdini. In the timeless standoff between man and cockroach, it remains to be seen who wins.

CHAPTER 4

THE SPARROW

FRENCH toast was a sacred part of our Sunday morning ritual. We would sit down with warm toast glazed with honey, as the morning sun bathed our cosy balcony. One Sunday, as I was about to tuck into this heavenly breakfast, a sparrow swooped in, with an audacity that would make a seasoned thief blush, and made off with a piece of toast, warm butter and all. Soon I found myself in a standoff with this bread bandit every Sunday morning. All attempts to prevent my balcony from turning into a gourmet restaurant for this brazen bird went futile. Finally, we decided to move our Sunday breakfast ritual indoors, with the balcony door shut determinedly.

My sentiments about this breakfast disruptor were captured back in the day by the nineteenth century Irish writer Robert Lynd. He wrote in his book *Solomon in All His Glory*, 'the sparrows, if you have so much as a crust of bread on you, will gather round you like guttersnipes demanding mouldies … How charming a little dancer he is, as he hops in scores and fifties round a Londoner who has bread—hops backwards and forwards like a marionette or like a small child hopping up and down in sheer excitement.'[1]

Sparrows, it seems, are the original urban pioneers. They've mastered the art of city living with a nonchalance that puts even the most seasoned city-bred man to shame. These tiny birds have proven themselves to be remarkably adaptable, intelligent, and, mischievous creatures. The tale of the house sparrow's association with humans, is perhaps as old as time, or at least as old as the time when humans first tilled the land.

The house sparrow's origins trace back about 11,000 years to the Fertile Crescent in the Middle East, the cradle of civilization. Coinciding with humanity's shift from hunting and gathering to agriculture, these birds likely thrived on the early grains cultivated by our ancestors. Seeking refuge and a steady food source, sparrows moved into human settlements, eventually spreading across much of Eurasia and North Africa. Currently, its natural habitat ranges from the West Coast of Ireland to the East Coast of Siberia in the north to the Arctic Circle in the south to North Africa, Middle East, India and Sri Lanka. It has also successfully adapted to North America and Western Europe where it was introduced by humans[2].

Scientists think that house sparrows have become so successful because of two genes, COL11A and AMY2A, that have helped them adapt to living near humans[3]. The COL11A gene makes their beaks and skulls stronger, which helps them eat tougher seeds. This is useful because human settlements had lots of seeds from plants like wheat and corn. The AMY2A gene helps them digest starchy foods, just like humans and dogs did when we started farming. This means they can eat a wide variety of food, including bread, rice, and other grains. Interestingly, a remnant population of early sparrows confined to the Central Asian steppes lacks these two genes. Unlike their urban counterparts, these birds migrate, consume only natural grass seeds, and are cautious around humans.

The house sparrow's remarkable adaptability has allowed it to colonize nearly the entire world within 170 years. It is now found on every continent except Antarctica. This rapid expansion took place due to intentional or accidental introductions by humans. The first successful deliberate introduction took place in New York City in 1851[4]. It began as a desperate attempt to curb the devastating impact of the linden moth, which was destroying the city's greenery. Believing these sparrows would prey on the moth larvae, officials introduced the birds from England, hoping for a natural solution to the problem. And indeed, the sparrows proved equal to the task. The house sparrow spread across the American continent from the north-west of Canada to Southern Panama, excepting Alaska. The house sparrow has adapted to eating many different kinds of food. For example, newer populations of house sparrows like those in Panama are more willing to try new foods than the established ones in New Jersey. This makes it easier for them to live in new places[5].

This unassuming bird is now found in every human habitat from the plains to the mighty Himalayas. The only terrestrial habitats that the house sparrow does not inhabit are dense forest and tundra. The house sparrow can put any global jetsetter to shame. It can travel over 230 kilometres in a year! However, as a result, it has become an invasive pest, competing with native birds, harming them in the process. In the US, after it was introduced, house sparrows took over nest sites and food from native birds. This led to dramatic decline of the indigenous bluebird population by the 1980s[6].

The house sparrow was one of the first animals to receive a formal scientific name, bestowed upon it by the renowned naturalist Carl Linnaeus in his groundbreaking 1758 work, *Systema Naturae*[2]. Linnaeus initially classified the sparrow as *Fringilla domestica*. However, later it was reclassified into its own genus, Passer, and family, Passeridae, and named Passer domesticus. The name 'domesticus' meaning 'belonging to the house' came about because of its close association with humans. It is a bird of many names, known as the English sparrow in North America and the Indian sparrow in Asia. Its common name derives from the Old English 'speerwa', meaning 'little flutterer'. While the term 'spar' is applied to various bird species, the house sparrow stands out as the most successful member of the Passer genus.

The house sparrow is a tiny compact bird with a rounded head and full chest. While both males and females exhibit a predominantly grey and brown plumage, there's a striking difference between the sexes. Males boast a bolder appearance with a dark grey crown, chestnut brown sideburns, a reddish back and a black bib below the beak. In contrast, females have a more subdued, buff-coloured plumage. The black bib adorning the male house sparrow is more than just a fashion statement. Its size is a crucial indicator of social status, age, and reproductive success. Males with larger bibs enjoy a higher social rank, often securing mates earlier in the breeding season and engaging in more frequent copulations, including extra-pair matings. These dominant males typically control territories with a greater number of suitable nesting sites[7].

They are highly sociable creatures, forming flocks year-round, often mingling with other bird species. These flocks can range from small groups to massive colonies of up to 50,000 pairs, as seen in golden sparrows, or even a million pairs like those of the Spanish sparrow. They also engage in communal activities such as dust bathing, water splashing, and social singing, creating a harmonious chorus.

Because of their small size, sparrows are conducive to study in experiments. The bird is widely used by scientists to study urban wildlife, to understand life history and body size evolution, sexual selection and many other biological phenomena. Sparrows were also used in early studies on the effects of high altitude on the body. In 1878, French scientist Paul Bert conducted laboratory experiments on sparrows and other animals in hypobaric chambers (chambers where the inside pressure is lower than the outer atmospheric pressure). This study was the first to explain the relationship between atmospheric pressure and blood oxygen levels—that living beings cannot survive at high altitudes without supplemental oxygen[8].

The Gambel's white-crowned sparrow, native to North America, has provided a fascinating model for studying depression. During mating season, a part of its brain called the HVC grows super-fast, expanding from around 100,000 neurons to nearly 170,000![9] It's like adding a whole bunch of new rooms rapidly to a house. This is extraordinary because it's usually hard for brains to grow so quickly without causing problems, such as inflammation and increased pressure.

But the sparrow's brain has remarkable flexibility. It seems to know how to make room for the new cells, when required. After mating season, the extra cells die off, and the brain goes back to its normal size. This process is like cleaning up a room after a party. Special brain cells called astrocytes help clean up the dead cells. Researchers believe that this cycle of growing and pruning neurons could provide valuable insights into depression. When the sparrow loses neurons, it exhibits symptoms similar to depression, such as a loss of motivation to sing. Understanding how the bird recovers from this phase could potentially offer clues for developing new treatments for depression.

For centuries, we've known that the company we keep can significantly impact our lives. Scientists in Hungary conducted a fascinating experiment on 240 wild house sparrows to check if sparrows, being social birds, could influence each other's behaviour just like we humans do[10]. They assessed each bird's personality by observing its behaviour in a solitary cage. Some birds were fearful and frantic, others passive and contemplative, while still others were curious and exploratory. Based on these observations, the researchers categorized the birds into groups of similar or diverse personalities.

Over a nine-day period, the researchers monitored the birds' health by tracking their weight, stress levels, and tissue damage. They discovered a surprising trend: birds in mixed-personality groups consistently outperformed those in homogeneous groups. These birds exhibited better overall health, lower stress levels, and less cellular damage. This was true regardless of individual personality traits. The study suggests that social diversity can have a significant positive impact on the health and well-being of birds. It highlights the importance of considering personality when studying animal behaviour and ecology.

Just as ancient humans were constantly on the lookout for predators, and their fear of them became instinctual, sparrows too have this fear embedded in them. A Canadian study found that the mere fear of predators can dramatically reduce sparrow populations. The researchers exposed one half of the population of song sparrows residing in five islands in British Columbia to calls of predators such as hawks, raccoons and ravens through speakers hung on trees. The other half was exposed to calls of non-predator birds such as geese. Sparrows that heard the predator calls had significantly fewer offspring, likely due to increased vigilance and reduced foraging time[11].

The legendary chirping of sparrows eulogised by Mozart and Henry Van Dyke, has been the subject of many studies. Song sparrows use their voices to defend their territories and attract mates. During the harsh winter months, these feathered crooners belt out their tunes to claim their turf. As spring arrives, their melodious performances reach a crescendo, a symphony of sound that fills the air. However, it's not just the males who sing. Female song sparrows, though less vocal, also contribute to the chorus. Their songs, while less frequent, play a crucial role in social interactions and territorial defence. Interestingly, song sparrows from different regions have their own unique dialects. They can recognize their neighbours' songs and even discriminate against those from distant lands, showcasing the complexity of their vocal communication[12].

A team of researchers studying Savannah sparrows on Kent Island, Canada, for over six years, discovered that these birds are not only able to learn new songs from distant populations, but also pass this knowledge on to future generations. Savannah sparrows, found across North America, have slightly different dialects depending on their location. They introduced West Coast sparrow songs to Kent Island birds and found that many of the male sparrows quickly picked up the new tunes. Even more surprising, some of these birds then taught their young the new songs, demonstrating a remarkable capacity for vocal learning. These findings suggest that sparrows may be more adaptable and socially connected than previously thought[13].

Back in the 1980s, the hustle and bustle of my childhood Mumbai mornings was often punctuated by a cheerful chorus—the chirping of sparrows. I often wondered how these tiny birds adjusted to the city's cacophony. It seems US scientists were asking a similar question. They studied how urban noise affected white-crowned sparrow songs in San Francisco over almost a thirty-year period from 1969 to 1998. They examined songs of the birds in three neighbourhoods-one urban and two less urbanised. They found that the birds' songs in urban areas increased in frequency, perhaps in response to the loud city noise. While some song dialects disappeared, the urban dialect thrived, suggesting that noise is driving the evolution of bird song in cities[14].

If the noise of our cities can affect the song of sparrows, could we humans be affected by sparrow song? Java sparrows, native to Indonesia, perhaps inspired the evolution of modern music, especially beatboxing. A fascinating discovery by Japanese scientists has revealed that these birds are natural beatboxers, clicking their bills in perfect synchronization with their songs. Just like a human percussionist provides the rhythm for a vocalist, male Java sparrows use their bills to create a rhythmic backdrop for their musical performances. The scientists found that the birds carefully time their bill clicks to match specific notes and patterns in their songs. This rhythmic accompaniment is not just for show; it plays a crucial role in the birds' mating rituals. The synchronized clicking and singing are followed by dancing and, ultimately, copulation[15].

House sparrows are loyal to their mates, and typically mate for life. They start breeding very young, sometimes in the very first breeding season, between April to August, after they hatch. Unmated male house sparrows initiate courtship by constructing nests of dried grass or twigs with linings of feathers, either in a hole or in branches of trees. They engage in frequent melodious calls to attract females. When a female shows interest, the male performs an elaborate display. This involves bobbing up and down, while simultaneously drooping and shaking his wings. He also accentuates the display by raising and spreading his tail, pushing up his head, and prominently showcasing his black bib[16].

After mating, the female sparrow lays clutches of four or five eggs, with hues of white, blue or green, speckled with brown or grey. Both parents share incubation duties, and the eggs hatch after approximately eleven to fourteen days. The newly hatched chicks are blind and featherless but quickly develop, opening their eyes within four days and sprouting their first down feathers around eight days old. The hatchlings remain in the nest for about fourteen to sixteen days, and are fed by both parents[16]. Young house sparrows often struggle to successfully raise offspring in their first breeding season. Breeding success tends to improve with age and experience. In a particularly aggressive reproductive strategy, widowed female house sparrows have been observed destroying the eggs, or killing the young of other pairs, potentially to coerce the male into partnering with them[16].

Sparrows live for just about three years. Perhaps to make up for this short life, they reproduce often, raising two to four broods in a year. Sparrows are therefore considered as symbols of lust and fertility. In ancient Greek mythology, sparrows were considered a symbol of love. The sparrow was the sacred bird of Aphrodite, the goddess of love, and symbolized true love and spiritual connection. Both Roman and Chinese cultures held sparrows in high esteem. The Romans believed they were bearers of good fortune, while the Chinese associated them with happiness and the arrival of spring. Dreaming of sparrows in Chinese culture is seen as a lucky sign, often linked to upcoming marriages or births and representing strength and happiness[17].

In ancient Egypt, sparrows were closely linked to the goddess Isis, the divine mother of nature. They symbolized spirituality and were seen as signs of hope and rebirth. Egyptians often kept sparrows in cages to represent their own spiritual knowledge and understanding. The sparrow holds a special place in Japanese culture, symbolizing joy and prosperity. Sparrows are portrayed in Japanese art, literature, and poetry as lively and hardy creatures, representing simplicity and the appreciation of life's small joys[17].

'The Plover's Eggs', a Vedic story from ancient India, speaks of the determination and personal endeavour of the sparrow[18]. According to the story, a tiny sparrow built her nest on the ocean's edge, but the mighty waves washed away her precious eggs. Heartbroken, the sparrow pleaded with the ocean to return her eggs, but the ocean ignored her pleas. Undeterred, the sparrow vowed to dry up the ocean, one tiny beak-full at a time. Everyone laughed at her seemingly impossible task. News of the sparrow's determination reached Garuda, the vehicle of Lord Vishnu. Moved by her courage, Garuda decided to help. He approached the ocean and demanded the sparrow's eggs be returned, threatening to take on the task of drying up the ocean himself. The ocean, fearing Garuda's power, quickly complied and returned the eggs to the grateful sparrow.

The Bible, on the other hand, did not think that sparrows are worthy. The verse Matthew 10:29–31 mentions sparrows, saying, 'Are not two sparrows sold for a penny? Yet not one of them will fall to the ground outside your Father's care. And even the very hairs of your head are all numbered. So don't be afraid; you are worth more than many sparrows.' Yet, the phrase conveys that even the smallest, most ordinary creatures are worthy of God's care and should be treated with humility.

It is believed that this biblical verse inspired Shakespeare to write the last act of *Hamlet*, where he replies to his friend Horatio, warning him of a plot to kill him: 'Not a whit, we defy augury. There's a special providence in the fall of a sparrow. If it be now, tis not to come; if it be not to come, it will be now; if it be not now, yet it will come. The readiness is all.' In this quote, Hamlet argues that fate is inevitable and cannot be avoided. He suggests that everything happens according to a predetermined plan, and that even the smallest events (fall of a sparrow) are part of a larger cosmic order that we cannot fully grasp.

Before Shakespeare, the first reference to the bird in literature appears in 'The History of the English Church and People' by the seventh-century English historian and monk, St. Bede the Venerable. He writes, 'When compared to the stretch of time unknown to us O King, the present life of man on earth is like the flight of a single Sparrow through the hall where, in winter, you sit with your captains and ministers. Entering by one door and leaving at another, while it is inside, it is untouched by the wintry storm; but this brief interval of calm is over in a moment, and it returns to the winter whence it came, vanishing from your side. Man's life is similar, and of what follows it or went before we are utterly ignorant.'

Thijs Porck, an associate professor of medieval English at the Leiden University Centre for the Arts in Society, the Netherlands, writes on his blog that Bede's intent was to compare the life of a pagan with the fleeting flight of the sparrow through the hall, arguing that the life of a Christian is better. In my opinion, we could also interpret that our life on Earth is as brief as the flight of a sparrow, and we should make use of this limited time to find work that is meaningful for us.

William Wordsworth perhaps had the same idea when he wrote in his poem, 'Persuasion":

Man's life is like a Sparrow, mighty King!
That—while at banquet with your Chiefs you sit
Housed near a blazing fire—is seen to flit
Safe from the wintry tempest ...

Wordsworth writes again about the bird in 'The Sparrow's Nest', where he recreates a childhood memory of discovering a sparrow's nest with his sister. The simple beauty, resilience, and the intimate connection they share with nature have inspired several poets to pen heartfelt tributes that celebrate their presence in our lives. Henry Van Dyke explored the joy of knowing a sparrow and celebrates its resilience in 'The Song Sparrow'.

Latin lyric poet Gaius Valerius Cattulus (84 to 47 BCE) wrote of a pet sparrow[19].

Sparrow, my lady's pet
whom often she teases and holds on her lap
and pokes with the tip of a finger, provoking
counterattacks with your mordant beak,
whenever my luminous love desires ...

Sparrows also inspired Mozart to compose *Sparrow Mass*, a delightful composition that's as light and airy as a summer breeze and is supposedly inspired by the chirps of the bird. Composed in the mid-1770s, this masterpiece is one of a series of five masses Mozart penned during that time. It's earned its name, 'Sparrow Mass,' from the playful violin melodies that dance and flit about, evoking the chirping of birds[20].

Legend has it that a sparrow played an inspiring role in the completion of a cathedral. The Bavarian city of Ulm, in Germany, renowned as the birthplace of Albert Einstein, is also steeped in local lore, the legend of Der Ulmer Spatz (The Ulm Sparrow). The town cathedral's spire, reaching a towering 160 metres, is one of the tallest in the world. However, its construction was not without obstacles. When the builders arrived with the long oak beams needed for the spire, they discovered a problem: the beams were too long to fit through the city gate. A local citizen, observing a sparrow building its nest in a niche in the gate tower, had a stroke of genius. The sparrow was carrying a long straw sideways in its beak. But upon reaching the narrow opening, it dropped the straw, picked it up by the end, and pulled it lengthwise through the gap. Inspired by the sparrow's ingenuity, the builders realized they could do the same with the oak beams. By placing the beams lengthwise in their carts, they were able to successfully transport them through the gate and complete the construction of the cathedral. The sparrow has been honoured by installing a copper likeness of the bird armed with its straw on the roof of the tower[2].

Elsewhere in Europe, sixteenth-century residents of London and the Netherlands began to regard the sparrow as a pest. To manage them, a peculiar trend emerged: the sparrow pot. These unglazed earthenware vessels, shaped like miniature rugby balls, were hung from house walls, offering a unique nesting site for the city's feathered inhabitants. The pot, with its small entrance hole and flat bottom, was designed to be accessible to both sparrow and human. Once the birds had laid their eggs or hatched their chicks, the pot could be taken down, and the contents removed. It was thought that the intention was twofold: to protect thatched roofs and walls from the sparrows' industrious nest-building and to potentially control their population, which was considered a nuisance in agricultural areas[2].

Some even believed that sparrow pots served as a source of food for poor peasants. The birds were harvested for their meat, which was then turned into a hearty sparrow pie. This culinary curiosity was particularly popular during World War I, and was supposedly mind-sharpening dish. 'How sharp you are! You have been eating sparrow pie', was a common refrain back then[2].

Beyond the confines of north-west Europe, the sparrow pot trend extended to other parts of the world. In Alexandria, Egypt, earthenware gin bottles were repurposed as avian accommodations, hung on the walls of houses to provide cozy nesting sites. Malta, France, and other regions adopted a more inventive approach. Cavities were carved into stone building blocks, which were then incorporated into the walls of houses. If the blocks were unsuitable for construction, they were simply placed loose on the rooftops[2].

These sparrow nesting sites were not mere afterthoughts but carefully planned elements of the built environment. In Malta, evidence of industrial-scale nest production still exists. Towers erected between 1550 to 1650 have been found having a number of nesting stones. Some blocks are said to have contained over a hundred holes, rivalling the dovecotes of the Middle Ages in terms of capacity. In Sri Lanka, however, the sparrow pot took on a different meaning. Earthenware chatties (cooking pots) were put up on the walls of the houses in villages and towns as a Buddhist gesture of goodwill as it was considered good luck to have sparrows around the house[2].

In the eighteenth century, sparrows became a scourge of European agriculture, wreaking havoc on grain crops. In response, parish councils in grain-growing regions of the United Kingdom instituted a bounty system, offering rewards for the birds and their eggs. The result was a mass culling, with tens of thousands of sparrows killed. Despite these measures, the sparrow population remained resilient. The bounty system eventually proved ineffective and was abandoned in the nineteenth century. Undeterred, the war against the sparrows continued, this time with the formation of 'Sparrow Clubs'. Members of these clubs were required to deliver a specific number of sparrow heads to the secretary, or face a fine. Prizes were given to members killing the most number of birds[2].

In 1958, Chairman Mao in China advocated for a similar campaign to kill as many sparrows as possible. They were considered as one of four evils, the other three being mosquitoes, rats and flies. Millions of birds were killed and while initially this led to higher crop yields, this effect was short-lived. A surge in insect pests, particularly those that preyed on rice and other staple crops, quickly overwhelmed the agricultural system. The resulting crop failures and widespread starvation led to the deaths of an estimated thirty-five million people[2].

It was only later, after the devastating consequences became apparent, that Chinese scientists began to reconsider the role of sparrows in the ecosystem. Research conducted before the extermination campaign revealed that while adult sparrows primarily consumed grains, their young relied heavily on insects for sustenance. By eliminating sparrows, the government had inadvertently created a population imbalance that favoured insect pests, ultimately leading to the destruction of crops. In response to the crisis, Mao eventually ordered the conservation of sparrows, acknowledging the critical role they played in maintaining ecological balance[2].

Sadly today, due to rampant development and urbanization, sparrows have vanished from many parts of the world. Agricultural intensification, characterized by habitat destruction and the excessive use of pesticides, has led to a significant decline in insect populations. This, in turn, has had a cascading effect on sparrow populations, as many species rely on insects as a primary food source. Additionally, the design of modern homes often provides little or no suitable nesting space for birds, further contributing to their population decline.

House sparrow populations have dwindled by half in Europe. In 2021, there were 247 million fewer house sparrows in Europe than there were in 1980[21]. In coastal India, and major cities of South Asia—Delhi, Karachi and Lahore—the house sparrow has almost vanished, with populations declining by 70 to 80 per cent[22]. This once abundant bird is on the red list of endangered species in some countries. To raise awareness about the decline and to save the bird from extinction, World Sparrow Day is celebrated every year on 20 March. The year 2010 marked the launch of this global official campaign thanks to the efforts of Nature Forever Society of India, the Eco-Sys Action Foundation of France, and other global organizations.

As a result of these efforts, the bird was declared as the state bird of Delhi, and the city has also taken great steps to revive the bird population. Goraiya Gram in Garhi Mandu forest, on the banks of the Yamuna, is an urban forest built to bring back the sparrow. Artificial nests made from natural materials like bamboo, jute, coir, and earthen pots and a steady supply of pesticide-free caterpillars, worms, and other insects to feed on have enticed the sparrow to nest here[23]. Across India, sparrow-loving households are adorned with bird baths and decorative wooden and terracotta nesting boxes in an effort to bring them back to our cities.

Sparrows, as ordinary as they come, are simple creatures of the sky, seeking their daily bread in our shared space. Sadly, today, despite my garden welcoming many birds such as the Himalayan bulbul and the tiny flittering sunbird, there are no sparrows. I long to see the day when they make an appearance, even if it means losing a piece of my bread. Our tangled relationship with this little bird is well summarized by the American biologist, Rob Dunn, who writes in the Smithsonian magazine, 'when sparrows are rare, we tend to like them, and when they are common, we tend to hate them. Our fondness is fickle and predictable and says far more about us than them. They are just sparrows.'[24]

CHAPTER 5

THE SQUIRREL

IN a languid May afternoon, a sudden flurry of rustling and chirping drew my attention to the tree outside our new Bengaluru home, a secluded haven nestled amidst lush greenery. Expecting a bird, I peered out only to be greeted by a playful troupe of squirrels. They raced up and down the branches, engaged in what seemed like a spirited game of tag.

This was my first close encounter with these creatures, and I watched in awe as they frolicked through the branches. In a fleeting moment, one squirrel seemed to pause and glance up at me before vanishing with lightning speed. I soon got used to their company, and their raucous antics. They reminded me of my favourite childhood cartoon characters, chipmunks Chip and Dale, who get into skirmishes with Mickey Mouse, Donald Duck and Pluto the dog. These battles, which usually occurred while the chipmunks hunted or stored food, often ended with Chip and Dale outwitting Mickey and Donald with their mischief and humour.

Their antics have even caught the attention of social media and TV channels, when one pet squirrel in the USA staged a dramatic death scene. The clever creature, after tripping over a pole, pulled it up to its chest, and splayed its arms on the floor, adding a touch of theatrical flair to its performance. Squirrels seem to have mastered the art of human psychology. They seem to know exactly when to be cute and when to be a nuisance. I suspect that the squirrels outside my home steal tomatoes from my garden, for a mid-day snack in between their playful antics. Like stealthy thieves, they seem to know when exactly to conduct their raids without being caught.

The squirrels' tryst with humans have occurred since time immemorial, or at least since the story of Lord Rama has been around. According to the Ramayana, as the monkey army led by Sugreeva and Hanuman was constructing the bridge from India to Sri Lanka to assist Rama to rescue Sita from the clutches of Ravana, a small squirrel came along with its own contribution of small pebbles. It is said that some monkeys made fun of the squirrel as the pebbles were too tiny to be of any value. But Rama stroked the squirrel in recognition of its effort, with three fingers, resulting in the three stripes seen today on the Indian palm squirrel.

The small act of a squirrel helping to build a bridge continues to be celebrated in India. As a tribute, in 2024, a fifteen-foot metallic sculpture was installed at the inauguration of a new railway station in Ayodhya, the birthplace of Lord Rama. Sculptor Kalyan S. Rathore explained that he was inspired by the popular Kannada phrase 'alilu seve' (squirrel's service) while creating this artwork[1].

Apart from the Ramayana, the story of how the squirrel got its stripes is found in other cultures too. In an American Indian tribe, the Iroquois, the story goes that a chipmunk asked a bear if it could stop the sun from rising. When the bear failed, the chipmunk mocked the bear, and barely escaped as the irate bear's claws raked its back, leaving the three stripes. In a Seneca myth, a grandmother chipmunk and her granddaughter shared what they thought was a bearskin blanket, which came alive, and chased them leaving the three stripes on their backs[2].

The squirrel holds a significant place in various cultures and mythologies worldwide. In Irish mythology, the goddess Medb is depicted as having a bird perched on one shoulder and a squirrel on the other. These creatures serve as her messengers, connecting her to the celestial realm and the earthly world, respectively. During the Middle Ages in Europe, bestiaries often portrayed squirrels as symbols of greed and avarice due to their habit of storing nuts. The Ainu people of Japan have a fascinating myth about squirrels. They believe that squirrels are actually discarded sandals belonging to the ancestral deity Aioina. This belief may stem from the way squirrels move in short bursts, resembling footsteps[3].

In Norse mythology, the squirrel Ratatoskr plays a pivotal role in the cosmic tapestry4). It inhabits the World Tree, Yggdrasil, whose roots and branches connect the Nine Worlds. Ratatoskr scurries up and down the tree, relaying messages between the wise eagle perched atop it and the evil serpent Níðhöggr beneath its roots. While its role might seem mundane, Ratatoskr's mischievous nature adds an intriguing dimension. Just like the divine mischief monger, Sage Narada, the son of Lord Brahma, Ratatoskr delights in sowing discord. The squirrel often embellishes or twists the messages it carries, exacerbating the animosity between the eagle and Níðhöggr. This cunning manipulation, however, serves a broader purpose. By maintaining tension between the two creatures, Ratatoskr inadvertently contributes to the cosmic balance. Its tale serves as a reminder that even the smallest players can have a profound impact on the grand mythological narrative. Perhaps due to this myth there was a practice of burning squirrels during Easter in medieval times and J.R.R. Tolkien incorporated squirrels as evil characters in his epic book *The Hobbit*, which describes the squirrels of Mirkwood as black and bad tasting[5].

In the original tale of Cinderella, it is believed that she wore squirrel slippers to the ball, and not glass slippers, as told in the modern version of the story. In the book *Squirrels: The Animal Answer Guide*, the authors explain that in the past, fur of Russian squirrels was used to adorn the clothes of royalty and it's likely that the slippers were made of fur rather than uncomfortable glass. When the story was written down, this confusion may have been caused by the similarities in the French words, 'verre' meaning glass and 'vair' meaning squirrel5).

Squirrels belong to the animal group Rodentia. These arboreal creatures may have been the ancestors of a vast array of rodent species. The earliest known rodents, Ischyromyoidae, date back to the late Paleocene of Asia. With their beaver-like skulls, squirrel-like teeth and feet, and skeletal features indicating a tree-dwelling lifestyle, these ancient rodents laid the foundation for the incredible diversity of rodent forms that have evolved over time[6].

Squirrels later evolved as a distinct lineage of rodents thirty-six million years ago. These furry creatures belong to the Sciuridae family, and are distinguished from other rodents by their bushy tails and unique skull features, including premolar teeth. Squirrels were originally known by the Old English word, ācweorna, until the Middle English period, after which it was replaced by the word 'squirrel' from the Latin word, sciurus, meaning 'shadow-tailed', referring to the long bushy tail.

Squirrel DNA studies have shown that the most ancient squirrel is the pygmy tree squirrel of South America and the giant tree squirrel of South Asia. The Indian giant tree squirrel is considered to be one of the most beautiful squirrels in the world. With a coat of dark maroon and black on its back and tail, contrasting cream-coloured legs and tail tip, and distinctive maroon ear tufts, it could be the poster child of rodent fashion[5].

An astounding 278 species of squirrels exist worldwide. This diverse family encompasses tree squirrels, ground squirrels (such as chipmunks and prairie dogs), and flying squirrels. Tree and ground squirrels live and nest in trees, while ground squirrels live in underground burrows. They live in a wide range of habitats, from lush tropical rainforests to arid deserts, avoiding only the harshest polar regions and the driest deserts. Native to the Americas, Eurasia, and Africa, squirrels were later introduced to Australia by humans[7].

Squirrels come in a wide range of sizes, from the tiny African pygmy squirrel, which is as small as your palm (10 to 14 centimetres in length), to the enormous Bhutan giant flying squirrel, which can grow as long as a ten-year-old child (4 feet). Even larger are several marmot species—the grey marmot native to Siberia and Kazakhstan can weigh over 8 kilograms. The largest flying squirrel is the woolly flying squirrel found in northwestern India and Pakistan. The Himalayan marmot is the only squirrel living high in the mountains at elevations of 4,000 to 5,000 metres above sea level. The best known species is the groundhog, in whose honour the United States and Canada observe Groundhog Day on 2 February every year. If a groundhog emerges from its burrow on this day and see its shadow, winter will go on for six more weeks; if it does not see its shadow, spring will arrive early[7].

Apart from the Indian palm squirrel, the one with three stripes on its back commonly found in cities, India is home to about forty species of squirrels including sixteen flying squirrels[8] and three rare giant squirrels. Most of the flying squirrel species are found in northeast India, and two in south India. The Travancore flying squirrel, one of the rarest squirrel species in India, was thought to be extinct till the 1980s, when it was rediscovered in a Kerala coconut field[9]. Among the three giant squirrels, the Indian giant squirrel is found only in India. This colourful marvel, often referred to as the 'shekru' in Marathi, is the state animal of Maharashtra. Its coat can vary widely, ranging from burgundy and maroon to black and cream, depending on its location and individual variations. The black giant squirrel or Malayan giant squirrel is predominantly found in northeast India. It is easily recognizable by its dark brown or black upper parts and lighter underparts. The grizzled giant squirrel is the rarest and smallest of the three giant squirrel species found in India. Its distinctive grey-brown coat is speckled with white hairs, giving it a grizzled appearance[10].

Squirrels have some unique features that helps them adapt to their habitat. Both flying squirrels and scaly-tailed squirrels have developed remarkable adaptations for gliding. This extraordinary ability is bestowed by the patagium, a thin, stretchy skin flap that connects their front and back legs. By spreading their limbs and flattening their bodies, they can glide gracefully through the air, covering long distances in a single leap. One of the most striking features of tree squirrels is that they can descend trees headfirst by rotating their ankles 180 degrees, allowing their hind feet to grip the bark from the opposite direction. No other mammal in the world has the ability to do this. If a human had to attempt this movement, they would have to stand on their tiptoes, rotate the ankles so that the soles of the feet face each other, then keep rotating them until the soles of the feet face forwards without moving the rest of the leg. Many tree squirrels have yellow-tinted eye lenses. These lenses act as sunglasses, and reduce the glare of the sunlight and increase the contrast between colours. This gives them clear sharp vision, essential for their life in trees[7].

The squirrel's bushy tail is as functional as it is stylish. For protection, a squirrel can wrap its tail around its body to shield itself from the elements, whether it's rain, snow, or the chill of night. In warmer weather, the tail can be used to regulate body temperature. By increasing blood flow to the tail, a squirrel can lower its body temperature and effectively cool down. The tail also plays a crucial role in balance. As a squirrel leaps through the trees, its tail acts as a counterbalance, helping it maintain stability. The bushy nature of the tail can also function as a makeshift parachute, slowing a squirrel's descent if it happens to fall. Squirrels use their tails as a form of communication. A rapid flicking of the tail three times in succession is a clear warning signal, alerting nearby squirrels to potential danger, such as a predator. Other squirrels are always vigilant for this signal, and their alertness increases upon observing it[11].

Male squirrels are veritable Casanovas, mating with several females during the mating season. Typically, squirrels mate once or twice a year, and after a brief gestation period, they give birth to a litter of tiny, furless bundles of joy. The timing of their breeding season depends on the weather and food availability. So, while most squirrels have their babies between late December and late August, there are exceptions. You might find a squirrel mom nursing her young as early as mid-February or as late as mid-November[12].

The female squirrel, ever the industrious builder, constructs a cozy nest called a drey. This is where her babies, known as kittens, will be born. When they arrive, they're completely helpless—no fur, no teeth, and no vision. After about two weeks, their skin starts to darken, and tiny hairs begin to appear on their backs. Within three weeks, they're fully covered in fur and look like miniature adults[12].

Squirrels are fiercely protective of their offspring. The mother squirrel is the sole caretaker, providing warmth, food and protection. If threatened by predators or disturbed by humans, a mother squirrel will do everything in her power to defend her young. She might even move her kittens to a different drey, a safer location away from danger. However, many young squirrels succumb to the challenges of their first year. Those who make it, are ready to start their own families by their first birthday. Adult squirrels can survive for five to ten years in the wild, with some reaching ten to twenty years in captivity[12].

Humans and squirrels may seem worlds apart, but they share a common trait: the urge to hoard. While hoarding in humans is considered problematic, it's a vital survival skill for squirrels. A single squirrel can bury up to 3,000 nuts in a season in a process known as caching. As winter approaches, these animals go into overdrive, searching and collecting food to survive the cold season. Unlike other small mammals whose brains shrink as winter approaches, squirrels brains actually expand during this time! It's a fascinating adaptation that helps them navigate the challenges of winter, and remember where they hid all their nuts[13].

Squirrels take their food storage very seriously. They don't just bury nuts randomly; they have a well-thought-out plan. They have two ways to store their food. In larder hoarding, they stash all their food in one place, making it easier to remember. However, this can be risky, as other animals might find it. Some squirrel species opt for a more scattered hoarding approach. They bury nuts in many different locations. This is safer, but they need to remember where they put everything. These squirrels seem to have developed a system to help them recall the exact spots where they've hidden their treasures. They have an impressive geographic understanding of their area, and can use visual cues to find their food[13].

Grey squirrels in particular have great memory of their surroundings[14]. They can remember up to twenty-four locations where they stored food, for as long as two months. They are able to recover a remarkable 95 per cent of the nuts they bury. They can also locate buried nuts by their odour. This ability is important for their survival, as it allows them to efficiently retrieve their stored food. Studies have shown that lab-reared squirrels can use landmarks, like bushes and trees, to navigate to their hidden stores of food. Squirrels can also memorize specific tree routes, typically the fastest route to and from their favourite feeding place. The BBC documentary

Daylight Robbery showed wild squirrels mastering a complicated obstacle course to reach food.

Some squirrels, though, seem to forget about half of their stashes. This seemingly forgetful behaviour actually has a positive impact on the environment. Forgotten nuts and acorns often grow into new trees, helping to replenish forests and expand their range. It's still a mystery whether squirrels genuinely forget about some of their food stores or simply abandon them in favour of easier-to-find food. Regardless, their absent-mindedness plays a crucial role in the ecosystem[15].

A 2017 study further revealed the impressive memory capabilities of squirrels. In the experiment, lab-reared squirrels were presented with a puzzle box that required them to manipulate the correct levers to obtain hazelnuts. After twenty-two months, the squirrels were given a new puzzle box with a different shape, colour and lever layout. Despite the changes, the solution to the puzzle remained the same. To the scientist's amazement, the squirrels immediately applied the strategy they had learned two years earlier. This showed their remarkable ability to remember information for a long time[13].

Just like humans, squirrels have distinct personalities. Some are bold and active, while others are shy and quiet. Researchers at the University of California, Davis, studied squirrels to learn more about their personalities. They observed squirrels' behaviour in various scenarios—placing them in a confined space, showing them their reflection, approaching them in the wild, and capturing them gently in a trap. They found that bolder squirrels were generally more active, aggressive and sociable. They also covered more ground and were more successful in gathering food compared to their shyer, less active counterparts. Understanding squirrel personalities could be crucial for predicting how these animals will respond to changes in their environment, such as habitat destruction[16].

Just like human children, young squirrels love to play! This playful behaviour may be solitary or social. Solitary play involves activities like running, jumping and tumbling. Squirrels might even engage in playful fights with twigs and leaves. Social play, on the other hand, is all about interaction. Siblings and friends may wrestle, chase, and box each other, strengthening their bonds and learning important social cues. Research suggests that play is essential for a squirrel's physical and social development. It helps them improve their motor skills, build strong bones, and enhance their lung capacity. Additionally, social play can establish hierarchies and strengthen relationships, setting the stage for successful adult life[5].

Squirrels are incredibly adaptable creatures, thriving in a wide range of habitats. From lush tropical rainforests to arid deserts, you can find squirrels making themselves at home almost everywhere, except for the coldest polar regions and the driest deserts. However, at one time, they almost went extinct in New York, where these animals have a long entwined history[5].

In the 1700s, grey squirrels were abundant in New York's forest. Later that century, as their populations surged, the state of Pennsylvania announced a bounty of three pence per squirrel. Many men quit their jobs and went squirrel hunting. They used the Kentucky long rifle developed referred to as the 'squirrel rifle' by the pioneers. The hunt cost the Pennsylvania treasury a whopping 8,000 pounds sterling[5]. Even today, many states have squirrel seasons for hunting that run from September to January, with some states including a limited spring season.

Squirrels were also commonly sold in markets and popularly kept as pets by wealthy citizens of America. Portraits of well-to-do children proudly displayed their reserved, upper-class squirrel companions, tethered to gold chains. An 1851 book *Domestic Pets: Their Habits and Management*, highlights their beauty, agility, and playful habits such as leaping around rooms and peering out from eaves. The book describes how squirrels could be trained to perform tricks, like jumping between hands or responding to their names. There's also a story of a squirrel hoarding an impressive number of treats, including sugar lumps and nuts, in the cornice of a drawing room[17].

In the nineteenth century, rapid deforestation and urbanization posed a significant threat to squirrel populations. These changes in their habitat should have spelled doom for New York City squirrels. Their presence had become such a novelty that when a pet squirrel escaped, it attracted hundreds of curious onlookers. *The New York Daily Times* once reported on an 'unusual visitor' spotted in a downtown tree, causing quite a stir among the locals[18].

In the 1870s, with squirrel population on the decline, a few grey squirrels were introduced to Central Park. With an abundance of nuts, trees, and winter nesting boxes provided by the city, these squirrels quickly thrived. Visitors were even encouraged to feed them peanuts, further contributing to their population growth. By the 1880s, Central Park was home to at least 1,500 squirrels. Unfortunately, their booming numbers led to problems, as the squirrels began destroying trees to build their nests. Despite opposition from the American Society for the Prevention of Cruelty to Animals, the city organized early-morning squirrel hunts to control the population. It was a controversial solution, but it helped to manage the squirrel population in Central Park[18].

By the late nineteenth century, the feeding and care of municipal squirrels in Central Park had become a social issue, often seen as a metaphor for broader societal responsibilities, particularly towards the poor. The squirrels, as small, vulnerable creatures, were seen as a symbol of those who needed protection and support. Squirrels served as moral educators, especially for children. Feeding squirrels was often seen as a way to foster humane behaviour and compassion. Marian Longfellow, niece of H.W. Longfellow, wrote a poem titled,

'Pensioner in Gray' which was published in the children's magazine *St. Nicholas* in 1908. The poem's theme was that the squirrel is as deserving of charity as humans[18].

In 1967, a particularly abundant acorn harvest along the East Coast led to a remarkable event: the Great Squirrel Migration. Driven by the need to find more storage space for their plentiful food, squirrels embarked on a mass exodus. These adventurous rodents were spotted swimming across the Connecticut River and other bodies of water, demonstrating their remarkable adaptability. Unfortunately, the migration also resulted in a tragic toll, with countless squirrels becoming roadkill or drowning. In a single New York reservoir, over 100,000 drowned squirrels were recovered[18].

In the 1980s, as human-squirrel interactions became more frequent, there was a shift in the attitude towards squirrels. Parks began posting 'No Feeding' signs to discourage people from providing food to these furry creatures. This approach aimed to reduce the potential for conflict and to encourage squirrels to rely on natural food sources, and live out life 'as nature intended'. Additionally, natural predators, such as birds of prey, were welcomed in order to control squirrel populations[19].

The grey squirrel has a similar history in the UK. In 1876, Victorian landowners shipped the first grey squirrels from North America. The native red squirrel was considered a pest to forestry and actively hunted by 'squirrel destruction clubs' in the eighteenth and nineteenth century in the UK. Later the red squirrel found a champion in Beatrix Potter. In her acclaimed children's book series, *The Tale of Squirrel Nutkin*, published in August 1903, Potter immortalized the red squirrel's mischievous adventures. The story follows the daring exploits of 'Nutkin' as he tests his luck with the Old Brown Owl. Inspired by Potter's observations of squirrels during a summer holiday at the Lingholm estate in the Lake District in 1901, this charming tale helped to popularize the red squirrel and shed a more positive light on this often misunderstood creature[20].

But the red squirrel population continued to decline and was replaced by invasive grey squirrels. Concerns about their decline led to unique campaigns such as the 'Save Our Squirrels' campaign, launched in 2006. To combat the threat posed by invasive grey squirrels, the campaign encouraged people to consume grey squirrel meat. With the slogan 'Save a red, eat a grey!', the campaign sought to create a market for culled grey squirrels, reducing their population and thereby benefiting the native red squirrels[21]. In 2017, thousands of volunteers came together to form the Red Squirrels United to cull the grey squirrel. This campaign was the largest programme to eliminate an invasive species in Europe, supported by more than thirty conservation groups[22].

Despite the mercurial relationship with humans, their independent nature and fortitude has been extolled in several poems such as 'The Squirrel and the Mountain' by Ralph Waldo Emerson, 'An Appointment' by W.B. Yeats and 'In Springtime' by Rudyard Kipling. And then there are some that have been immortalized through letters and poetry. In January 1772, while residing in Britain, Benjamin Franklin, the founding father of the US, gifted a grey squirrel to a daughter of a bishop, Jonathan Shipley. The daughter, Georgina, named the squirrel Mungo, who lived on the Shipley country estate. However, in September 1772, Mungo met an untimely demise at the paws of the Shipley estate dog[23].

Franklin went on to include an elegy to celebrate Mungo's life:

Alas! poor *Mungo*!
Happy wert thou, hadst thou known
Thy own Felicity!
Remote from the fierce Bald-Eagle,

Tyrant of thy native Woods,
Thou hadst nought to fear from his piercing Talons;
Nor from the murdering Gun

....

Too soon, alas! didst thou obtain it,
And, wandering,
Fell by the merciless Fangs,
Of wanton, cruel Ranger.
Learn hence, ye who blindly wish more Liberty,
Whether Subjects, Sons, Squirrels or Daughters,
That apparent *Restraint* may be real *Protection*,
Yielding Peace, Plenty, and Security.

And who can forget that charming sabre-tooth squirrel in the *Ice Age* film series? The clumsy squirrel, named Scrat, ended up causing catastrophic events with his obsession for collecting acorns. Another famous squirrel who became a bit of a celebrity in the US, was an eastern grey squirrel, Tommy Tucker[24]. Tommy led a luxurious life, rivalling many Hollywood and Bollywood divas. He was adopted in 1942 by Dr Bullis and his wife, who dressed him in fashionable dresses and jewellery. In 2014, the story of Tommy was featured in *Time* magazine. The article titled 'A Squirrel's Guide to Fashion' noted that Tommy had thirty specially made costumes, including a 'coat and hat for going to market, a silk pleated dress for company, a Red Cross uniform for visiting the hospital'. If Tommy had been alive today, he would probably be an Instagram influencer, and have his own line of fashion merchandise.

Duke University in North Carolina had its fair share of squirrel celebrities. In the 1930s, Pee Wee the Squirrel was a frequent visitor to the offices of the Duke University Press. He became a campus legend, often captured in photographs enjoying his midday meals. In 1966, the university security division chief W.C.A. Bear had an encounter with another squirrel which he recounted in a letter to the director of operations. He found the squirrel resting after having torn and consumed a number of packaged goodies. He then arranged for a photographer and reporter to document the 'theft' and noted that this was the first vending machine thief he personally apprehended[25].

While squirrels were persecuted in the US and UK, in other parts of Europe, they were exploited for the purpose of trade and commerce. In the fourteenth century, squirrel fur, particularly from northern Russia, became highly sought after in Europe. Russian towns like Novgorod developed economies centred around the trade of this valuable commodity. Squirrel fur served as a form of currency in Novgorod, collected as tax or rent. Merchants exchanged food, clothing and silver for squirrel skins, which they then sold in European markets. The significance of squirrel fur extended beyond Russia, as it was also used as currency in Finland. The modern Finnish word for money, 'rahaa' originally meant 'squirrel skins'. Even today, North American Inuit tribes use the fur of the Artic ground squirrel to make coats and boots[5].

In India, the tails of squirrels are in demand to make brushes for painting and cosmetics. In Rajasthan, northern palm squirrels are captured in the spring. Their long tail hairs are carefully removed, and the squirrels are then released back into the wild. The collected hairs are selected and bundled into a thin tube called a ferrule. These bundles are adjusted to create a suitable brush shape, then glued in place. Finally, a handle is attached to the other end of the ferrule, completing the artist's brush[5].

Besides the fur and tail, squirrel meat is also popular in some cultures. It was once a common ingredient in the original recipe for Brunswick stew, a popular dish in southern United States. Other regional stews such as burgoo were also traditionally based on squirrel meat. Native Americans hunted squirrels and ate them. The Hopi and Navajo tribes have recipes for baked Prairie dogs. Marmots are also hunted because of their large size and are popular among those who like to eat wild game. In Mongolia, squirrel hunts are conducted on horseback and are a popular pastime.

Squirrels are proving to be valuable subjects for medical research. Scientists at the Institute of Arctic Biology at the University of Alaska are studying the physiology of hibernation in Arctic ground squirrels. During deep hibernation, blood flow to the heart, brain and lungs of these squirrels is significantly reduced by 90 per cent. Remarkably, despite this drastic decrease, the squirrels experience no tissue, muscle or nerve damage. Given that heart attacks and strokes in humans can also result in reduced blood flow, researchers hope that by unravelling the secrets of squirrel hibernation, they can develop treatments for these conditions as well as neurodegenerative diseases[5].

Squirrels even play a crucial role in law enforcement. A unique training program in southwestern China has successfully trained a team of six Eurasian red squirrels to detect drugs! As part of a national initiative, the squirrels were taught to signal the presence of drugs by scratching. Their ability to navigate tight spaces and a keen sense of smell to sniff out illicit substances and detect drugs hidden within packages makes them ideal for this unusual task[26].

Like a puppy who likes to cut its teeth on shoes, squirrels are infamous for gnawing on cables, wires, garden chairs and crops. In North America, some ground squirrels are considered as agricultural pests as they are known to damage many grain crops. Belding's ground squirrel caused damages worth $400 per hectare by feeding on alfalfa crops in Northern California. In 1953, squirrels in Mississippi knocked out twenty transformers in a month. In 1969, a single squirrel caused $1 million in damages to an electrical substation in Pennsylvania when it ventured into a generator, causing explosions and fire. Between 1983 and '84, it was reported that there were 579 squirrel related electrical outages in Washington D.C.[5].

Prairie dogs are also vilified by ranchers in the US. Ranchers claim that they compete with livestock for food and their burrowing poses a danger to machinery and farm animals. At the beginning of the twentieth century, prairie dogs were killed by the thousands with the support of the US government. Today, very few prairie dogs remain in the US. Biologists say the damage caused by them were overstated and are attempting to gain protection for these species[5].

While grey squirrels are abhorred, their cousins, the white squirrels seem to have caught the imagination of Americans. These squirrels have snow-white fur and pink paws as a result of a recessive gene that limits pigmentation. The residents of Olney, Illinois, proudly call themselves the 'White Squirrel Capital of the World.' With a population of over 8,000 white squirrels, this town is home to the largest known colony of these adorable creatures. These squirrels have the right of way on every street! Hit one, and you'll face a hefty $500 fine. To show their love for their furry friends, the Olney Police Department even features a white squirrel on their officers' uniform patches[27].

White squirrels aren't just a quirky phenomenon in Olney, Illinois. They've made their presence felt on university campuses across North America too. One such campus is the University of North Texas at Austin, where a white squirrel population has sparked a fascinating superstition. According to the myth, spotting an albino squirrel before an exam is a surefire way to ace it. This legend has taken on various forms over the years, but the core belief remains the same: the white squirrel is a lucky charm[28]. The University has also established the Albino Squirrel Preservation Society in 2001. This society has since gained global recognition, with chapters springing up around the world.

In India, the Indian palm squirrel, once a common sight in cities, is now facing a decline in population. As urban development continues to encroach on their natural habitat, these adorable creatures are losing their homes. Their wild cousins also face numerous challenges. The Malayan giant squirrel, a crucial indicator of forest health, is facing an alarming decline. A recent study by the Zoological Survey of India predicted a 90 per cent drop in their population by 2050, potentially leading to their extinction in the country if urgent conservation measures aren't taken. These majestic creatures, native to India's Northeast, are threatened by habitat loss and other factors, highlighting the urgent need for their protection[29].

Recognizing the threats to giant squirrels, the Kerala Forest Department has taken some measures. The have constructed bamboo canopy bridges along the Marayoor-Udumalpetta Road to save the giant grizzled squirrel. This innovative solution was implemented to prevent tragic road accidents involving wildlife, including the majestic giant squirrels. The first such bridge was erected at the Chinnar Wildlife Sanctuary. These elevated pathways serve as safe corridors for giant squirrels and other animals, reducing human-wildlife conflict and ensuring their long-term survival[30].

Whether we find them endearing or a nuisance, there's no denying the enduring appeal of squirrels. To celebrate their unique charm, 21 January has been designated as National Squirrel Appreciation Day worldwide. This nimble acrobat, is a creature of contrasts—a hoarder and sharer, solitary and social, just like us. Behind the playful antics lies a more serious task. By dispersing seeds, they play an important role in our ecosystems, as 'gardeners of our landscape'. Who wouldn't want such an adorable gardener, even if it means losing a few tomatoes?

CHAPTER 6

THE RAT

THERE'S something primal about rats, a fear that runs deep in our collective psyche. They've been our literary and cinematic antagonists for centuries, their presence often signalling impending doom or moral decay. In Arthur Conan Doyle's story 'The Adventure of the Sussex Vampire', Sherlock Holmes mentions the 'Giant Rat of Sumatra' as a creature so horrifying that even he, the world's greatest detective, shies away from discussing it. It's a tale, he claims, that the world isn't ready to hear. The master of horror Stephen King depicts a character enjoying a cold hamburger just moments before a gruesome encounter with a swarm of rats in his book *Graveyard Shift*. The juxtaposition of pleasure and impending horror is chilling, and masterfully created[1].

George Orwell's dystopian classic, *1984*, employs rats as a tool of psychological torture. Winston Smith, the protagonist, has a primal fear of rats due to a recurring nightmare. The fear is used against him as a potent weapon by the authoritarian regime. His torturer confronts him with a cage full of starving rats, playing on his fear, to compel him to give in to avoid being devoured alive.

George Orwell's fascination with rats extends far beyond the pages of *1984*. His personal experiences and writings reveal a deep-seated fascination with these creatures that often serves as a metaphor for the darker aspects of human nature. In his memoir of the Spanish Civil War, *Homage to Catalonia*, Orwell writes about the Fascist regime, 'If their machine-gunners spotted you, you had to flatten yourself out like a rat when it squirms under a door.' This imagery draws a parallel between the vulnerable human being and the scurrying rodent, both seeking to survive in a hostile environment[2].

Orwell's letters also reveal a more fascinating side to his interest in rats. In a letter from Suffolk in 1921, he describes the pleasure he takes in trapping and shooting rats. 'It is also rather sport to go at night to a corn-stack with an acetylene bicycle lamp, & you can dazzle the rats that are running along the side & whack at them, or shoot them with a rifle.' This could perhaps be a reflection of the violence and cruelty he had witnessed in his life, writes D.J. Taylor in his biography, *Orwell: The Life* (2003). He argues that Orwell's obsession with rats can be seen as a symptom of his broader interest in exploring the complexities of human nature. Rats, with their adaptability, cunning, and often-repulsive appearance, serve as a powerful metaphor for the darker aspects of humanity[2].

If you have ever looked up 'rat' in a thesaurus, you'll find a whole bunch of unsavoury synonyms: tattlers, tattletales, betrayer, and turncoats. For instance, take Scabbers, the rat, aka Peter Pettigrew, the seemingly innocent pet of Ron Weasley. He turned out to be a total turncoat, once best friends with Harry Potter's father and the good wizards, Sirius Black and Lupin, but later betraying and switching loyalties to the evil wizard, Voldemort's camp.

This less-than-stellar reputation comes from serious health risks they pose, as rats carry dangerous viruses and bacteria and transmit numerous diseases. The fourteenth century plague, known as Black

Death, was caused by rat-borne fleas, which claimed the lives of millions of people. From the medieval plague to the modern-day laboratory, the rat has played a significant role in shaping human history. It has been both villain and victim, a bane and a boon to our species. Rats are the poster child for filth and disease, a nocturnal nuisance whose scattering and shrieking sounds disturb the peace of the night. Despite their negative portrayal, the rat possesses qualities that are worthy of admiration. For one, the rat is a survivor with its ability to navigate complex environments with ease, and its knack for finding food in the most unlikely of places.

Rats always seem to be in a hurry, scurrying away to some unknown destination. Perhaps that's how the term rat race came about—people hurrying to get somewhere, with no clear destination or goal. I suppose, we've all been rats in our own way … gym rats, club rats, lab rats. Back in the day, I was a young lab rat (pun intended) myself, trained to work not with rats but with their tinier cousins—white mice. These mice, smaller than my palm, would scurry timidly around their cages. The rats in the lab, on the other hand, were like mini-dogs, scratching away at their cages like they owned the place. I was grateful that I did not have to work with them.

Although their presence is unsettling, they still have a place in our homes, albeit only on the auspicious day of Ganesh Chaturthi. Many Hindus pay homage to this little creature, the faithful steed of the Hindu god, Ganesha, the remover of obstacles. According to the Hindu scripture, the Matsya Purana, Ganesha's rat was originally a heavenly singer named Krauncha. The story goes that one day as Indra, the king of the gods, held court, he summoned Krauncha to approach him. As Krauncha rushed from his seat, he accidentally stepped on the foot of a sage named Vamadeva. The furious sage cursed Krauncha to turn into a giant rat! As Mushak, the giant rat, he wreaked havoc on the land, destroying crops and causing all sorts of trouble. One day, Mushak stumbled upon the hermitage of Sage Parashar. Little did he know, Lord Ganesha was also there. The lord, tired of Mushak's antics, decided to teach him a lesson. After a fierce battle, Mushak finally realized the error of his ways. With a humbled heart, he surrendered to Lord Ganesha and begged to be his vehicle. And so, Mushak became the loyal companion we know of today.

Across the world, rats are associated with several myths. In ancient Greece and Rome, rats were actually considered symbols of prosperity! Since rats are found in places with plenty of food, a rat infestation meant a bountiful harvest. The obscure and mysterious Greek god, Arimanius, associated with darkness, akin to Hades, the God of the underworld, had a preference for water rats, making them his chosen creatures. In Japan, there's a god named Daikoku who is the deity of wealth and farming. He's always pictured surrounded by rats, and piles of riches and other symbols of prosperity. In Japan, rats are seen as symbols of hard work, fertility, and good luck, and are therefore associated with the god of wealth[3].

In France, a fifteenth century bishop put a formal curse on rats. He supposedly took inspiration from the ancient Indian text, the Atharva Veda, in which a prayer extols Ashwini, the Hindu god of medicine, to destroy rodents: 'O Ashwini, kill the burrowing rodents, which devastate our food grains, slice their hearts, break their necks, plug their mouths, so they cannot destroy our food'.[4] South African warriors believed that weaving rat hair into their own hair would give them the agility and stealth of a rat, helping them evade enemy spears.

In the Chinese zodiac, the rat, a clever and resourceful creature, is known for its curiosity and imagination. According to a popular tale, the Jade Emperor decided to rank the animals based on their speed and agility. The first twelve animals to cross a river would be assigned a year in the Chinese zodiac calendar. Recognizing its limitations due to its size, the rat proposed a partnership with the strong ox: the rat would navigate while the ox carried it across the river. The plan worked perfectly until they neared the shore. With a quick leap, the rat jumped off the ox's back and sprinted to the finish line, securing the first position. The ox came in second, followed by the other animals[3]. As the first animal of the twelve year cycle, the rat is believed to herald a new dawn. Those born under its sign are often seen as quick-witted, and effortlessly adaptable to life's twists and turns[5].

The term 'rat' typically refers to rodents in the genus Rattus, including the common brown and black rats. These medium-sized creatures have thin tails and are native to Asia, Southeast Asia, and Australia. Rats are adaptable creatures that can thrive in various environments. While some species prefer the wilderness, like forests and meadows, others have adapted to living near humans. These opportunistic rodents can be found on every continent except Antarctica, as they seek out places with food, water and shelter. Rats have developed remarkable adaptations based on the habitat they live in. Their coat colour often mirrors their environment, providing camouflage against visual predators. This pattern has evolved repeatedly, with dark coats appearing on rats living on dark substrate, and light coats in rats living in sandy deserts. Aquatic rodents, like marsh rats and fish-eating rats, have developed webbed feet and furry tails for efficient swimming. Mole rats, adapted for burrowing, have reduced eyes, ears, tails and fur, but powerful claws[6].

Rats are breeding machines, churning out multiple litters a year, each litter teeming with tiny, squirming offspring. These social creatures thrive in the company of their kin. They groom and sleep together, forming strong family bonds. If separated from the colony, a rat's stress levels increases. However, they can be territorial and aggressive towards unfamiliar rats[6].

The most common rat species found living near humans are the house or black rat (*Rattus rattus*), Wroughton's or brown rat (*Rattus norvegicus*), and the bandicoot rats (*Bandicota bengalensis* and *Bandicota indica*). These species are major pests, causing major economic damage, contaminating food supplies, damaging crops, and destroying electrical equipment. Rats continue to threaten human health, transmitting diseases like leptospirosis, Lyme disease, and salmonellosis through direct contact or contaminated environments.

Rat infestations are a serious issue in all major cities around the world. In Mumbai, leptospirosis has claimed seventy lives in Mumbai since 2015, surpassing the death toll from both dengue and malaria[7]. To combat this relentless menace, the city wages a nightly war. A dedicated army of rat killers, hired by the civic body, prowls the streets under the cloak of darkness, killing a total of about 1,000 rats each night. Around fourteen of Mumbai's twenty-four wards are under constant surveillance by these nocturnal hunters. Each day, the killed rodents are collected and transported to a facility in Parel, where they are meticulously counted and recorded. A select few are dissected to detect the presence of yersinia pestis, the insidious bacteria responsible for the dreaded plague.

New York City, renowned for its large rat population, even appointed a rat czar in 2023 to address the problem[8]. In 2024, Katie, a four year old dog in New York rose to fame for having killed nearly 500 rats in the year. In Chicago, named the rattiest city in America, an animal shelter has introduced over 1,000 sterilized and vaccinated feral cats to homes and businesses since 2012. These cats act as natural deterrents, hunting and catching rats while their mere presence scares them away[9].

The city of Alberta in Canada is perhaps the only one that has managed to get rid of rats since 1950 when the Rat Control Program was established. There is no resident rat population, however when the city does get an occasional infestation of rats, they are immediately identified, isolated and eradicated[10].

The brown rat, also known as the common rat, Norway rat, Norwegian rat, or wharf rat, is one of the most familiar and largest rat species. The brown rat originated in China, and made its way to Southeast Asia during the southward migration of people between 800 and 1550 CE. Eventually it spread globally, through trading ships, becoming the dominant rat species in Europe and much of North America[11].

Genetic adaptation likely played a role in the spread and adaptation of rats to urban areas. By comparing the genetic makeup of New York City rats to their Chinese ancestors, researchers have uncovered significant genetic differences. These changes, particularly in genes linked to diet, behaviour and movement, suggest that urban rats have evolved to thrive in our concrete jungles[12].

Despite their role as disease carriers, rats ironically serve as invaluable models in biomedical research. Laboratory mice and rats have been instrumental in studying virtually every human disease. In 1895, Clark University in Worcester, Massachusetts, established a population of domestic white rats through selective breeding of the brown rat for scientific research. Over time, several rat strains such as the Wistar rat, Sprague Dawley, Holtzman albino strains, and the Long-Evans, have been established. These have been used in numerous experimental studies, advancing our knowledge of genetics, diseases and drug effects, that have significantly improved human health and well-being[13].

Naked mole rats, while less commonly known than brown rats, are increasingly used in medical research. Their unique underground lifestyle, where they are exposed to high levels of carbonic acid, (formed from the reaction of carbon dioxide with moisture), has led to an extraordinary adaptation: insensitivity to acid. This resilience to an acidic environment could offer insights into human conditions involving inflammation, such as arthritis, where localized acidity often occurs. By understanding how naked mole rats tolerate acid, researchers may uncover new ways to manage pain associated with these conditions[14].

Another intriguing aspect of naked mole rats is their remarkable resistance to cancer. While their healthy cells transform to cancerous cells with age, just as in mice or humans, cancer cases are much rarer in these rodents. This is because mutations in naked mole rat DNA occur at a much slower rate than in mouse DNA. Additionally, it's possible that naked mole rats possess a highly effective immune system capable of identifying and eliminating cancerous cells. These findings suggest that naked mole rats could be valuable models for studying human diseases like cancer and inflammation, and the development of new treatments[14].

Amami spiny rats, endemic to the subtropical forests of Amami Oshima Island in Japan, have provided clues to the gradual shrinking of the Y chromosome in many mammals, including humans. One of the most intriguing aspects of Amami spiny rats is their unusual chromosomal arrangement. Unlike most mammals, both male and female spiny rats possess only a single X chromosome. This phenomenon is relatively rare among rodents and has significant implications for sex determination. In Amami spiny rats, the Y chromosome has been lost entirely. This loss has also resulted in the disappearance of the SRY gene, which is considered the 'master switch' for male development in many mammals. Surprisingly, the rat's other chromosomes have evolved to take over this role[15].

Research has further revealed that other genes involved in male rat development have not been lost but have moved from the Y chromosome to other chromosomes. This suggests that the genetic mechanisms underlying male development can be more flexible than previously thought. The story of the Amami spiny rat offers a glimmer of hope for human males, especially given the discovery that the human Y chromosome has lost 1,393 of its original 1,438 genes over the past 300 million years and is steadily diminishing[16].

Rats are eerily similar to us humans. They have a sense of what they know, get tickled and even have imagination. A study from the University of Georgia shows that rats can think about what they know and what they don't know. This finding challenges the long-held assumption that only humans and primates have this ability[17].

The researchers conducted experiments where rats were presented with a sound, and they had to determine if it was short or long. Some sounds were easier to distinguish and others more difficult. The rats were rewarded for a correct answer, but faced the risk of no reward if they made incorrect guesses. They were also given a choice of declining the test for which they received a smaller reward than that for a correct guess. The study revealed that the rats were more likely to decline difficult tests. They seemed to know when they wouldn't be able to solve a problem, so they chose easier tasks instead to maximize their rewards.

Rats can remember places they've been and imagine going to new places. Scientists at Janelia Research Campus have created a way to read the thoughts of rats, through a real-time 'thought detector'[18]. They can see what a rat is thinking about by looking at its brain activity, through a brain-machine interface (BMI). The researchers found that rats can control their thoughts in a very precise way. They can focus on a specific place for a long time, just like humans do when they remember or imagine something. This discovery could lead to the creation of better brain-controlled devices, like robotic limbs, that people can control more intuitively and precisely with their thoughts.

Like many other social animals, rats indulge in play and 'laugh' when tickled. Rat laughter is distinct from the other sounds they make. Rats are especially ticklish in their neck area. When young rats playfully pin each other down and tickle the other in this area, they make high-pitched squeaks that sound like laughter. Neuroscientist Jaak Panksepp at Washington State University, found a correlation between ticklishness and playfulness[19]. The more rats laugh, the more playful they are. They even remember those who tickle them and like to play with them again. Though this does not mean that rats have a sense of humour, it only indicates that they can express laughter similar to children having fun while playing.

Although these findings that rats can laugh were initially debated, recent research showed that a rat's laughter is encoded in a part of the rat's brain called the PAG (periaqueductal gray). When scientists at the Humboldt University of Berlin tickled rats on their backs and bellies, they let out delighted shimmying and endless 'giggles'[20]. As they monitored the rats' brain activity, the team observed that when rats are tickled, the PAG part of their brain becomes more active. But when rats are scared or stressed, this part of the brain becomes less active and they stop laughing.

Rats can even engage in complex play behaviour similar to that of humans. In a previous experiment, the same scientists taught rats to play hide-and-seek. One rat was placed in a box while a researcher hid in the room. Upon release, the rat would search for the hidden researcher, receiving a tickle as a reward for success. The rats also could hide effectively, often finding creative hiding spots.

Rats have been shown to be good Samaritans. They have great empathy for their fellow rats, even giving up a reward in favour of helping a rat in trouble. Empathy was till recently only associated with intelligent animals such as dolphins, primates and elephants. A scientist from the University of Chicago conducted an experiment where rats were kept in pairs for two weeks[21]. One rat was then placed in a cage, with the other having the ability to free them by pushing a restraining door. Despite taking a week to learn the technique, the rats consistently freed their partners. When offered chocolate chips, surprisingly, the rats chose to free their cage-mate over seeking food, often sharing their chocolate bounty afterward. In today's material world, this is a quality that is on the decline in humans.

Rats have an incredible sense of smell. They can even pinpoint the exact location of a smell by comparing the signals from each nostril. This amazing ability has led to some surprising uses. For example, a group called APOPO, a Belgian organization, has trained African giant pouched rats to detect tuberculosis (TB) in people's saliva. They were trained to recognize the distinctive smell of TB caused by chemicals known as volatile organic compounds (VOCs). For this, rats were motivated by occasional sips of a banana and avocado smoothie. These trained rats can check a hundred samples in just twenty minutes, while a lab technician might take four days[22].

Rats were domesticated and bred long before they were used in laboratories. The origin of rat breeding can be traced to Japan's Edo period(1603–1868), when they bred fancy rat species. Two breeding guides from the late 1700s, the *Yoso-tama-no-kakehashi* and the *Chinganso-date-gusa*, give details on breeding fancy rats from brown rats. Fancy rats were probably also bred in China around this time or earlier, as hinted by old Chinese stories referenced in the *Yoso-tama-no-kakehashi*[23].

These days, there are even competitions for fancy rats, similar to the ones held for pet dogs and cats. Fancy breeds such as agouti, cinnamon, dumbo, chocolate, mink, russian blue, pearl, and russian blue agouti, are noted for their exquisite fur quality and rare colours. The American Fancy Rat and Mouse Association (AFRMA), a non-profit organization,   hosts competitions in Southern California several times a year, where pet rats are judged based on their coat colour, shine, markings and other features. They also provide information to encourage the breeding and exhibition of fancy rats[24].

In England, France, and later North America, brown rats were bred for sport in rat-baiting events from the early 1800s, with dogs competing to kill the most number of rats. Among the earliest captive rat colonies are those established in 1856 at the Jardin des Plantes in Paris. This colony, consisting of hooded brown rats, was initially created to feed the reptiles housed in the gardens and was maintained until 1988[23].

While rats are abhorred in most places, they form an important part of the socio-cultural fabric of several tribal communities, especially in India. The Adi people, residing in the central part of Arunachal Pradesh, celebrate Aran, an important festival in March. During Aran, they engage in hunting and rodent trapping in forests, with the harvested animals being shared among family, relatives and friends. Prior to the Aran festival, male villagers prepare various indigenous traps using locally sourced bamboo. This practice helps control the rodent population in the region before the planting season, thereby minimizing potential damage to crops[25].

In Adi tradition, rodents play a symbolic role in marriage arrangements, as wedding dates are often decided during Aran. The hunted rats are exchanged and seen as a gesture of goodwill and settlement during the marriage process. Rats are considered to be a messenger between the deities Doying Bote (god of wisdom) and Kine Nani (goddess of agriculture and prosperity).

The Irulas, a Particularly Vulnerable Tribal Group, in Tamil Nadu, consume rat meat, which they cook fresh after capturing rodents in paddy fields. They usually obtain these rats from nearby farmers who hire them to eliminate pests from their fields. Rats steal paddy, ragi (finger millet), or groundnuts and store them in underground tunnels[26].

Rats create intricate tunnel systems, resembling a city's road network, both above and below the ground. These intelligent creatures cleverly close their burrows with mud, making them difficult to detect. To capture them, Irula rat-catchers often work in pairs, although individuals or teams of three may also hunt. They carefully observe and block the entrance with a stone, then dig from the opposite end. If the ground is too hard to dig, they use smoke from burning cow dung to suffocate the rats. Occasionally, rat-catchers encounter baby rats in the tunnels. Many Irula families adopt these young rats as pets and companions[26].

Irula rat-catchers can find up to eight to ten kilos of paddy stored in rat burrows, yielding approximately three kilos of rice. The Irulas have described the rice from rat tunnels as having a distinct earthy aroma and a sweet flavour. Some even use it to make modaks, a sweet dish made with freshly pounded rice flour filled with jaggery and coconut. Rats are known to select mature groundnuts for storage. These groundnuts are prized for their sweetness and can be used to extract oil. So the Irulas look forward to hunting rats in fields planted with groundnuts[26].

In Belize, a former colonial country, indigenous farming communities hunt a native rat, called the gibnut. It's a large rat weighing 30 pounds and growing up to 30 inches in length. In 1985, during a national celebration, Queen Elizabeth II was a guest of honour. At the state banquet, she was presented a rather unusual but unique local delicacy—the gibnut along with other traditional dishes. Since then the gibnut has also been referred to as the royal rat. While it is the unofficial national dish of Belize, and a staple protein source for many indigenous communities, due to its 'bush meat' status, it's less commonly found on the tables of the wealthier population. The gibnut is typically served stewed or grilled, and occasionally makes an appearance on the menu of fancy restaurants[27].

While rats are often portrayed as villains or pests in popular culture, E.B. White's *Charlotte's Web* introduces us to Templeton, a rat who defies this stereotype. Templeton is a complex character, often seen as selfish and unlikable by the other barnyard animals.

However, beneath his gruff exterior lies a surprising depth of loyalty and resourcefulness. Despite his reputation, Templeton plays a crucial role in the story. The other animals rely on him to do their dirty work, and he always comes through, albeit reluctantly. One of Templeton's most significant contributions is his ability to provide the protagonist, Charlotte, the spider, with the words for her messages. By scavenging through the dump, Templeton finds old magazine ads that Charlotte uses to weave her inspiring messages on her web. This unexpected talent showcases a hidden intelligence and creativity that belies his rough exterior.

But the one rat in my opinion that redeemed the reputation of all rats is Remy, the protagonist of *Ratatouille*. Unlike the stereotypical portrayal of rats, Remy is presented as a lovable and intelligent character. His journey to become a renowned chef challenged stereotypes and redefined our perception of both rats and French cuisine. Remy's passion for cooking is fuelled by his admiration for the legendary chef Gustav, whose mantra 'Anyone can cook' inspires him to pursue his dreams. As a rat, Remy is the last creature anyone would expect to see in a kitchen, yet his exceptional culinary skills and unwavering determination allow him to overcome adversity and achieve success.

Ratatouille uses Remy to represent the simple, yet delicious, country-style cooking that had been overlooked by high-end restaurants, and challenges the elitist and prejudiced world of French gastronomy. His presence in the kitchen serves as a reminder that true talent and passion can come from unexpected places, regardless of social status or background. When the movie came out in 2007, I did not consider myself a great cook. Remy's journey and passion in some ways inspired me to look beyond traditional recipes and find other ways of cooking, particularly for my children.

Another lovable fictional rat is Splinter, the adoptive father and mentor to the Teenage Mutant Ninja Turtles. Known for his wisdom, intelligence, and exceptional martial arts skills, his calm demeanour and unwavering determination make him a truly inspiring figure. Splinter's wisdom and guidance are invaluable to the Turtles. He serves as their teacher, philosopher and friend. Even in the face of adversity, Splinter maintains his composure, offering his young charges words of encouragement and support. His ability to remain calm under pressure is a testament to his strong willpower and self-control.

As an elderly martial arts master, Splinter possesses a wealth of knowledge and experience. He trains the Turtles in various martial arts disciplines, equipping them with the skills they need to protect their city. Splinter's teachings extend beyond combat, as he also imparts valuable life lessons about honour, loyalty and perseverance.

In the action-packed superhero film *The Suicide Squad*, rats take centre stage as a crucial element of the team's mission. Ratcatcher II, a supervillain with the ability to control rats, is a unique and compelling character who challenges traditional notions of heroism. Unlike many superhero films, *The Suicide Squad* focuses on a group of anti-heroes, or supervillains forced to work for the government. Ratcatcher II, a second-generation supervillain, brings a surprising depth and vulnerability to the team.

An inflatable rat, often called 'Scabby', has become a recognizable symbol of labour disputes in the United States. These oversized rodents are used by unions to protest companies that employ non-union labour. The first inflatable rat was introduced by the International Union of Operating Engineers Local 150 in Plainfield, Illinois, in 1989. Other unions soon adopted the use of Scabby to draw attention to labour issues. The inflatable rat served as a visual reminder of the union's grievances. By placing Scabby outside a non-union company's workplace, the union aimed to shame the company and encourage it to negotiate with workers[28].

In literature, while most of the early nineteenth century authors used rats to create fear or to symbolize horror, a twenty-first century author spent an entire year studying rats in an alley in New York. Robert Sullivan, the critically acclaimed American author, came across a street, Edens Alley, not far from Wall Street, which was littered with food waste, garbage, and several rat holes. He started making nightly visits to the alley and met with exterminators, sanitation workers and community activists, working on the frontlines of the age-old battle between human and rats. He documented his impressions in the book, *Rats: Observations on the History and Habitat of the City's Most Unwanted Inhabitants.* In his book, he writes 'in New York City, the bulk of rats live in quiet desperation, hiding beneath the table of man, under stress, skittering in fear, under siege by larger rats … Rats live in man's parallel universe, surviving on the effluvia of human society; they eat our garbage.'[29]

There is no doubt that rats are every city's most unwanted inhabitant. Every household and every city goes into 'rat-elimination' mode, as soon as one is spotted. The internet is filled with rat control guides and DIY steps to rid homes of this pest. While many cities have attempted to control rat population, rather unsuccessfully, one city has been making headlines for its innovative approach to urban rat control. Since 2021, Paris has been exploring the possibility of cohabitation with rats, a concept that challenges traditional methods of extermination of these often-maligned creatures[30].

The city has recognized that extermination rarely eradicates rat populations completely. Rats are highly adaptable and reproduce rapidly, making it difficult to eliminate them permanently. Instead, Paris is focusing on managing the rat population through sustainable and humane methods. One key strategy is to improve waste management practices. By properly disposing of garbage, Paris aims to reduce the availability of food and water for rats, limiting their population growth. The city hopes to foster a culture of coexistence (not in homes, but in the city), and promote a more positive attitude towards these creatures.

Whether we like it or not, rats are an integral part of the human ecosystem. While we cannot upend the centuries-old battle between man and rats, perhaps one day both humans and (controlled populations of) rats can thrive in the urban environment without causing harm to each other.

CHAPTER 7

THE FROG

I'VE often pondered on the fate of the countless frogs that met their end in high school biology labs. It was a rite of passage, a gruesome initiation into the world of science. The poor school attendant, a veritable frog-catcher extraordinaire, would scour the nearby ponds, returning with a bag full of quivering amphibians, destined for the dissection table. While some of my classmates revelled in the macabre task, dissecting with the precision of a surgeon, I couldn't shake the feeling of unease. The thought of cutting into a creature, even if it was a tiny frog, filled me with dread. I imagined the animal waking up mid-procedure, its eyes wide with terror, its limbs flailing in a desperate attempt to escape. My worst fears almost came true one fateful day. As I delicately sliced through the frog's skin, I noticed a strange movement. Its front limb began to twitch up and down, almost as if it were dancing to the beat of John Travolta's iconic dance in, *Saturday Night Fever*. My heart pounded in my chest, and I couldn't help but think that the frog had a strong urge for '*Staying Alive*'.

Panic set in, but as I looked closer, I realized my nightmare wasn't quite reality. The frog did not miraculously come alive. I later learnt that the movement was caused by a post-mortem twitch, a result of electrochemical reactions in the nerves. It was a chilling reminder of the strange and often unexpected ways science can manifest itself, even in the most mundane settings.

Frogs, often seen as humble creatures of ponds and marshes, have played a surprisingly significant role in scientific advancement. These amphibians have served as invaluable model organisms, providing insights into fundamental biological processes that have shaped our understanding of life itself. As early as the eighteenth century, scientists began studying frogs to understand their biology and natural history. With the growing knowledge of amphibian reproduction and development, researchers started experimenting with frog embryos, laying the groundwork for future discoveries[1].

Frogs have been at the centre of several Nobel Prize-winning experiments. Their role in shaping the fields of stem cell research and cloning is particularly noteworthy. Scientists John Gurdon and Shinya Yamanaka used frogs to study how cells can be reprogrammed to become stem cells, a breakthrough that has revolutionized regenerative medicine[2]. For this discovery, they jointly won the Nobel Prize for physiology in 2012.

In the early twentieth century, a groundbreaking discovery involving frogs had a profound impact on diagnostics. Scientists Lancelot Hogben, Hillel Shapiro, and Harry Zwasrenstein found that injecting urine from pregnant women into African clawed frogs could induce ovulation[1]. Millions of these frogs were exported to labs worldwide for testing pregnancy. This simple test was widely used from the 1930s to the 1960s. Women, however, had to mail their urine samples to one of these labs, through a doctor, and that too, only if there was an urgent need to know about the pregnancy, and they had to wait for weeks to know the result.

The African clawed frog, belonging to the genus Xenopus, became a global model organism. Humans and Xenopus frogs shared a common ancestor about 360 million years ago. By studying these animals, scientists can trace the evolution of DNA which can help improve the understanding of human biology. These flat brown frogs, with a small fish-like head and webbed toes with claws, can live for up to thirty years. Its ease of breeding, rapid development, and large eggs made it ideal for laboratory studies[3]. From the humble pond to cutting-edge laboratory work, these frogs have made a remarkable contribution to scientific progress. Their unique characteristics and adaptability have made them indispensable tools for researchers, helping to unravel the mysteries of life.

African clawed frogs have helped scientists create the first of its kind living machine. Using a computer algorithm, scientists from Tufts University and the University of Vermont sculpted cells extracted from African clawed frog embryos into unique shapes. These miniature robots, named 'xenobots' after the frog's scientific name *Xenopus laevis*, are roughly the size of a grain of sand, and are capable of surprising feats. They can move around petri dishes, manipulate microscopic objects, and even self-heal after being cut[4].

The potential applications for xenobot technology are vast. With further development, these machines could be used to deliver drugs, clean up environmental pollutants, and perform tasks that traditional robots are unable to accomplish. And best of all, unlike traditional robots, xenobots are biodegradable, leaving no harmful footprint on the planet.

Frogs have held profound symbolic significance in ancient Indian cultures. In Sanskrit texts and the Vedas, they were associated with beauty, aspiration and wisdom. The etymological root of the Mandukya Upanishad, a key text in Hindu philosophy, is the word 'manduka', meaning frog. It is the shortest of the 108 Upanishads but is one of ten principal Upanishads. The Mandukya Upanishad encourages the reader to 'leap like a frog' into a higher state of awareness through meditation and gain enlightenment of the true reality—that we are all the one unchanging consciousness. Several theories exist on the symbolic choice of the frog for the Upanishad. One theory is that the rishi Varuna, to whom the Upanishad was revealed, may have once taken the form of a frog[5]. Swami Sarvapriyananda, head of the Vedanta Society of New York, beautifully elucidates the meaning of the Mandukya Upanishad in his talks. Despite listening to him many times, I haven't yet 'leaped' into awareness. Perhaps I need to appease the frog-gods and seek their blessings to gain enlightenment.

After all, frogs have long been associated with various beliefs and superstitions across India. In the agrarian communities of India, where rainfall is crucial for agricultural prosperity, a unique and fascinating ritual has been practised for centuries: the frog wedding. This ritual, believed to appease Indra, the Hindu rain god, involves marrying two frogs. It is thought that this unusual union will bring forth much-needed rains. The ritual typically involves capturing two frogs, often from a nearby pond or field. A makeshift wedding ceremony is then performed, complete with traditional rituals and blessings. The frogs may be adorned with miniature wedding attire, and vows are exchanged, albeit symbolically[5].

In 2019, a village in India experienced an unexpected consequence of this ritual. The rains, which were intended to alleviate drought, became so torrential that they posed a threat to the community. In a desperate attempt to curb the excess rainfall, the villagers decided to divorce the frogs, believing that this would reverse the effects of the wedding[5]. The frog wedding is a fascinating example of how traditional beliefs and superstitions can shape cultural practices. While the scientific basis for this ritual is debatable, it remains an important part of the cultural heritage of many Indian communities, reflecting their reliance on the monsoon rains for their livelihood.

In some regions, frogs are linked to tantra and dark magic, while in others, they are believed to have an impact on pregnancy. In Kerala, for example, it is said that if a pregnant woman sees a green frog, she may face a higher risk of miscarriage. However, in neighbouring Karnataka, encountering a tree frog during pregnancy is believed to be a sign of good fortune[6].

The Western Ghats of India, a renowned amphibian biodiversity hotspot, is home to the pig-nosed purple frog, an unusual frog with an elongated snout. This unique creature spends most of its life underground, only emerging during the monsoon rains to breed. Its secretive nature and association with thunderstorms have made it a significant part of local folklore and culture. The Nadukani-Moolmattom-Kulamaav tribal people of the Western Ghats have a long-standing tradition of harvesting pig-nosed purple frogs and their tadpoles as a delicacy. This practice, while controversial, reflects the deep connection between these communities and their natural environment. Due to its elusive nature and emergence during stormy weather, the pig-nosed purple frog is often associated with thunder and lightning. In some local beliefs, adult frogs are preserved and made into amulets to protect children from the fear of storms[6].

The elusive pig-nosed purple frog, endemic to Kerala's Western Ghats, is a rarity even among amphibians. Listed as endangered by the IUCN red list, this unique creature spends most of its life underground, emerging only briefly during the monsoon season. Named Mahabali, after the legendary Asura king, it's like a mythical figure of the Western Ghats, appearing annually for a fleeting moment, just as Mahabali rises from the netherworld for Thiruvonam[7].

According to the Katha Sarita Sagara, a classical eleventh century collection of Indian folk tales, the frogs gained their distinctive croaking voice as a result of a divine intervention. The story goes that the gods, concerned about the passionate play between Shiva and Parvati, which threatened to destroy the world, sought help from Agni, the god of fire. Afraid to intervene, Agni fled and took refuge in the waters. However, the frogs, scorched by the heat of Agni's presence, betrayed his location to the gods. As punishment for their betrayal, Agni cursed the frogs, making their speech inarticulate and forcing them to croak. This curse, according to the tale, is the reason why frogs have such a unique and distinctive sound[5].

In South Africa, frogs are often viewed with fear and superstition. There is a widespread belief that they are poisonous and that touching one can cause warts. As a result, frogs are frequently persecuted and killed on sight. However, in some indigenous cultures, frogs may be seen as messengers from ancestors or valuable rainmakers. The Venda people of the Bantu tribe consider them sacred and integral parts of their waterbodies, while the Khoi-San have cave paintings depicting Xenopus species as symbols of fertility[6].

The frog held a profound symbolic significance in ancient Egyptian culture. Ancient Egyptians considered the frog to be a symbol of life creation. It was associated with fertility due to the annual flooding of the Nile River, which brought fertile silt to the otherwise barren lands. As a result, the frog-goddess Heqet emerged as a powerful deity representing fertility and childbirth. Heqet was often depicted as a frog, a woman with a frog's head, or, less commonly, a frog atop a phallus, emphasizing her connection to fertility. She was believed to assist in the birthing process and was invoked to ensure healthy babies[8].

Another lesser-known Egyptian deity, Kek, was sometimes depicted in the form of a frog. He was associated with darkness, the underworld, and the primordial waters. The Ogdoad of Hermopolis, a group of eight primeval gods, were often portrayed with the heads of frogs (male) and serpents (female). This depiction reflects the dual nature of creation, with the frog symbolizing life and fertility, and the serpent representing the earth and its generative powers. The god Nu, associated with the primordial waters, was sometimes depicted with the head of a frog surmounted by a beetle. This combination further emphasizes the frog's connection to creation and the origins of life[8].

Frogs are ancient creatures with a long history on Earth. They have been around for at least 200 million years, since the time of dinosaurs. Soon after the extinction of dinosaurs, three major lineages of modern frogs evolved which then gave rise to the immense diversity of frogs we see today[9]. There are over 6,000 known species of frogs worldwide, in a wide variety of sizes and colours. The world's largest frog, the goliath frog of West Africa, can grow as large as a cat. On the other hand, one of the smallest frogs is the Cuban tree toad, about the size of a fingernail[10].

Frogs and toads belong to the order Anuran, which means 'without tail' in ancient Greek. They make up nearly 90 per cent of all amphibians and can be found on every continent except Antarctica. These amazing creatures have adapted to a wide range of habitats, from the tropics to subarctic regions[11]. India is a hotspot for frog biodiversity, with over 400 species of Anurans[12]. The Indian bull frog, with tiger-like stipes and vocal sacs that turn indigo-blue during the breeding season, is the largest frog in India[13].

If frogs were to participate in any of the *Extreme* television series, they would win hands down. These creatures have adapted to survive in extreme weather conditions. The wood frog that lives north of the Arctic Circle is one of few animals that can endure weeks of freezing temperatures. The frog freezes its entire body during winter, using glucose in its blood to protect its vital organs from damage. It does not show any heart, lung or brain activity, and resumes normal activity in spring after its body thaws. Scientists are studying this miraculous ability of the wood frog to develop new ways to freeze organs for transplants[14].

The Australian water-holding frog with a hard rock-like body, burrows deep underground to survive the harsh heat of the desert. It secretes a transparent cocoon that forms a hard shell and helps it to conserve moisture underground as it waits patiently for the next rainfall[15].

Like Harry Potter's cloak of invisibility that renders the wearer invisible, glass frogs can seamlessly blend into their environment, appearing invisible. But their most impressive trick lies beneath their skin. Flip them over, and their organs, including their heart, liver, and intestines, are clearly visible. It's like a living dissection without the knife! When these frogs sleep, they siphon off almost 90 per cent of their brightly coloured red blood cells into crystal-lined sacs in their liver. This magical feat not only makes them nearly invisible, but also helps them avoid predators[16].

The real magic, however, lies in the implications for human medicine. Normally, when the body makes too many red blood cells, it can cause the blood to thicken with the risk of forming blood clots, a serious health risk. Yet, the glass frog can seemingly condense and expand its red blood cells at will without any adverse effects. Scientists have been searching for decades for a biological mechanism that prevents excessive bleeding while also preventing excessive clotting. This discovery could lead to groundbreaking advancements in medical research.

Today, we humans are the only ones to use complex language to communicate. But frogs and toads were the first land animals to develop vocal cords and communicate not just with sounds, but with syntax as well. Male frogs possess vocal sacs, which are pouches of skin that inflate with air. These sacs act like megaphones, amplifying the frog's sounds, which can be heard from a distance of over a mile[10].

Frogs and toads can produce intricate calls by repeating the same note or using different notes depending on the situation. Indian scientists studying the calls made by two frog species in the Western Ghats, the Bombay night frog (*Nyctibatrachus humayuni*) and the Amboli bush frog (*Pseudophilautus amboli*), found that they each had a unique repertoire of calls, modified for different social contexts[17].

Bombay night frog males produce two types—ascending and descending notes. The ascending notes are produced when alone, while descending notes are added when in the presence of another male. Amboli bush frog males on the other hand produce six distinct note types, some of which are more frequent than others. When alone, they call with three different notes, and when with another male—two different notes. It's possible that these different notes play a crucial role in territorial defence, mating, and other social interactions.

Some frogs also let out a loud scream, like that of a startled baby. The sound, lasting for more than five seconds, could be a distress call to startle attackers, or to attract secondary predators. The pint-sized leaf litter frog, *Haddadus binotatus*, when threatened, raises its upper body, opens its mouth wide, and throws its head back, as if about to unleash a mighty roar. But instead of a deafening sound, the frog emits a high-pitched scream completely inaudible to the human ear. Scientists, intrigued by this peculiar behaviour, used specialized equipment to detect the frog's hidden cry. They discovered that the frog was screaming at a frequency far beyond human hearing[18].

However, there's one frog that's as quiet as a mouse. In 2023, researchers discovered a new silent frog species in the Ukaguru Mountains in central Tanzania. Unlike its vocal counterparts, the spiny-throated reed frog (*Hyperolius ukaguruensis*) has no croak, chirp, or ribbit. Scientists believe that in place of a vocal call, the males' distinctive throat spines might play a role in attracting females[19].

When it comes to mating, the act isn't a serene affair, but a high-stakes battle. That's the reality for Charles Darwin's frogs, a tiny species endemic to India's Andaman Islands. These tiny amphibians have developed a truly unique mating strategy that's as dramatic as it is unusual. Rather than the traditional underwater or land-based rendezvous, these frogs prefer to mate in a vertical, upside-down position on the walls of tree cavities. But it's not just the unusual pose that sets them apart. The mating process is a veritable battleground, a constant struggle against rivals vying for the same female. When a male frog spots a potential mate, he begins a complex courtship ritual, calling out with a series of unique vocalizations. If a female responds, the pair will climb up the tree cavity wall, clinging to each other in a precarious upside-down embrace. But this romantic ambience is far from peaceful. Other males may attempt to disrupt the mating, using aggressive tactics that can include biting, kicking, and even trying to wedge themselves between the coupled pair[20].

The defending male must fight off these intruders to protect his mate. The female, meanwhile, must climb higher up the wall to avoid being separated from her partner. Charles Darwin's frogs are facing a loss of habitat and lack of adequate breeding sites. Scientists think this upside-down spawning behaviour in unnatural human-made sites may have evolved as a tool for survival and to ensure that the eggs are laid safely.

Frog sex can sometimes take a bizarre turn. Some males have been observed attempting to mate with inanimate objects like shoes, coconuts, and even dead frogs. This peculiar behaviour, known as 'misdirected amplexus', has been documented over 370 times in the past century. Scientists think that this quirk likely originated millions of years ago, suggesting that even the earliest frogs were prone to these unusual mating attempts[21].

Some species engage in explosive breeding, where thousands gather for a brief window of opportunity to reproduce[22]. The stakes here can be incredibly high, especially for females. With multiple males vying for a single female, the situation can quickly turn deadly, leading to the death of the female. The European common frog has developed a clever survival strategy to survive this intense mating season. When faced with a horde of eager suitors, females will often fake death, resorting to a tactic known as 'tonic immobility'. They stiffen their limbs and remain completely still, mimicking the appearance of a lifeless frog. This deception can be remarkably effective, deterring potential mates who may be less inclined to pursue a seemingly lifeless partner. And tonic immobility is not the only tool in a female frog's arsenal. They also twist and turn their bodies to dislodge unwanted males, or emit 'release calls' that signal their displeasure and may discourage further advances[23].

Once they have successfully mated, frogs typically lay hundreds of tiny eggs, which clump together in groups known as frogspawn. These eggs, each a tiny black dot encased in a protective jelly, are often laid in shallow water among vegetation. After a week or two, the eggs hatch, revealing tiny, fish-like creatures known as tadpoles. These aquatic babies have gills for breathing underwater, a long tail for swimming, and a mouth for feeding on algae and plant matter. Their lives are entirely dependent on the water[24].

Over the next several weeks, tadpoles undergo a remarkable metamorphosis. First, they develop hind legs, then fore legs. Their bodies begin to change shape, and their diets shift from plant matter to insects. Their tails gradually shrink, and lungs and eardrums begin to form, preparing them for life on land. Finally, after a dramatic twenty-four-hour push, the tadpole emerges from the water as a tiny frog.

Tadpoles are not only remarkable for their transformation but also for their ability to adapt to their environment. These tiny creatures have evolved a fascinating strategy to ensure their survival: they can control the timing of their metamorphosis. If a tadpole finds itself in a dangerous pond teeming with hungry fish, it knows it's time to speed things up. By accelerating its development, the tadpole can quickly transform into a frog and leave the water, reducing its risk of becoming a meal. On the other hand, if the pond is a safe haven with plenty of food and few predators, tadpoles can take their time. They can delay their metamorphosis, remaining in the water for up to a year[24].

Inspired by the amazing life cycle of frogs, starting from swimming tadpoles to jumping frogs, scientists at Colorado State University developed three robot frogs. These robots can swim, walk, and crawl, just like real frogs. They can adapt to different environments by changing their movements. They can curve their legs to 'swim' through water, scale rocky obstacles, and even flatten themselves to squeeze through narrow openings. One of the key features of these robotic frogs is that they are lightweight, and don't require bulky batteries. This design allows them to move easily with greater manoeuvrability. With their impressive versatility and efficiency, these robotic frogs hold immense promise for search-and-rescue missions in challenging environments. Their ability to navigate through water, land and obstacles could make them invaluable tools in disaster relief efforts[25].

While these robots with their manoeuvrable legs may someday save humanity, real frog legs have been served to humans as a delectable dish for centuries. Archaeologists digging in an area in UK not far from Stonehenge found the charred bones of a toad, which dates back to the Mesolithic era, proving that humans were enjoying frog legs as far back as 7596 BCE![26]

Fast forward to today, frog legs remain a culinary delight in many parts of the world. France, for instance, proudly claims them as a national treasure. Every year, the town of Vittel in northeastern France organizes a two-day fair called 'Vittel Brotherhood of Frog Thigh Tasters', where over 6,000 kgs of frog legs are consumed[27]. Italy hosts lively festivals dedicated solely to frog-based cuisine. Frog legs are also popular in several parts of the world including East Asia, and southern US.

However, the demand for frog legs has had a negative impact on frog populations. The European Union alone imported millions of pounds of frog legs between 2011 and 2020, representing an estimated 814 million to two billion frogs. Overharvesting has led to declines in certain species, particularly in regions like Indonesia. To protect endangered frogs, countries have had to switch to exporting smaller, more common varieties[28].

Frogs, with their ability to transform from tadpoles to adults, have long been symbolic of personal growth and change. They often represent rebirth, fertility and wisdom, making them popular characters in children's literature. The most well-known story is 'The Frog Prince', a classic fairy tale written by the Grimm brothers and brought to life in a Disney animated film. The story follows a spoiled princess who encounters a frog, who unknown to her is actually a prince cursed by a witch. Despite her initial disgust, the princess eventually befriends the frog and helps him break the curse and regain his human form.

Kermit the Frog is one of the most iconic characters in the world of puppetry. Created by Jim Henson, this green amphibian is known for his wise-cracking humour and relatable struggles. Kermit's signature catchphrase, 'It's not easy being green', has become a popular expression for the challenges of standing out. He's often seen leading the Muppets through various adventures, showcasing his leadership qualities and comedic timing.

Although nothing to do with the animal, the 2023 Greek film *Frogs* is a tragicomedy based on the works of Aristophanes, Euripides and Plato. It's the world's first feature-length film spoken entirely in ancient Greek. The film explores themes of philosophy, comedy and tragedy, drawing inspiration from the original Greek texts. The 1972 horror film *Frogs* takes a much darker turn, telling the story of a family celebrating a birthday on an island estate being terrorized by frogs and other animals. The plot suggests that nature is seeking revenge for the family's mistreatment of the local environment. This horror film offers a unique twist on the classic man-versus-nature theme.

It's hard to imagine calling someone a frog as a compliment, but Frida Kahlo, the renowned Spanish painter, famously used this image to describe her husband. Despite her tumultuous relationship with her husband, Diego Rivera, she writes in a heartfelt tribute in the afterword to his autobiography[29]:

'Growing up from his Asiatic-type head is his fine, thin hair, which somehow gives the impression that it is floating in air. He looks like an immense baby with an amiable but sad-looking face. His wide, dark, and intelligent bulging eyes appear to be barely held in place by his swollen eyelids. They protrude like the eyes of a frog, each separated from the other in a most extraordinary way. They thus seem to enlarge his field of vision beyond that of most persons. It is almost as if they were constructed exclusively for a painter of vast spaces and multitudes … On rare occasions, an ironic yet tender smile appears on his Buddha-like lips. Seeing him in the nude, one is immediately reminded of a young boy-frog standing on his hind legs. His skin is greenish-white, very like that of an aquatic animal. The only dark parts of his whole body are his hands and face, and that is because they are sunburned.'

In Australian Aboriginal mythology, Tiddalik, a greedy frog, drinks up all the water in creeks, lakes and rivers, resulting in drought. Later, many animals come together to get Tiddalik to release the water. In the original story, the water released by Tiddalik caused a mighty flood, from which the animals are rescued by a pelican. Modern retellings of the story have a happy ending with the water bodies revived after the animals succeed in releasing the water from Tiddalik. This myth highlights the importance of the sustainable use of water, which is extremely relevant in today's era of global warming[30].

Today, global warming has emerged as the primary threat to frogs and all amphibians. According to a recent assessment, more than 8,000 amphibian species are at a higher risk of extinction compared to just two decades ago[31]. This alarming statistic places amphibians among the most imperilled animal groups on the planet. These delicate creatures are particularly vulnerable to rising temperatures, wildfires, drought and hurricanes, which are becoming more frequent and intense due to climate change. Their permeable skin, essential for respiration and water absorption, makes them susceptible to changes in temperature and humidity. Their aquatic life stages are also highly sensitive to alterations in water conditions and precipitation patterns. Additionally, they face increased disease risks, such as from the deadly chytrid fungus, which thrives in altered climates[32].

The Rabbs' fringe-limbed tree frog, a species native to Panama, was wiped out by this deadly fungus. Toughie, the last known Rabbs' fringe-limbed tree frog, died in September 2016 at the Atlanta Botanical Garden. Environmental journalist Jeremy Hance drew attention to the extinction of this tiny frog species in his *The Guardian* article dated 27 October 2016, 'Frog goes extinct, media yawns'. He lamented the lack of media coverage and public awareness surrounding the disappearance of species, even as the planet faces a biodiversity crisis.

The death of Toughie inspired a song that calls to attention the urgent need for conservation. Moved by Hance's article, musician Talia Schlanger composed the poignant song 'The Endling' as a tribute to Toughie[33]. An 'endling' is the last known individual of a species, marking the brink of extinction. The song's haunting refrain, 'You are the endling, the ending of a sound'—echoes the finality of this loss.

> *Long gone the daughter who left you in water*
> *The son of a song, a seed of tone*

There in the cavity with nothing to eat
You fought to grow limbs of your own
And yours would have done the same
But their chance never came around.

Over 40 per cent of India's frog species too face the threat of extinction[34]. One of the world's most threatened frogs are those belonging to the Micrixalus genus such as the dancing frogs of the Western Ghats. A recent assessment revealed that two-thirds of these unique amphibians are either critically endangered or endangered, with a staggering 92 per cent of its species facing extinction[35].

To combat the decline in frog populations, 26 April is designated as 'Save the Frog Day', a reminder of the importance of protecting these creatures. Various other innovative initiatives have also sprung up to create awareness about the frog's fragile status. One such effort is the International Bornean Frog Race, a unique competition that combines adventure, education and conservation. Held on the island of Borneo, home to 178 amphibian species, the race challenges participants to identify and photograph as many frogs as possible within two hours. While the race is a fun and exciting activity, it also serves a crucial purpose: raising awareness about the importance of amphibian conservation. Organizers provide guidelines to ensure that participants minimize their impact on the environment, avoiding physical contact with frogs and staying on designated trails. To prevent the spread of a deadly fungal disease, participants' shoes are sanitized before entering the forest[36].

Video games are another creative approach to promoting frog conservation. The organization On The Edge offers a playful yet thought-provoking experience with their video game, Save the Purple Frog. Players navigate their virtual frog through a perilous landscape, dodging owls, snakes, trains and other threats to reach the breeding ground. The game's objective is to emphasize the challenges faced by real-life frogs in their natural habitats[37].

Frogs are facing challenges not just in their natural habitats, but also in cities. They were commonly found in many Indian cities, from Pune to Pondicherry. Pune had thirty-one species of frogs, while my home town, Bengaluru, had sixteen[38]. I recall a time when we moved to a then-remote part of Bengaluru. Our home was a veritable frog paradise. Every evening, as the sun dipped below the horizon, a symphony of croaks and chirps would fill the air. Frogs, in countless varieties, hopped and leaped through the city's green spaces. Stepping out into the courtyard, after dusk, required navigating a maze of tiny hopping frogs as they chased after insects. It was a delightful, if slightly disconcerting, experience.

In recent years, frogs have vanished from my courtyard, and their absence is a stark reminder of the environmental degradation that has plagued our cities, too focused on building urban landscape. Hopefully, this will change and we will come together to reclaim our lost symphony and ensure that the chorus of frogs continues to fill our nights for generations to come.

CHAPTER 8

THE SPIDER

AT a resort in the green valleys of Chikmagalur in Karnataka, my husband and I woke up to a symphony of birdsong and the gentle rustle of leaves. But our tranquillity was quickly shattered when I spotted a monstrous black spider, as big as my hand, sprawled across our blanket. My heart pounded. I first grabbed my phone to capture a picture of this eight-legged intruder, then looked around to see how to evict it. As I reached for the intercom to call for help, the spider vanished. I wondered if it had slithered under the bed or scaled the wall? The thought of that spider lurking beneath the bed was enough to send shivers down my spine. But I was relieved that our stay at the resort was nearing its end, and I needn't worry about spiders crawling over me while I slept.

Spiders, often seen as symbols of fear and horror, have a profound psychological impact on humans. Arachnophobia, a debilitating fear of spiders, affects approximately 6 per cent of the population. This phobia is believed to have evolved as a survival mechanism, passed down through generations from our hunter-gatherer ancestors to whom spiders might have posed some danger[1].

But the vast majority of spider species are actually harmless, with less than 0.5 per cent posing a significant threat to humans[1], yet, our primal fear of spiders persists. The few spider species that are dangerous are found in regions like Australia and South America. Further, spiders do not transmit any disease to humans unlike other insects like cockroaches. Given these factors, the intense negative emotions often triggered by spiders seem somewhat incongruous. It's as if our ancestors developed a deep-seated fear of a creature that posed a minimal threat to their survival.

Scientific studies have explored the reasons behind this aversion, examining our perceptions of fear, disgust and beauty in relation to various insects such as cockroaches, locusts, and arachnids (spiders, scorpions). The results revealed a clear pattern: spiders and scorpions consistently scored high in both fear and disgust. Researchers hypothesize that our fear of spiders may stem from a more generalized fear of chelicerates, a group of arthropods that includes spiders and scorpions[1].

In my opinion, while it's understandable to be cautious around wild unfamiliar spiders, the ones that share our homes pose no real threat. They occupy a minuscule part of our world, and their homes (cobwebs) deserve a little peace. However, some people believe that cobwebs in a home bring bad luck and financial misfortune. According to folklore from southern Andhra Pradesh, if a house has cobwebs as big as an elephant's head, it's a sign of impending doom for one of the residents. These myths, born from fear and misunderstanding, have led to the needless killing of spiders, which are actually doing us a favour by eating mosquitoes and cockroaches[2].

Despite these ominous myths, they hold a special place in Hindu mythology. In many regions, spiders are revered as symbols of devotion, creation and spiritual transformation. In the same state, Andhra Pradesh, the Srikalahasti temple worships the spider as a devotee of Lord Shiva[2]. The spider's unwavering commitment to its deity is seen as a model for human devotion. Similarly, in Trichy's Jambukeswara temple, it's believed that Lord Shiva himself took the form of a spider to build the prakaram (the courtyard around the temple sanctum). The Chola king Kochengot Chola, who built the temple, claimed to have been a spider in a previous life. In coastal Karnataka, during the Navratri festival, removing cobwebs is considered a bad omen, believed to bring a curse upon the household. In Gujarat, the Girnar hill, a pilgrimage centre for Lord Dattatreya, recognizes the spider as one of the guru's teachers. This association further elevates the spider's spiritual significance[2].

In the Upanishads, the spider is used as a powerful analogy to illustrate the creation of the universe. The Mandukya Upanishad says, '*yathā ūrṇanābhiḥ sṛjate gṛṇhate ca*'—Just as a spider creates and withdraws (the threads), so did the Lord *īśvara* create this world out of himself[3].

Greek mythology describes the origin story of spiders. Arachne, a skilled weaver, challenges the goddess Minerva to a weaving contest. In the tale recounted by Greek poet Ovid in his magnum opus, *Metamorphoses*, Minerva, the goddess of wisdom and crafts, wove a tapestry depicting the glorious deeds of the gods. Arachne, however, chose to portray the sins and flaws of the gods, a bold and provocative act that angered Minerva. Unable to tolerate such audacity, Minerva defeated Arachne in the contest and punished her by turning her into a spider. Arachne was cursed to weave webs for the rest of her life, forever a reminder of her defiance. And so, the legend goes, the first spider came into existence[4].

Ananse, the spider, is a legendary figure in West African mythology known for his cunning and wit, and is portrayed as a trickster. In one telling of the story, Ananse approaches Nyame, the sky god and creator of the world, to make him the lord of stories and narratives. Nyame, amazed by his audacity, sets him up to a difficult task of capturing a number of dangerous animals and bringing them to him. Ananse tricks each of them, and succeeds in his task[5].

In the North coast of Peru 4,000 years ago, people belonging to the Cupisnique culture worshipped a spider god[6]. A temple, dating back to around 1500–1000 BCE, dedicated to the spider god was discovered in 2009 at the archaeological site, Ventarrón. To the Cupisnique people, the spider was a symbol of power, rain and even war. The spider god's image appears throughout the Cupisnique culture's archaeological sites. From the majestic temple dedicated to the deity in Ventarrón to the smaller Garagay temple in Lima, the spider's face, with its cat-like mouth and bird-like beak, adorns ancient walls and pottery. Spiders were associated with rain, as they often appeared before the rains. Moreover, their ability to spin intricate webs connected them to textiles, a crucial part of ancient Peruvian life. The spider god was also tied to power and warfare. Some depictions show spider deities holding nets filled with decapitated human heads, symbolizing the conquest of enemies, and considered a divine symbol of victory.

And who can forget the monstrous spider, Aragog, and his seemingly endless army of spiders, their tiny legs skittering across the walls? They not only terrified Harry Potter, Ron Weasley and Hermione, but all young movie watchers with the chilling voice 'Follow the spiders' adding to the intrigue. On the other end of the spectrum, there's the adorable spider, Charlotte, the protagonist of the book and movie *Charlotte's Web* who weaves positive messages in her web, to save her friend Wilbur the pig from slaughter.

Spiders have fascinated several artists through the ages. The Rolling Stones, wrote and released a song, 'The Spider and the Fly', in 1965. Meanwhile, The Who's bassist John Entwistle spun a different web with his 1966 song 'Boris the Spider', a rock anthem that became a live show staple. Even David Bowie, the 'Starman', couldn't resist the spider's allure. His backing band in the early '70s, The Spiders from Mars, later influenced the name of his iconic album *The Rise and Fall of Ziggy Stardust and the Spiders from Mars*, Bowie even revisited the spider theme with his 1987 song 'Glass Spider', which inspired his subsequent tour. David Bowie even has a spider species named after him, *Heteropoda davidbowie*[7].

In fact, several rock stars and literary icons have been immortalized in scientific names of these eight-legged creatures. *Bagheera kiplingi* is named after Rudyard Kipling's iconic *The Jungle Book* character. The Harry Potter series has also left its mark on the arachnid world. The *Eriovixia gryffindori*, with its distinctive hat-like appearance, is a nod to the sorting hat from the wizarding world. And then there are the spiders inspired by pop culture icons like Leonardo diCaprio, Angelina Jolie, Arnold Schwarzenegger, and even Pink Floyd! The ex-President of the USA, Barack Obama and his wife Michelle also have their own spiders *S.barackobamai* and *S.michelleobamaae*[7]. The golden orb-web spider *Tropazodium kalami* is named after Dr A.P.J. Abdul Kalam, and *Marengo sachintendulkar*, a jumping spider, is named after Sachin Tendulkar.

Spiders have been weaving their way through Earth's history for nearly 300 million years! The first true spiders emerged from their ancestors, who had tails and could spin silk, but were unlikely to weave webs. The fossil of one such early spider, *Chimerarachne yingi* has been found in Myanmar, dating back to the Cretaceous period, when dinosaurs walked the earth[8].

Currently, there are more than 50,000 recorded species of spiders worldwide[9], and close to 2,000 in India[2]. With such a variety of spiders, it stands to hold that they come in all shapes, sizes and abilities. The tiny Samoan moss spider and *Patu digua* of Columbia are the smallest spiders, barely visible to the naked eye with a mere length of 0.4 mm[10]. The colossal Goliath bird-eating spider is the largest by weight (175 grams) and length (13 centimetres)[11].

Spiders are found in every continent except Antarctica. One spider has even made it to space. In 2012, a jumping spider *Phidippus johnsoni* became the first arachnid astronaut. The spider spent 100 days aboard the International Space Station before returning home to Earth and settling into the Insect Zoo at the Smithsonian National Museum of Natural History. This pioneering spider was the first of its kind to venture into space and successfully adapt to life back on our planet[9].

Spiders are sometimes mistakenly referred to as insects. While both are arthropods, spiders are in a separate class from insects. Spiders belong to the class Arachnid, which includes scorpions, ticks and mites. Arachnids have eight legs as opposed to insects which have six. Carl Clerck, often regarded as the father of arachnology, was the first to distinguish spiders from insects. Prior to his work, spiders were commonly classified as insects. He made significant contributions to the study of spiders[12]. His groundbreaking work *Svenska Spindlar* (Swedish Spiders), published in 1756, is considered a cornerstone of the field. *Svenska Spindlar* includes a comprehensive classification of spider species, along with beautifully hand-coloured illustrations. This work remains a valuable resource for researchers and enthusiasts even today. Interestingly, Clerck's book was published just one year before Carl Linnaeus' seminal work, *Systema Naturae*. Both scientists played crucial roles in developing the modern system of scientific classification.

Much like the scientists studying them, spiders have remarkable achievements that have been entered in the Guinness Book of World Records. Spiders hold a whopping forty-four Guinness world records. The Moroccan flic-flac spider, a desert dweller, holds the title for the world's fastest spider. Capable of reaching speeds of up to 1.7 metres per second, this arachnid is a master of evading predators. The Sydney funnel-web spider, a venomous Australian species, holds the record for the most venomous spider. Its bite is incredibly painful and can cause a range of symptoms, including nausea, vomiting, confusion, and even unconsciousness. Just 0.2 mg/kg of the male's venom is a lethal dose for primates (including humans)[13].

Strength is another area where spiders excel. The Californian trapdoor spider, known for its underground burrow with a trapdoor-like covering, is the world's strongest spider relative to its body size. It can resist a force thirty-eight times its own bodyweight, a feat that would put even the best Olympic powerlifters to shame. Finally, there's the *Evarcha culicivora*, or 'vampire spider,' a jumping spider found near Lake Victoria in Kenya and Uganda. This unique species has a peculiar taste for blood, specifically that of female Anopheles mosquitoes. By feeding on these disease-carrying insects, the vampire spider plays a role in reducing the spread of malaria[13].

Female spiders are generally much larger than males. This makes spider mating a high-stakes game where the male often finds himself on the losing end. This size disparity is particularly pronounced in web-spinning spiders like orb weavers and widows. The female giant golden orb weaver is ten times the length of the male, and 125 times heavier. Male orb spiders often approach their partners cautiously, timing their advances when the female is less likely to attack, such as when she is eating or molting. Another interesting strategy is adopted by the Asian hermit spider. When it feels threatened, the male spider can detach its sexual organ, pedipalps, and run away. The organ can still release sperm, even without the spider[14].

Beyond the physical dangers, male and female spiders have conflicting evolutionary interests. While females seek to produce offspring with the best possible partner, and may mate with multiple mates, males are focused on producing many offspring with a single mate. This can lead to behaviours such as cannibalism and mate guarding, as males attempt to ensure their paternity and prevent females from mating with other males. The black widow is a notorious spider, known to kill and eat its male counterpart after mating. This gruesome act gave the insect its name. The male Australian black widow, also known as redback, sometimes allows himself to be eaten, by somersaulting directly on his partner's fangs during mating. This allows the male spider to deposit more sperms into the female to secure his paternity[14].

Despite its fearsome reputation, the black widow's bite is rarely fatal to humans. While its venom is potent, most people who are bitten experience only mild symptoms like muscle aches, nausea, and difficulty breathing. However, black widow bites can be serious, especially for young children, the elderly, or those with underlying health conditions. In rare cases, the venom can lead to death[15].

The black widow spider has captured the human imagination for centuries, appearing in various forms of media. Its venomous nature and striking appearance have made it a symbol of danger, mystery, and female empowerment. In music, the black widow has inspired songs that explore themes of revenge, betrayal and feminine strength. The song 'Black Widow' by Australian rapper Iggy Azalea is a prime example, delving into the complexities of a failed relationship and the consequences of being wronged. The black widow has been featured in numerous movies, with the most notable being the 2021 Marvel film, *Black Widow*. The protagonist, a skilled assassin and former member of the Avengers, embodies the black widow's reputation for both danger and resilience.

Despite its notorious reputation, the black widow spider is a dedicated mother. After mating, she creates massive webs where she hangs her egg cocoons, each filled with hundreds of tiny eggs. Once the spiderlings hatch, they quickly disperse, leaving behind the intricate web. Black widows also rely on their webs to capture prey, including flies, mosquitoes, grasshoppers, beetles and caterpillars[15].

Spiders make their webs from silk, a natural protein. While all spiders produce silk, not all spiders weave webs. Those that do, make intricate webs designs that are a marvel of engineering. From the iconic orb webs to the funnel webs and the ingenious trapdoor nests, each web design is tailored to the spider's hunting style and habitat. These webs are not only beautiful but also highly functional, serving as both hunting tools and homes[16].

Spiderwebs have not only fascinated scientists but have also inspired artists, architects and designers. The intricate patterns and delicate structures of these webs have been a source of inspiration for centuries. Beyond their aesthetic appeal, spiderwebs have also proven to be incredibly functional. The shape of a spiderweb is highly efficient, allowing it to cover the maximum surface area with the minimum amount of material. Architects have adopted this principle in their designs, using steel cables to mimic the spider's silk and creating lightweight, durable structures[17].

The Estadio de la Plata, a stadium in Argentina, is a prime example of this architectural innovation. Inspired by the spiderweb, the stadium's design incorporates a structure that can withstand seismic activity. The web-like pattern allows the structure to absorb shocks without affecting other parts of the building. Another notable example of spiderweb-inspired architecture is the Fiero Milano shopping centre in Italy.

Spiderwebs possess excellent sound insulation properties. The intricate structure of the web absorbs or deflects sound waves, reducing noise pollution. Inspired by this natural phenomenon, scientists have developed 'metamaterials'. These artificially engineered materials can be produced in large quantities and used to improve sound insulation in homes and other buildings.

Frei Otto, a renowned architect, was inspired by spiderwebs. After being released as a prisoner during World War II, he attempted to create makeshift tents from sheets and blankets. This experience sparked his interest in lightweight, sustainable structures. Otto became a pioneer in the field of biometric construction, designing buildings that mimic the natural forms of living organisms[18]. He studied the intricate patterns and structures of spiderwebs, finding inspiration for his own architectural designs. Two of Otto's most notable works are the Munich Olympic Stadium and the Montreal Expo German Pavilion. The Munich Olympic Stadium, with its iconic translucent roof, resembles the web of the grass spider (genus Agelenopsis). The German Pavilion at the Montreal Expo, known for its innovative and sustainable design, was also influenced by spiderweb structures.

Spider silk is a material stronger than steel, yet lighter than a feather. A substance so delicate it can float on the wind, yet so resilient it can withstand the toughest of storms[19]. Spiders use this extraordinary material for everything from cozy cocoons and sticky traps to daring aerial adventures. They can balloon on the wind, sailing for miles, like tiny sailors of the sky. Humans, too, have recognized the incredible potential of spider silk. In the Solomon Islands, clever fishermen use a kite, a line, and a spider-silk lure to catch elusive needlefish, whose small mouths would be impossible to snare with a traditional hook. Even in ancient Greece and Rome, warriors relied on spider silk to staunch their wounds, its natural antiseptic properties aiding in healing[19].

In the nineteenth century, a French Jesuit missionary, Paul Camboué, became captivated by the golden orb weaver, a magnificent creature with webs as large as a human hand and silk that shimmers a vibrant saffron yellow. Camboué envisioned a future where this incredible material could be harnessed for industrial purposes. To achieve this, he invented a grim contraption dubbed 'the guillotine'. Resembling a miniature medieval stock to restrain people, the device held the spider securely, with its abdomen protruding from one side. With a gentle touch to the spider's spinnerets, the silk producing organ on the spider's abdomen, Camboué could extract the silk directly from its abdomen. Camboué's innovative approach led to the establishment of a spider-silk farm in Madagascar[19].

Young Malagasy girls were tasked with capturing the spiders, placing them in the guillotine, and reeling out their golden threads. Each spider produced between 150 to 600 meters of brilliant yellow silk thread before dying, after being milked five to six times in a month. The resulting silk was used to create a bed-canopy, which was proudly displayed at the 1900 Paris Exposition[19].

More recently, in 2012, a cape woven from the finest spider silk was displayed at the Victoria and Albert Museum[20]. This cape, the largest piece of spider silk cloth ever created, was the culmination of a three-year project involving a massive team of artisans. The silk was harvested from more than one million female golden orb weaver spiders, collected from the wild. The spiders' golden threads were carefully extracted, then woven into intricate patterns that showcased the vibrant colours and delicate textures of the natural material. The cape, in particular, was a stunning work of art. Its sunny gold hue was complemented by images of web-casting spiders, a fitting tribute to the creatures that had provided the raw material for this extraordinary piece. Despite these efforts, spider silk has not yet been commercialized to the extent as silk from silkworms.

Spider venom, on the other hand, often feared for its potency, is proving to be a treasure trove for the benefit of humans. This complex cocktail of toxins, composed of thousands of components, is revealing promising applications in the treatment of a wide range of human diseases. Scientists are particularly interested in the venom of the Australian funnel-web spider. This potent mixture has shown potential in treating neuronal damage after strokes and improving heart function for organ transplants. Additionally, components of spider venom are being explored for their antibiotic and pain-relieving properties[21].

Professor Glenn King from the University of Queensland has made significant strides in this field. He developed eco-friendly insecticides from spider venom, that are not harmful to bees[22]. His more recent research has led to the discovery of Hi1a, a compound found in the venom of the K'gari funnel web spider. Hi1a has shown promise in reducing heart and brain damage during heart attacks and strokes by preventing cell death caused by oxygen deprivation[23]. This drug candidate is currently undergoing preclinical trials and could soon become a valuable treatment option.

King's team also screened spider venom for its potential to alleviate pain. They discovered that over 40 per cent of the 206 spider venoms they examined contained compounds that could block human pain by inhibiting nerve activity[24]. One standout was the orange-fringed tarantula, whose venom showed particular promise for developing a non-addictive painkiller. Beyond pain relief, spider venom is being investigated for its potential to treat heart arrhythmia, neurodegenerative diseases, epilepsy, cancer and erectile dysfunction. Additionally, its antibacterial, antimalarial and drug delivery properties are being explored. To date, over forty patents have been filed for therapeutic uses of spider venom in humans[25]. As research continues to unravel the mysteries of spider venom, it is becoming increasingly clear that this often-overlooked substance holds immense potential for improving human health.

Spiders are not only helping humans here on Earth but are also playing a role in space exploration. Six spider-inspired robots, called ReachBot, designed by scientists at Stanford University, have landed on Mars, and could unlock new mysteries about the Red Planet. ReachBot's design is modelled after 'daddy longlegs', a type of arachnid known for its long, spindly legs. The design allows the robot to navigate through tight spaces and grasp uneven surfaces with ease. In a recent test in California's Mojave Desert, ReachBot successfully demonstrated its ability to climb and explore a natural cavern. ReachBot will explore the underground network of Mars including its caves and tubes which could contain clues of past or present alien life[26].

While spider robots crawl over Mars looking for clues, spiders of a different nature have been found on another space object, the moon. Recent discoveries have revealed intriguing features known as 'spiders,' which are believed to be indicators of vast underground cave networks[27]. These spider formations are characterized by a central indentation (spider's body) surrounded by radiating gullies (spider legs). Scientists believe these structures formed when molten lava flowed into surface depressions, creating an underground network of tunnels. The discovery of a large lunar pit with a hidden cave beneath it further supports the theory that these spider formations could conceal extensive underground cave systems. With hundreds of spiders known to exist on the moon, it's possible that a vast network of caves stretches beneath its surface.

From extraterritorial space to our cities, spiders have adapted and thrived in various environments. One spider that is particularly making sensational headlines is the Joro spider (*Trichonephila clavata*), a large jumping spider. Native to East Asia, Joro spiders made their way to the United States in 2014, likely stowing away in shipping containers. But they are not the monstrous creatures as they've been portrayed in the US and UK media who have referred to them as 'gag-inducing' and 'giant flying venomous spiders'. These large orb weaving spiders with a striking yellow-and-black body are actually quite calm and gentle.

Known for their impressive web-building skills, Joro spiders often create communal webs, living together in harmony. Researchers have discovered that Joro spiders' tolerance for city life may be due to their physiological makeup. Unlike other spider species, Joros maintain a steady heart rate even under stress. This ability to remain calm and collected helps them cope with the hustle and bustle of urban environments. When faced with threats, Joros are more likely to wait out the danger rather than resorting to aggression or flight[28].

With their toxin and silk producing abilities, it may be hard to imagine any similarities between humans and spiders. The truth is that they are as cunning and intelligent as us. Jumping spiders, particularly those in the Portia genus, have defied the notion that size matters when it comes to intelligence. In spite of having brains that are barely the size of a pinhead, scientists think these tiny arachnids are super smart because they have sharp eyesight, the best among animals their size. This allows them to spot, track, and strategically outwit their prey with incredible precision. Unlike their web-weaving cousins, jumping spiders are active hunters, using their visual prowess to stalk and pounce on their targets[29].

To lure a web-building spider into their clutches, Portia spiders often mimic the vibrations of a trapped insect, tricking the unsuspecting spider into approaching. But if the target is too large or dangerous, they may employ a more subtle approach, gently disturbing the web in a way that mimics a fruit fly lightly landing on the web. Once the target spider comes close to inspect, the Portia pounces with lightning speed, delivering a venomous bite.

A recent study has revealed that jumping spiders, particularly the Portia africana species found in Kenya, possess a surprising ability to estimate quantities[29]. Scientists at the University of Canterbury in Christchurch, New Zealand conducted an experiment to test the spiders' numerical abilities. They showed a specific number of prey items from a viewing tower to Portia spiders and then changed the number while the spider was traveling to the target. They discovered that the spiders were less likely to attack if they found more prey items than they were initially shown. While the spiders couldn't count in the traditional sense, the research suggests they have a rudimentary understanding of quantity, similar to a one-year-old child. This ability is likely crucial for survival, as it helps them assess the risks and rewards of an attack.

Jumping spiders, with their large, expressive eyes and curious demeanour, have captured the hearts of many. These tiny creatures have become popular pets, leading to a booming cottage industry of specialized habitats and accessories. One of the most endearing aspects of jumping spiders is their playful behaviour. Videos of them grooming their fangs, wrestling mealworms, and tilting their heads at their owners have gone viral, sparking the hashtags #jumpingspider and #spidertok, which have amassed over 1.5 billion views combined. While these videos have helped to improve the public perception of spiders, they have also fuelled a growing demand for exotic species in the pet trade. Unfortunately, this demand can have negative consequences for some rare and endangered spiders[30].

Tarantulas have become popular to keep as pets because of their large colourful bodies and long life. The Indian ornamental tree spider, a species of arboreal tarantula, for example, is highly sought after by collectors and is threatened by habitat loss and illegal smuggling. The peacock tarantula (*Poecilotheria metallica*) known for its vibrant blue coloration is another species that has become a popular choice for the pet trade. It is classified as critically endangered by IUCN, primarily due to habitat loss in its native deciduous forests of Andhra Pradesh, India and illegal pet trade.

The United States imports thousands of tarantulas each year, contributing to their decline. To address this issue, fifteen species in the *Poecilotheria* genus, including the Indian ornamental tree spider, have recently received strong trade protections under the Convention on International Trade in Endangered Species (CITES) treaty. These measures aim to curb the illegal pet trade and protect these vulnerable species from extinction[31].

Despite the fear they evoke, spiders are far from the villainous monsters they're portrayed as. In fact, they're a vital cog in the ecological machine. Spiders are found in nearly every land-based environment, acting as nature's pest-control unit, keeping insect populations in check and maintaining a healthy ecological balance. Together, spiders consume a staggering 400 to 800 million tons of prey annually[32]! But their role goes beyond just pest control. Spiders themselves become food for a variety of birds, reptiles and other animals. Their presence helps maintain a diverse food web, ensuring a healthy balance within ecosystems.

Spiders also make significant contributions to public health. Some species are specialized to prey on mosquitoes[32], and help reduce the transmission of dangerous diseases like malaria, dengue fever and West Nile virus. These diseases are carried by mosquitoes, which can infect humans when they bite. By reducing the number of mosquitoes, spiders play a vital role in protecting communities from these debilitating and potentially fatal illnesses.

Spiders, despite their long history on Earth, have been relatively understudied. There isn't enough information about the conservation status of spiders, nor are there many scientists studying them. In India, P.A. Sebastian from Kerala was a rare scientist who dedicated his life to studying spiders. He established India's oldest arachnology lab at Sacred Heart College, Kochi, in 1998 and has identified nearly sixty new spiders[33]. Saaliga, a group in Karnataka, has been working with school students and citizens to raise awareness about spiders, and documenting them.

Documentation of the different species of spiders could help provide more information about these relatively unknown creatures. I think it would be a great idea if resorts and hotels near forest areas could have a catalogue of the various spiders and insects found in the vicinity. For example, I would have loved to know the species of spider I encountered in the Chikmagalur resort, whether it was venomous or a threatened species. Only when we know more, we can shed our fears and give this ancient critter a chance. After all, its presence in popular culture serves as a testament to its enduring impact on the human imagination.

CHAPTER 9

THE MONKEY

AS I was driving through the lush Bandipur National Park on my journey to Ooty from Bengaluru, I was treated to a once-in-a-lifetime encounter. A gray langur materialized from the dense foliage and gracefully perched on my car's side mirror, right beside me! My heart pounded with a mix of excitement and apprehension. Would this curious creature damage my window or demand a feast of snacks? But to my surprise, it simply sat there, seemingly content to enjoy a free ride. I drove cautiously, keeping a watchful eye on my unexpected passenger, fearing it might lose its balance and tumble off. As we neared the end of the forest, I knew I couldn't take the monkey away from its natural habitat. I stopped and gently tried to coax it back into the woods. Thankfully, a helpful forest guard arrived and gently shooed it away, ensuring its safe return to the jungle.

Gray langurs, with grey fur, and black face and hands are found in the forests, savannas and some urban areas of the Indian subcontinent. Langurs are considered to be less aggressive than other monkeys, and are regarded as sacred, due to their religious-cultural connections. They belong to the genus Semnopithecus, and as of 2005, there are seven species of gray langurs in India: Nepal gray langur, Kashmir gray langur, Tarai gray langur, Northern plains gray langur, Black-footed gray langur, Southern plains gray langur and Tufted gray langur[1].

The Northern plains langurs are also known as Hanuman langurs. They are named after the Hindu god Hanuman, the deity of courage, loyalty and devotion. In the Ramayana, Hanuman, a loyal devotee of Lord Rama, helps him to fight a war against King Ravana, who had kidnapped Rama's wife Sita. There are different stories as to why the langurs are named so. In one version, the langurs rushed to help Hanuman when his tail was set on fire by Ravana, when he went as a messenger of Rama to Sri Lanka.

Monkeys hold sacred and cultural significance in many countries around the world. A symbol of agility, intelligence, and a touch of trickery, the monkey held a prominent place in the Chinese zodiac. The year of the monkey is the ninth of the twelve-year cycle of animals.

One of the most iconic representations of the monkey in Chinese mythology is Sun Wukong, the Monkey King[2]. Sun Wukong first appeared in the classic novel *Journey to the West*, which was published in the 1590s. This novel, attributed to writer Wu Cheng'en, reimagines the historical journey of the Buddhist monk Xuanzang to India. In the novel, Xuanzang is joined by three mythical companions, including the mischievous and powerful Monkey King, Sun Wukong, who protects the monk on his perilous pilgrimage. The story goes that Sun Wukong, born from a stone egg, possessed supernatural powers. Through this perilous journey, Sun Wukong faced numerous obstacles, battling demons and overcoming other dangers. Some experts believe that the legend of Sun Wukong was inspired by Lord Hanuman, as there are references to the Ramayana in the Buddhist monk Xuanzang's travel account, *Records of the Western Regions*.

In Chinese mythology, Sun Wukong's mischievous nature often led him to cause trouble and even consume life-saving fruits from the Jade Emperor's garden. To curb his unruly behaviour, the Jade Emperor sought the intervention of Buddha, who imprisoned him in a mountain. Hundreds of years later, Sun Wukong is released from the mountain and ultimately finds enlightenment. The Monkey King's transformation from a mischievous troublemaker to a devoted follower of Buddha, protecting Buddhist scriptures, has captivated readers for centuries. Even today, the Monkey God Festival remains a vibrant tradition in China and Hong Kong, celebrating the legacy of this legendary creature. The story of Sun Wukong has inspired many films, TV series and video games[2].

In fact, the term 'monkey mind' popularly used in psychology and the mindfulness field originated from this story. As Sun Wukong learns to control his restlessness and capriciousness through meditation and self-reflection, it gave birth to the metaphor 'monkey mind' to describe a state of restlessness. The term originates from Chinese *xīnyuán*, a word that literally means heart-mind monkey[3].

Mark Schumacher, a scholar of Japanese Buddhist statuary, notes on his blog, On Mark Productions, that in Japan's mythological landscape, the monkey became intertwined with the native Shinto religion, taking on a dual role as both a messenger to the gods and a physical manifestation of divine power. Mahatma Gandhi's famous Three Wise Monkeys: 'See no evil, hear no evil, speak no evil' are believed to originate from Japan. They were named Mizaru, Kikazaru and Iwazaru. These iconic figures are often associated with the Hiei Shrine on Mount Hiei, a significant Buddhist site. The central figure at Mt Hiei is Sanno, the Mountain King. The Sanno deity, represented by three important Buddhas, has a monkey as a messenger.

The Mayans of Guatemala and Mexico revered a howler monkey god, often depicted as twin deities, Hun Batz and Hun Choven.

American anthropologist and Mayan expert M.D. Coe's research on Maya funerary vases from the Late Classic period (600–900 CE) has revealed a recurring theme of these gods in acts of writing and carving. They are also prominent figures in the Popol Vuh, a sixteenth century Quiché-Mayan text. In this narrative, they are portrayed as the antagonistic stepbrothers of the heroic twins Hunahpu and Xbalanque. The association of the howler monkey god with the number 'one' in the Popol Vuh is significant. It suggests a connection to the thirteen-day unit of the Maya calendar, hinting at the deity's cosmic and creative power[4].

The 'White City' (Ciudad Blanca) in Honduras is also known as the legendary 'Lost City of the Monkey God'. In the 1940s, American explorer Theodore Morde claimed to have uncovered this lost city hidden deep within the Honduran rainforest. According to him, local indigenous people described a colossal statue of the monkey god, now buried beneath the jungle floor[5].

While the term 'monkey' is often used generically, there are actually over 300 distinct species of monkeys. These primates can be broadly categorized into two main groups: (a) Old World monkeys: From the intelligent macaques, and acrobatic langurs to the powerful baboons, this group found in Africa and Asia, boasts a diverse range of species and (b) New World monkeys: Their most distinctive feature is their prehensile tails, which they use as an extra limb to grasp branches and swing through the canopy. Native to Central and South America, this group includes howler monkeys, spider monkeys, and capuchin monkeys[6].

The term 'monkey' became increasingly common in English language usage, particularly around the time Shakespeare began his playwriting career in the 1590s. Until then, the terms 'ape' and 'monkey' were used interchangeably with little distinction between them. Besides the words ape and monkey, Shakespeare also used the terms baboon and marmoset to describe primates.

Sachi Sri Kantha, a Sri Lankan scientist and historian, suggests that Shakespeare was likely unaware of the existence of 'real apes', such as gibbons, orangutans, chimpanzees and gorillas. These smaller and higher apes were not as well-known in Europe at the time[7].

The word 'monkey' is thought to be derived from a German proper name Moneke, a variant of the Italian name, Monna. Interestingly, the Italian variant 'Monna' is thought to have evolved into a colloquialism for a prostitute. This connection stems from the practice of courtesans keeping imported monkeys as pets. The association of monkeys with sexual freedom and unrestrained behaviour may have contributed to their use as a metaphor in literature[7]. In his book *Life of Primates,* Adolph Schultz, a Swiss anthropologist, highlights the intriguing role primates played in Western European culture during the Middle Ages and Renaissance. They were seen as embodying negative human traits like vanity, lust, and other abhorrent qualities. Shakespeare himself used the term monkey and its variants to convey contempt, endearment, imitativeness, and even sorcery[7].

These fascinating creatures were often portrayed in folklore, art and literature as fools, imitators, tricksters and sinners. J. Sheridan le Fanu, a nineteenth century Irish writer, writes in his short story 'Green Tea' about a clergyman named Mr Jennings who is haunted by the spectre of a small black monkey with glowing red eyes that follows him everywhere. Invisible to others, the monkey disrupts the reverend's religious lifestyle and even develops the ability to speak to Jennings inside his head, bombarding him with evil urges to harm others and himself. Jennings becomes convinced that this monkey is an agent of hell. However, a detective, Dr Hesselis, argues that Jennings's excessive green tea consumption, combined with his hereditary suicidal mania, exacerbated his condition, suggesting that the monkey is a manifestation of his own dark side.

The frequent use of primates as human caricatures in satirical writing reflects their perceived similarity to humans. Their ability to mimic human behaviours and expressions made them a natural choice for satirists seeking to expose societal flaws and hypocrisy. Edgar Allan Poe's 'The Murders in the Rue Morgue' tells the story of a primate that learns violence from its owner. The story revolves around a brutal double murder of a mother and daughter locked in a room. The murderer is initially assumed to be a human, described by witnesses as speaking in an unfamiliar language. The daughter's throat bears marks resembling a human handprint. However, investigation reveals that the culprit is an orangutan with a similar hand shape. Captured by a sailor in Borneo and brought to Paris, the creature is intelligent and capable of breaking free from confinement. It has learned violent behaviours from its owner, who frequently beats it with a whip. The orangutan's animalistic nature manifests in violent brutality when enraged or frightened. The story also serves as a cautionary tale about the dangers of removing such creatures from their natural habitat[8].

In recent times, monkeys have been portrayed with an entire gamut of characteristics ranging from horror such as in *Planet of the Apes* to cuteness such as the *Curious George* series. Curious George, the beloved character created by Hans and Margret Rey, has captured the hearts of children and adults alike for generations. His innocent adventures and endearing antics have dispelled any negative stereotypes about monkeys, turning them into lovable, playful creatures. From his early days exploring the jungle to his life in the big city, George's curiosity and playful nature have made him a timeless icon. The Reys' original seven books, published during Hans' lifetime, laid the foundation for a vast universe of stories, films, cartoons and board games featuring the lovable monkey. I still fondly remember reading George's adventures to my own little monkeys when they were young. There's something truly magical about sharing these stories with children and watching their eyes light up with excitement as they follow George on his escapades.

Capuchin monkeys have become popular figures in popular culture, with notable appearances in films and television shows like *Pirates of the Caribbean, Night at the Museum* and *Friends.* One famous capuchin monkey is Jack, the pet of Captain Hector Barbossa in the *Pirates of the Caribbean* franchise. Named after the series' protagonist, Captain Jack Sparrow, this mischievous primate participates in various pirate adventures, including the climactic battle of Calypso's maelstrom where he plays a crucial role in distracting the enemy pirate Maccus.

Besides their popularity in culture and art, monkeys, particularly the rhesus macaques have played a crucial role in scientific research[9]. Rhesus macaques are Asian monkeys, sharing a common ancestor with humans roughly twenty-five million years ago. The use of monkeys in medical research began in the 1920s with Robert Yerkes, an American psychologist and primatologist, establishing a primate research laboratory at Yale University. Around the same time, the Carnegie Science Institute in Washington D.C. established a breeding population of rhesus macaques to study embryology and fertility. These primates were relatively easy to maintain and breed in captivity and were readily available from colonial India. However, it wasn't until the founding of the National Foundation for Infantile Paralysis (NFIP) founded by US President Franklin D. Roosevelt in 1938 (later renamed as March of Dimes) that the demand for primates skyrocketed. The NFIP's mission to find a polio vaccine required the use of non-human primates, as the polio virus did not infect the commonly used laboratory rodents and rabbits. Hundreds of thousands of rhesus macaques were imported into the United States to support polio vaccine research. India emerged as a primary source for these monkeys, but concerns about cost, public health, and the stability of supply led to a brief halt in exports. Through diplomatic efforts, the United States secured a resumption of monkey shipments with the condition that a US diplomat would personally verify each shipment's intended use for critical medical research.

In 1949, scientists John Enders, Thomas Weller and Frederick Robbins at Boston Children's Hospital were able to grow the polio virus in human cells, that won them the Nobel prize in 1954. This led to the development of the successful polio vaccine by John Salk in the early 1950s[10]. The success of the polio vaccine program paved the way for further studies using primates to understand various diseases and develop new treatments. Until 1978, India was a significant exporter of monkeys to the United States, supplying approximately 20,000 individuals annually at a price of $50 each. These monkeys were primarily used for biomedical research purposes. However, in 1978, India imposed a permanent ban on the export of monkeys following revelations that some of these animals were being utilized in the development of biological weapons[11].

Indian-origin rhesus macaques were also introduced to Cayo Santiago, an island off the coast of Puerto Rico, for behavioural research. In 1938, the American primatologist Clarence Ray Carpenter released 400 free-ranging rhesus macaques in Cayo Santiago. Despite facing a population decline in the 1950s, these monkeys have become a goldmine for scientific research. With thousands of individuals genotyped and their family trees meticulously recorded, these monkeys have been extensively studied. Their accessibility and the wealth of data collected have made them a prime subject for research across multiple fields. Studies on behaviour, physiology, demography, ecology, genetics and psychology have significantly advanced our knowledge of rhesus macaque biology dend behaviour[12].

In the early days of space exploration, when even the most basic questions about survival in space were unanswered, Miss Baker, a squirrel monkey, stepped in to provide crucial insights.

Accompanying her on a historic 1959 mission was a rhesus monkey named Able. Together, they became the first primates to return alive from space[13]. Prior to their flight, only small animals like mice and flies had ventured into the cosmos. Miss Baker and Able's fifteen-minute journey, reaching a height of over 1,700 miles, was a crucial step in understanding the physiological effects of space travel. The rockets' powerful g-forces during launch and splash down were a big problem that needed to be solved for future space travel. Their successful flight paved the way for further space research, demonstrating that humans could potentially survive the rigours of interstellar travel. Following their mission, Miss Baker and Able embarked on a year-long press tour, captivating audiences across the country.

Tragically, Able passed away during the tour due to complications from an infection. Miss Baker, however, continued to serve as an ambassador for space exploration, spending her later years at the Space & Rocket Centre in Huntsville, Alabama. Visitors from around the world would often leave bananas on her grave, a tribute to her pioneering spirit. Miss Baker lived an exceptionally long life for a squirrel monkey, passing away at the age of twenty-seven. Her legacy as a trailblazer in space exploration endures, inspiring future generations of scientists and astronauts.

In the 1960s, S.D. Singh, a professor of psychology in Punjab University, studied how monkeys living in cities and forests differed from each other behaviourally. He captured rhesus macaques from both habitats and studied them in a lab. Singh was able to observe a variety of differing behaviours[14]. He found that city monkeys were more curious and active than forest monkeys. They liked to play with things and solve puzzles. However, city monkeys were more aggressive. Forest monkeys were calmer and spent more time grooming each other. Even though city and forest monkeys behaved differently, they were equally smart at solving problems. This showed that while the city shaped new adaptive behaviours, it didn't change their basic intelligence.

Dr S.D. Singh also studied how mothers, friends, and social groups influenced the behaviour of baby monkeys. Infant monkeys were separated from their mothers and raised either alone or in groups of six infant monkeys. He wanted to understand how each of these factors affected the infant monkeys' behaviour. He found that monkeys raised with other infants, even without their mothers, showed signs of distress and aggression. This suggests that social interaction, both with mothers and peers, is crucial for healthy development in rhesus macaques. Social isolation can lead to serious behavioural problems, emphasizing the importance of social bonds for primate well-being.

The critical role of social bonds, particularly touch and affection, in human and animal development was first demonstrated in rhesus macaques by American psychologist Harry Harlow in the 1950s[15]. He separated baby monkeys from their mothers and provided them with artificial mothers made of cloth or wire. Surprisingly, the baby monkeys became attached to the artificial mothers, even though they didn't provide food. This demonstrated the crucial role of comfort and touch in infant development. His findings also informed research on child abuse and neglect, mental health, and the importance of human connection.

Research has consistently shown that social bonding is a crucial aspect of primate behaviour. Physical touch, in the form of social grooming, plays a significant role in strengthening these bonds. Primates spend a considerable amount of time grooming each other, engaging in rhythmic plucking, pinching, and pulling at skin debris. While self-grooming serves hygienic purposes, social grooming appears to be more about relationships and affection. The grooming partners are often stable over time, suggesting a deeper connection beyond mere physical maintenance. This ritualistic behaviour helps to reinforce social bonds, reduce stress, and maintain group cohesion[15].

However, Harlow's experiments were highly controversial. The 'pit of despair', a small, isolated chamber where monkeys were confined for extended periods, was widely condemned for its cruelty. These monkeys exhibited severe psychological distress, highlighting the devastating effects of social isolation. The ethical implications of Harlow's research sparked a debate and contributed to the rise of the animal rights movement. While his work provided valuable insights into the importance of early social experiences, it also underscored the ethical responsibilities of researchers to minimize animal suffering.

Even today, research on monkeys continues to provide insights into behaviour and psychology. To investigate what happens in the brain during a high-stakes situation, scientists from Carnegie Mellon University trained monkeys to complete a task on a computer, rewarding them for quick and accurate movements. However, they introduced a twist: occasional 'jackpot' rewards, much larger than the usual ones. This created a high-stakes scenario that could potentially induce anxiety[16].

By monitoring the monkeys' brain activity, the scientists discovered that when faced with a jackpot, the brain region responsible for movement became less active. This led to slower and less accurate movements. In other words, the monkeys' nerves got the better of them, just like a cricketer might miss a catch under pressure when the stakes are high. This fascinating study reveals that just like us humans, even monkeys, our distant relatives, can experience performance anxiety and underperform in high-pressure situations, highlighting the universality of this emotion.

Another emotional function shared by humans and monkeys is the ability to understand another person's thoughts and intentions.

Imagine you're watching a movie. You can not only see the actions on the screen but also understand the characters' thoughts and feelings. This ability, known as theory of mind, is a cornerstone of human social intelligence. To explore the origins of this ability, researchers at The Rockefeller University studied rhesus macaques using a neuroimaging technique—functional magnetic resonance imaging (fMR)[17]. They studied the brain activity of rhesus macaques as they watched different videos. The videos showed physical interactions between objects, social interactions between monkeys, and a combination of both. Interestingly, the researchers found that the mirror neuron regions in the monkeys' brains were active not only when watching social interactions but also during physical interactions and even when observing objects colliding. This suggests that the mirror neuron system, which has been known to help animals and humans observe others' actions and mimic them, might have a broader role in understanding not just social but also non-social interactions.

When it comes to social interactions, marmosets, those pint-sized primates from South America, have an amazing level of social complexity. These tiny monkeys, barely 8 inches tall, have a high-pitched whistle-like call known as 'phee calls'. Scientists from the Hebrew University of Jerusalem discovered that each marmoset has its own unique phee call, much like a personal nickname[18]. When separated, they use these calls to address each other directly. This is a groundbreaking finding, as only dolphins and elephants were previously known to use vocal communication to address each other. This suggests that marmosets might possess a level of social intelligence that we hadn't imagined. It's like they're having secret conversations, calling out to each other by personal nicknames, just like we do!

The use of monkeys in research has been further strengthened by the successful cloning of a monkey. In January 2024, scientists at the Chinese Academy of Sciences reported the successful cloning of a rhesus macaque that for the first time made it to adulthood, surviving for more than two years[19]. Cloned animals can provide a more consistent and controlled experimental environment, allowing for more accurate and reliable scientific studies.

However, the use of primates in laboratories continues to be a contentious issue. The US, Europe, and the UK use thousands of monkeys for medical research each year. These monkeys are used to study diseases like AIDS, hepatitis, malaria, for clinical trial toxicology tests, and tuberculosis. Because they're similar to humans, monkeys are useful to understand and find cures for these diseases. However, there's a growing concern about 'monkey laundering'. This practice involves capturing wild monkeys and falsely presenting them as being born in captivity to avoid rules and regulations[20].

Scientists have called for more stringent oversight mechanisms to verify the true origins of research animals. Animal rights activists have also raised serious ethical concerns about the use of primates in laboratory experiments. They argue that these intelligent and social animals deserve protection from unnecessary suffering and exploitation. Critics point to the potential for pain, stress and psychological distress experienced by primates in laboratory settings. The debate over primate research is complex and multifaceted. While the scientific benefits are undeniable, the ethical implications cannot be ignored.

Another dark side to monkey use is the pet trade. Although in India it is illegal to keep monkeys as pets, in other parts of the world, such as the UK, an estimated 5,000 primates are being kept as pets, including marmosets, capuchins, squirrel monkeys and lemurs[20]. Keeping pet primates is unsafe for the animals and their owners. Some primates are used to roaming across large areas in the wild. Imagine confining them to a small cage or apartment. This seriously impairs their development and can lead to behavioural problems.

Primates are social creatures, just like us. But most people only keep a single monkey for a pet, not an entire troop. This means primate pets are not only physically cramped, but they're also socially deprived. Additionally, researchers have linked the pet trade to instances of demand for violent online content involving monkeys and other primates[20]. Such criminal acts not only violate animal cruelty laws, but pose a danger to wild primates that are at risk of extinction.

The threat of extinction looms large over some monkey species that are declining in numbers due to deforestation, hunting and illegal trade. Lemurs, rhesus monkeys, spider monkeys, howler monkeys, woolly monkeys and capuchin monkeys, among others, are reported to be traded for meat, traditional medicine and small scale commercial uses. Long-tailed macaques and pig-tailed macaques are captured and traded for experimental purposes. In some regions of India, the body parts of rhesus macaques, such as hands, fingers, or skulls, are employed as amulets to ward off evil spirits[20]. This practice, along with the widespread use of primates in traditional medicine throughout Asia, poses a significant threat to primate populations. A staggering 86 per cent of primate species utilized in traditional medicine are classified as endangered, highlighting the urgent need for conservation efforts and ethical alternatives[20]. One subspecies of African red colobus, known as Miss Waldron's red colobus, is believed to be extinct due to hunting and loss of habitat from logging[21].

In India, the loss of monkey habitats has led to escalating conflicts between humans and primates. The rhesus macaque, bonnet macaque and Hanuman langur, once considered part of the cultural landscape, are now increasingly viewed as pests. In Bengaluru, where I live, complaints about bonnet macaques entering flats and stealing food have surged in recent years. On the city outskirts, there are reports of these monkeys becoming aggressive, snatching food from children and even biting people[22]. In some apartments, such as my friend's, monkeys have practically become permanent residents. 'All they need is an Aadhaar card,' my friend quipped humorously.

However, this intrusion isn't always tolerated. In Belur taluk, 220 kilometres from Bengaluru, thirty-eight monkeys were poisoned to death and left in a bag on the roadside in 2021. While the perpetrators and motive remain unclear, experts opine that it's likely connected to conflicts arising from the monkeys raiding crops in nearby villages. Following the discovery of the carcasses, the high court initiated a suo moto case, instructing civic authorities to develop a scientific approach to capture and relocate monkeys. Despite this, activists claim that clear guidelines are still lacking, and many forest rangers remain ill-equipped to handle the monkey issue[23].

The city of Delhi in particular has had a history of conflict with monkeys. In 2007, the tragic death of S.S. Bajwa, then the deputy mayor of the city, following an attack by monkeys, sparked a swift response from the Delhi High Court[24]. The court directed authorities to capture and relocate the monkeys to Asola Bhatti wildlife sanctuary in the city. Iqbal Malik, a wildlife expert, advised the Delhi government to sterilize the monkeys and fence off the sanctuary to prevent their escape. While the government followed Malik's advice regarding sterilization, the fencing solution proved inadequate. Along with a fibreglass barrier, the authorities relied on iron rods and bars to hold it together. However, the ingenious monkeys would use these joints as a ladder to climb over the fence. To keep them inside, the Delhi Municipal Corporation procured fruits and vegetables from a wholesale market for the monkeys, spending a whopping Rs 14 lakh per month on food from 2007 to 2018[25].

The increasing presence of monkeys in Delhi is primarily attributed to the destruction of their natural habitats and the proliferation of monoculture forests. Previous attempts by the Delhi government to relocate monkeys to neighbouring states like Uttar Pradesh and Madhya Pradesh proved unsuccessful as the primates returned to urban areas in search of food. The monkeys' adaptability to urban environments has contributed to their population explosion. Residents offering food items like chapatis and rice have inadvertently encouraged their presence. To address the problem, the Delhi government has explored various strategies, including hiring individuals who imitate langur sounds to scare away monkeys[26].

During the G20 summit in 2023, the New Delhi Municipal Council (NDMC) deployed life-size cutouts of gray langurs and trained workers to mimic their sounds, deterring rhesus macaques from G20 venues[27]. The Uttar Pradesh Cricket Association (UPCA) also employed langurs to protect the Green Park Stadium from monkey intrusions. The practice of using langurs to control rhesus macaque populations is based on the belief that these two species are natural enemies. While this notion is widely accepted, there is no scientific evidence to support it. In fact, in natural settings, langurs and rhesus macaques often coexist peacefully[28].

We humans too can coexist peacefully with our cousins, in shared spaces in cities. Recently, Indian politician Shashi Tharoor shared a picture on social media of a monkey that sat on his lap while he was enjoying a cup of morning tea in his garden. The monkey sat quietly, ate a few bananas and then left quietly. We need to be cautious about seemingly kind acts like feeding wild primates which can create dependency and aggression, leading to conflict. By educating communities about the negative consequences of feeding monkeys and promoting understanding of monkey-human interactions, we can foster empathy and coexistence.

CHAPTER 10

THE CROW

AS a young girl growing up in the bustling city of Mumbai, I had a rather unusual neighbour: a mischievous crow. This bird had made its home in a tree within our apartment complex, and tales of its territorial antics swirled among the residents. It was said that this feathery guardian would swoop down upon any unsuspecting soul who dared to venture too close to its nest, pecking at their heads with alarming precision.

Every evening, we children would gather in the courtyard, eager to engage in games of tag, hopscotch, and hide-and-seek. But if our games brought us near the crow's domain, fear would grip us. We'd dash past the tree, shielding our heads, dreading the sharp peck of its beak. At other times, it would frequently perch on my windowsill, its beady eyes fixed upon me. Its caws, sharp and insistent, seemed to carry a hidden message. Its stern gaze, however, always filled me with a sense of unease.

It's no surprise that unlike the beloved sparrows and pigeons, often fed and cherished, the crow has never enjoyed the same level of affection. Perhaps its reputation for mischief has earned it a less than favourable reputation. This oft-neglected common bird, annoying us with its hoarse 'caw-caw' is, however, one of the most successful among birds to adapt to cities.

Crows belong to the Corvidae family, which encompass 117 species including jays, magpies, and their relatives. Crows (genus Corvus) make up about one-third of this diversity, found on every continent except South America and Antarctica. Recent research suggests that the ancestral Corvidae originated in an archipelago north of Australia during the late Oligocene/early Miocene period, about thirty million years ago, and spread throughout the Indo-Pacific before reaching other parts of the world[1].

Common crow species include the American crow (North America), carrion crow (Europe and Asia), hooded crow (western Europe to eastern Asia), house crow (Indian subcontinent), pied crow (tropical Africa), and fish crow (southeastern and central North America). India is home to four resident crow species, with the house crow and jungle crow being the most widespread[2]. While they may look similar, there are key differences between them. The house crow has a distinctive grey patch on its nape, neck, upper breast and upper back. The jungle crow, on the other hand, lacks this grey colouration. A third species, the jackdaw, is smaller than the house crow and has less grey in its plumage. It also has a white iris around its eye. The jackdaw is primarily found in Kashmir and northern Punjab. The raven, while similar in appearance to the jungle crow, is larger and has a different call. Instead of the familiar 'caw-caw,' ravens emit a hoarse 'pruk-pruk' sound. They are found in parts of Punjab, western Rajasthan, and Kutch. In addition to these resident species, India also welcomes two winter visitors from the northwest: the rook and the carrion crow, both of which closely resemble the jungle crow.

The ubiquitous house crow is a constant presence in our lives, with its incessant crowing and cawing. The names given to this bird—corvus, crow, kaka, kawwa, kaage—all stem from its characteristic calls. The house crow is notorious for its impudence, frequently harassing people, dogs, and bullying smaller birds. It's a bird that demands attention, whether you appreciate its striking looks or find its behaviour annoying.

House crows travel significant distances each day, much like humans commuting to work, but remain deeply rooted in their local communities[2]. This strong sense of place is a defining characteristic of these birds. Another interesting aspect of house crow behaviour is their communal roosting. It's not uncommon to find massive mixed roosts of Indian mynas, jungle mynas, house crows and jungle crows gathering together at specific locations. Crows are highly social birds, living in close-knit families that hunt, forage, defend territory, and care for young together. They usually mate for life, and build their own nests, but some gather in large roosts during winter for warmth, protection and information sharing. Crows can live up to thirteen years in the wild[2].

Crows are known for their impressive aerial acrobatics, but they can also be quite territorial, especially when it comes to protecting their nests. These clever birds typically build their homes once a year, starting around spring. Using twigs, grass and other soft materials, they construct open, shallow-cup nests in a variety of locations, from towering skyscrapers to hidden tree branches. They build their nests close to human habitations, taking advantage of readily available food sources. The breeding season for house crows varies slightly depending on local conditions, but typically occurs between January and September. However, these adaptable birds can breed throughout the year in areas with favourable conditions[2].

A typical house crow lays three to six bluish-green eggs, which are incubated for approximately sixteen to seventeen days[3]. The young crows stay in the nest for about thirty days before fledging. Once the eggs hatch, crows can become particularly aggressive, engaging in 'dive bombing' tactics to defend their young. These aerial assaults can be startling and even dangerous. Crows in urban areas tend to be more aggressive than their rural counterparts. So, if you hear frog-like croaking from a tree, catch a sight of a pink mouth or beautiful blue bead-like eye, it may be a crow baby—it's best to stay away, give them some space and avoid any unnecessary encounters.

Both crows and ravens belong to the family songbirds; though one might find it hard to imagine the iconic 'caw-caw' as a song unlike the melodious tunes of other songbirds such as a robin or sparrow. The reality is that songbirds are not just about the pretty sounds they make. The designation is based on both their foot placement and, more importantly, the anatomy of their vocal area. Most songbirds, including crows, have a syrinx, a specialized organ that allows them to produce complex sounds.

So why don't crows sound more like their songbird counterparts? Unlike many birds that sing loudly to attract mates from afar, crows have a more subtle courtship ritual. They prefer close-range interactions, using soft coos, rattles and growls, accompanied by gentle bowing and nuzzling behaviours. Crows have their own unique social dialects. Studies of captive crow groups have revealed that each group develops its own distinctive sounds. These sounds become a sort of cultural tradition, a dialect, which crows use to identify and bond with members of their own group[4].

Crows have remarkable memories. Once threatened or harmed, they can remember a human's face for their entire lives. Not only do they personally scold their tormentors, but they also rally their family and even strangers to join them. This collective hostility allows inexperienced crows to learn about dangerous individuals indirectly, associating certain faces with danger and responding accordingly[5].

These interesting findings were discovered by scientists conducting experiments near Seattle to study crow intelligence[5]. Volunteers wore a unique mask while trapping crows, and crows associated the masks to a 'dangerous face'. When exposed to the masks after they were released, the crows immediately scolded the mask. Uncaptured crows that witnessed the event also responded in the same way, suggesting social conditioning. Later, even crows that had not witnessed the event recognized the dangerous mask, indicating horizontal social learning. Young crows whose parents had taught them to scold the mask exhibited vertical social learning. Within two weeks of the trapping event, 26 per cent of crows scolded the person wearing the 'dangerous mask'. Over five years, the hostility towards the mask grew, suggesting that captured crows had warned others. The number of crows reacting to the dangerous mask steadily increased, including new birds, while the response to a neutral mask remained unchanged. Expectedly, crows that were initially trapped were better at distinguishing between dangerous and neutral masks than those who learned socially.

Crows are remarkably adept at recognizing human voices, and can distinguish between familiar and unfamiliar voices, even when the words spoken are the same. To test this ability, researchers recorded the voices of five people who regularly interacted with a group of carrion crows living in an aviary at the University of Vienna[6]. They then recorded the voices of five other people who were completely unfamiliar to the birds. When these recordings were played back to the crows, the birds displayed a much stronger reaction to the unfamiliar voices, immediately turning to investigate the source. The researchers believe that this heightened response is due to the crows' perception of the unfamiliar humans as potential threats. Any unfamiliar voice they hear needs to be carefully evaluated to ensure their safety. In a way, this behaviour can be compared to a child who may ignore their mother's constant nagging but quickly becomes alert to a new voice.

Crows are known for their intelligence and playful nature. A viral video from Russia perfectly captures this. The video shows a hooded crow picking up a jar lid, placing it on a snowy roof, and sliding down, carefully balancing on the lid. It then flies back up, tries another side, and repeats the process, clearly enjoying the thrill of sledding. This deliberate playfulness, using a toy, and maintaining balance, highlights the crow's intelligence and curiosity[7].

The remarkable intelligence of crows has long fascinated humans, leading to various attempts to train them for specific tasks. From picking up litter to sorting through discarded electronics, crows have demonstrated their potential to be valuable allies in addressing environmental challenges. Swedish startup Corvid Cleaning and US based company CrowBox have taken the lead in exploring the potential of crows for environmental cleanup. Both companies have successfully trained crows to perform specific tasks in exchange for food, such as picking up litter and collecting dropped coins.

Corvid Cleaning's approach involves providing crows with a bin/feeding station where they can dispose of litter and receive a food reward[8]. CrowBox, on the other hand, has trained captive crows to deposit coins they find on the ground into a designated container[9].

While these initiatives show promising results, scaling them up to a meaningful impact remains a significant challenge. The Dutch startup Crowded Cities had proposed a similar idea to Corvid Cleaning, but ultimately abandoned their project due to challenges in scaling and understanding the potential effects on crows and the environment.

In another remarkable display of intelligence, crows have been found to adapt themselves to using resources they find in urban areas. Crows were observed using traffic to crack walnuts in Sendai city in Japan. As David Attenborough noted in the 2007 BBC Wildlife documentary, 'Wild Crows Inhabiting the City Use it to Their Advantage', these clever birds have devised a unique solution to overcome the limitations of their beaks. Unable to open walnut shells with their beaks alone, crows have turned to the power of vehicular traffic. They carefully drop the shells at pedestrian crossings, timing their actions to coincide with the traffic lights. When the lights turn green, cars passing over the nuts crack them open, providing the crows with a convenient way to access the nutritious interior. Once the vehicles have done their work, the crows wait for the lights to turn red. Then, they safely retrieve their cracked walnuts from the road, avoiding the risk of being hit by passing vehicles.

New Caledonian crows, found in the Pacific Islands, are renowned for their impressive tool-making abilities, particularly their creation of hooks. These intelligent birds utilize a native plant called pandanus, known for its rigid, serrated edges. By carefully peeling off sections of the plant, they whittle them down to size and insert them into crevices of logs and rotting wood to extract grubs[10]. This behaviour is similar to that of chimpanzees, who also use modified twigs to extract ants. However, the New Caledonian crows' ability to create tools that meet the specific definition of a hook is truly remarkable. Tool use is a rare phenomenon in the animal kingdom, with only about 1 per cent of species exhibiting this behaviour. But the ability to actively modify objects to create tools is even more exceptional.

In fact, New Caledonian crows can even construct a complex tool combining two to three different tools[11]. In a study conducted by European scientists, these birds were presented with a challenge: retrieving food targets that were too far away to reach with a single tool. Surprisingly, four of the eight crows spontaneously combined different objects to create functional tools that allowed them to reach the food. This innovative behaviour was not just a one-time occurrence; each time the crows adjusted their tool-making strategies based on the position of the food. One crow even constructed tools with three and four elements when necessary. In humans, the ability to create complex tools is often linked to higher cognitive functions like planning, coordination, and even language. While these crows' behaviour cannot be fully explained, the study suggests that these birds are highly adaptable and can quickly solve novel problems.

Carrion crows possess a rudimentary form of counting ability. Scientists at the University of Tübingen in Germany trained these intelligent birds to associate specific sounds with a corresponding numbers of caws[12]. The crows in the experiment were taught to produce one to four caws in response to different audio cues. A frequency sound corresponded with four caws, a drum roll with three, a cash register noise with two and a guitar chord with one. To ensure accuracy, they were also trained to tap a screen after completing their vocalizations. This provided a clear indication of when they had finished counting. The researchers found that the crows were particularly good at counting lower numbers, achieving 100 per cent accuracy at counting to one and a 60 per cent success rate at counting to two. While their performance slightly decreased when counting to three, their overall accuracy was impressive. One of the most intriguing findings of the study was the crows' deliberate pauses before vocalizing higher numbers. This suggests that they were carefully planning their responses, indicating a level of cognitive sophistication previously thought to be exclusive to humans.

In fact some crows are even better than humans at calculating the likelihood of an imminent event. The same group of scientists at the University of Tübingen trained two crows to understand and apply probabilistic concepts[13]. The experiment began with a simple task: pecking at images on a touchscreen to receive food rewards. However, the scientists soon introduced an element of uncertainty—not every peck would result in a reward. This forced the crows to figure out the relationship between each image and the likelihood of receiving a reward. They quickly learnt to associate different images with varying probabilities of success. The next step involved a more complex decision-making task. The crows had to choose between two images, each representing a different reward probability. Despite the abstract nature of the task, the crows consistently selected the image with the higher chance of reward.

This showed that they could use statistical inference to make informed decisions. Over ten days of training and 5,000 trials, the crows became so skilled that they consistently outperformed their human counterparts in this task. With such impressive intelligence, one can't help but wonder if a crow's ability was to be used to train AI models, whether they would be more accurate than the current AI models that often falter.

Beyond their impressive statistical abilities, another trait crows share with humans is their response to death. When a crow dies and is discovered by another, the discovering crow emits an alarm call, attracting other crows from the area[14]. A large, noisy mob forms, seemingly gathering to take notice of the deceased crow. After about fifteen to twenty minutes, the group disperses. Unlike humans though, scientists think that these gatherings are a way to learn about danger. Scientists at the University of Washington conducted an experiment where crows were exposed to a person associated with a dead crow. In the following days, the crows avoided foraging for food in the area, as they considered it to be dangerous, suggesting that crows learn socially from such events and adjust their behaviour accordingly[15].

The crow is also associated with death ceremonies in Hindu culture, which holds the crow in high esteem. Hindu scriptures mandate offering food to lower beings first, with crows receiving the initial offering after God. This practice, particularly during death ceremonies (shraaddh), where food or pinda is offered to crows, symbolizes the belief that crows represent our ancestors. Another Hindu belief is that crows are messengers between the physical and spiritual realms. Offering food to these birds is seen as a way to spiritually connect with departed ancestors, as the crows are thought to carry the essence of the offerings to them. For this reason, crows are also fed during Amavasya, the new moon day, as an offering to ancestors. Lord Shani, often depicted with a crow, is associated with both challenges and rewards. Feeding crows is believed to appease Lord Shani and to seek his blessings for a smoother life journey[16].

Another Hindu practice of feeding crows occurs in January, during the harvest festival, Pongal. In Tamil culture, married daughters visit their maternal home to celebrate the 'Kanu Pongal' festival where the women offer a feast of coloured rice and cooked vegetables on a turmeric leaf to cows and crows. Chanting 'Kanu pidi kaka pidi' (we offer this to the cows and crows) during this ritual, women pray for the well-being of the family they are born into, and hope that the bonds will be as strong as the crow family. Like all Tamilians, my mother and I, along with her sisters and my girl cousins would visit our mama's (mother's brother) house on this festival day, where we would partake in delicious food, and receive gifts in the form of new clothes or money.

Apart from the Hindu religion, the crow is woven into the fabric of several cultures worldwide. Whether seen as a harbinger of misfortune or a wise and cunning creature, the crow's presence in myths, legends and religious texts is undeniable. In the Bible, the crow is often conflated with the raven and similar birds like the chough, daw, and rook. These predominantly black carrion birds are typically associated with negativity, yet some intriguing positive connotations exist. The first raven in the Bible, represented by the Hebrew word 'oreb', which can also signify a crow, is the first of four birds released by Noah to check if the ark is nearing land. It is said that the raven likely found some food and did not return to the ark, which was considered to be a good sign. In other parts of the Old Testament, the raven is referred to as a 'scavenger', an 'unclean bird'[17].

In Norse mythology, the raven is closely associated with the god Odin, often referred to as the 'Raven God'. Odin's two ravens, Huginn (thought) and Muninn (memory), fly across the world, gathering information and returning to Odin to share their insights. This connection highlights the raven's role as a messenger and a harbinger of wisdom[17]. Similarly, in Celtic mythology, the raven is linked to war and death. The Irish war goddess Badb Catha is often depicted as a 'Raven of Battle'. These mythological associations with ravens reflect their powerful symbolism. They are seen as both ominous and wise, representing the duality of life and death, knowledge and mystery. The raven's ability to soar high and observe the world from above has made it a symbol of insight and foresight. In both Greek and Roman cultures, these birds were widely used in augury, the practice of divination, by interpreting the behaviour of birds. Coupled with their habit of scavenging on corpses, this association solidified the perception of the raven as a harbinger of death and misfortune[17].

Kaeli Swift, an avian ecologist at the University of Washington writes on her blog 'Corvid Research' about various folklore that explain the crow's inky black plumage. In Greek mythology, Apollo was betrayed by his lover, Coronis who married a mortal named Ischys. A white crow, serving as a messenger, informed Apollo of the betrayal. Enraged, Apollo turned the crow's feathers black and punished Coronis with death. Other interpretations suggest Coronis herself transformed into a black crow, symbolizing the forbidden love between her and Ischys. The Greek word 'corone', meaning crow, is derived from the name of Coronis.

A popular Islamic legend recounts another incident for the crow's black colour. When Prophet Muhammad was hiding in a cave to escape his enemies, a white crow is said to have revealed his location by crying 'ghar, ghar!' (cave, cave!) to his pursuers. However, they failed to understand the crow's warning, allowing Muhammad to escape. But the enraged Prophet turned the crow's feathers black and cursed it to utter only those two words forever.

In Judaism, the thirteenth century *Yalkut Shimoni*, a compilation of the Hebrew Bible, offers a poignant tale about ravens. After the death of their son Abel, unsure of what to do with the body, Adam and Eve were shown the way by a compassionate raven. The raven sacrificed one of its own to show them the burial ritual. This set the practice of burying dead in many cultures.

The Quran presents an alternate account of the burial of Abel. A folklore researcher and retired professor from the University of Pittsburgh, D.L. Ashliman, writes on his blog that after Cain kills Abel, he was perplexed about how to dispose of the body. He observed two crows fighting, one killing the other. The crow dug a hole and buried the deceased crow, revealing the proper way to bury a body. The Quran narrates this event, '... And God sent a crow to scratch in the earth and show him how he might hide his brother's shame, he said, "Alas, for me! Am I too helpless to become like this crow and hide my brother's shame?"'

It was a widely held belief in antiquity that ravens would peck out the eyes of the deceased. Proverbs 30:17 of the Bible and the ancient Greek play, *Birds*, written by Aristophanes, attest to this grim belief[17]. Catullus, a Latin poet from the second century BCE, in a particularly cruel wish for an enemy, wrote: May your eyes be torn out and swallowed by a raven's black throat.' Similarly, Epictetus, a first century Greek philosopher, observed, 'Crows pick out the eyes of the dead, when the dead have no longer need of them.'

This macabre act of plucking out the eyes of the fallen perhaps inspired thirteenth century Sufi poet Baba Farid to write: '*Kaga re mori itni araj tose, chun chun khaiyo mans, arajiya re khaiyo na tu naina more, khaiyo na tu naina mohe, piya ke milan ki aas*.' The poet through these poignant lyrics asks the crow to eat the flesh of his body, but to leave his eyes alone because he is longing to see God, his loved one. These lyrics were also used in the song '*Nadaan parindey*' from the movie *Rockstar*.

These birds, with their dark plumage and often ominous calls, have long been associated with death and misfortune in folklore and literature. Shakespeare artfully employs these associations to create a sense of foreboding and impending doom and enhance the dramatic tension and psychological depth of his plays. The raven's croak, for instance, becomes a harbinger of violence and tragedy. Lady Macbeth predicts King Duncan's murder:

The raven himself is hoarse
That croaks the fatal entrance of Duncan
Under my battlements.

In Hamlet, the prince links the idea of revenge with the same birds:

Begin, murderer. Pox, leave
thy damnable faces, and begin! Come, the croaking raven doth
bellow for revenge.

Shakespeare mentioned crows and its cousins so frequently in his writings that Scottish illustrator Jemima Blackburn wrote a book titled *Crows of Shakespeare* in 1899, which had extracts of his plays and her illustrations of corvid birds.

The crow has even made its mark on human language. The Greek poet Theognis lamented, 'Everything here has gone to the raven and perdition,' a phrase similar to our English expression, 'to the dogs'. Similarly, characters in Aristophanes' plays often exclaimed, 'To the ravens!' as a curse or a dismissal[17].

The phrase 'I ate crow' is a humble admission of being wrong, often uttered after a strongly held belief is proven false. The etymology of this expression likens the experience of being incorrect to the act of consuming crow meat. Some language experts trace the origin of this phrase to English writer Rudyard Kipling. In his 1885 short story 'The Strange Ride of Morrowbie Jukes', the protagonist, a proud European colonist in India, is trapped in a sand pit. Desperate for survival, he eventually resorts to eating crow, a stark contrast to his earlier declaration of never doing so[18].

This vivid image of eating crow, a symbol of humiliation, likely contributed to the phrase's entry into the vernacular, alongside similar idioms like 'eating dirt', 'eating humble pie', and 'eating one's words'. Historically, crow meat was not considered a delicacy. In most accounts, it was consumed only out of necessity, highlighting the unpleasant nature of the act and its association with humiliation.

Yet, this misunderstood creature has captured the imagination of poets and lyricists. Tamil superstar Sivaji Ganesan immortalized the crow in the iconic song '*Ka Ka endrey ellorum ondraaga*' from the film *Parasakthi*, praising the crow's intelligence and resourcefulness. And who can forget the mesmerizing dance of Dimple Kapadia in '*Jhoot bole kauwa kaate*', a song from her debut movie *Bobby*, that catapulted her to stardom and captivated the nation.

Mary Oliver, a Pulitzer Prize winner, is full of admiration of the bird as she writes in her poem 'Crows'[19].

… they don't envy anyone or anything—not the tiger, not the emperor,
not even the philosopher.
Why should they?
The wind is their friend, the least tree is home.

I see them in trees, or on ledges of buildings,
as cheerful as saints, or thieves of the small job
who have been, one more night, successful—
and like all successes, it turns my thoughts to myself.

Should I have led a more simple life?
Have my ambitions been worthy?
Has the wind, for years, been talking to me as well?
Somewhere, among all my thoughts, there is a narrow path …

This heartwarming poem, celebrating the crow's simple yet fulfilling life, offers a valuable life lesson for us humans. It reminds us to appreciate the small joys, live in the moment, and find contentment in the ordinary. The next time a crow sits at my window, instead of feeling uneasy at its stare, perhaps I will remind myself to follow its path and appreciate the beauty of a life lived simply and authentically.

CHAPTER 11

THE ANT

CENTURIES ago, a small army, hailing from the lush rainforests of Central and South America, embarked on an epic global journey. Hitching rides on European ships, they navigated the vast oceans, from the bustling ports of the New World to the distant shores of the Old. Some even braved the treacherous Pacific, sailing on Spanish galleons laden with silver. As empires rose and fell, these intrepid beings adapted and thrived, building their societies to one of the largest in the world[1].

I'm talking about the tiny ant, ubiquitous in our homes and cities. There isn't a place without them. Every morning, I encounter a disciplined line of ants in my kitchen threatening to invade my pantry. On the other hand, they like to spread themselves in random order in the bathroom sink, perhaps ready to disperse at the first hint of danger—the rush of water from the tap. The garden, reminiscent of the rainforest they originated from, is of course a refuge for them, providing sustenance to thrive. They love my compost bin; ant after ant, dragging bits and pieces of the nutritious vegetable waste, clamber over the compost pot, yanking the booty for yards, eventually disappearing into the soil. They are famous for disrupting picnics, and outdoor events. Despite our efforts to rid ourselves of ants, they turn up relentlessly.

Ants are one of the most successful organisms on the planet. Scientists have estimated that there are a staggering twenty quadrillion ants on earth[2]; about 2.5 million ants for every human, roughly 200,000 times more than the 100 billion stars in the Milky way.

The first and most famous Cretaceous ant-like fossil, sphecomyrma, was found trapped in a ninety-two-million-year-old New Jersey amber. These exquisitely preserved worker specimens offer a glimpse into the early evolution of ants. Sphecomyrma displays a fascinating blend of ant and wasp characteristics, showcasing a transitional stage in ant evolution. While sphecomyrma is more closely related to ants than any other living organism, scientists think that the direct ancestor of modern ants probably emerged a bit later[3].

The history of ants is closely linked to the rise of flowering plants. Around a hundred to fifty million years ago, when flowering plants were rapidly diversifying, ants also underwent major evolutionary changes. Scientists from France studied fossils and ant genes to understand this relationship. They found that many older types of ants died out during a period of rapid environmental change. However, after this extinction event, ants began to diversify rapidly, likely because the rise of flowering plants created new habitats and food sources for them. Ants continued to evolve quickly during periods of climate change and the appearance of new plant communities[4].

It was during this Cenozoic era, sixty to seventy million years ago, ants became ecologically dominant. A pivotal shift during this time was the diversification of their diet. While their ancestors were primarily predators, ants began to exploit new food sources. As flowering plants diversified, they provided ants with a variety of new food sources, such as nectar, pollen and fruits. Some species even specialized in harvesting seeds, while others, in a remarkable feat, began cultivating fungi for food[3]. The close relationship between ants and angiosperms has been a driving force in their joint evolution. In turn, ants played a crucial role in pollinating flowers and dispersing seeds, contributing to the success of angiosperms.

Ants belong to the family Formicidae, which include about 15,000 species worldwide. They are present on every continent except the polar regions[5]. Ants are masters of eusociality, a complex social structure, which sets them apart from many other animals. Unlike bees and wasps, where social living evolved multiple times from solitary ancestors, it's believed that the very first ant ancestor was already eusocial. Essentially, ants haven't simply evolved socially; they've built upon a foundation of complex social behaviour that was already present in their ancient lineage. This unique evolutionary trajectory has played a significant role in shaping the incredible diversity and success of ant societies we see today[3].

Ant colonies are like extended families where multiple generations live together. From the youngest larvae to the wise old queens, they all play a role in the colony's success. In an ant colony, parenting is a communal effort. Workers tend to the young, feeding them, protecting them, and nurturing them until they're ready to join the workforce.

At the heart of every colony is the queen, the sole reproductive member. She lays countless eggs, ensuring the continuation of the colony. The rest of the ants, the sterile workers, dedicate their lives to serving the queen and her offspring. The queen produces specific chemical signals, known as cuticular hydrocarbons (CHCs), that act as a sort of royal decree. These pheromones are like a subtle perfume, carrying information that's vital to the colony. They signal the presence of the queen, reassuring the workers and suppressing any thoughts of rebellion. By controlling the release of these chemical messages, the queen maintains her dominance and ensures the smooth functioning of the colony[6].

While the queen is the traditional ruler of the ant colony, easily recognizable by her size and wings, in some species, a unique figure known as the gamergate takes the reins. A gamergate, though similar to a worker in appearance, possesses the ability to reproduce. However, she produces fewer eggs than a queen. To compensate and maintain the colony's growth, multiple gamergates often work together, ensuring a steady supply of new ants. Gamergates exhibit extraordinary longevity similar to a queen. While workers have a lifespan of about seven months, and queens can live for up to five years, gamergates can live for an astonishing three years. This extended lifespan allows them to maintain their role as the colony's reproductive leader for an extended period. This unique adaptation highlights the flexibility and resilience of ant societies. Whether ruled by a single queen or multiple gamergates, the colony's survival and prosperity depend on the collective efforts of its members[6].

For a long time, ant pupae were seen as passive members of the colony, merely waiting to transform into adults. However, recent research has revealed a surprising secret: these seemingly dormant creatures play a vital role in the colony's survival. During their pupal stage, ants secrete a nutritious fluid that is essential for the growth and development of young larvae. This fluid, similar to mammalian milk, provides the necessary nutrients for the larvae to thrive[7]. Adult ants actively consume this secretion as well, highlighting its importance for the entire colony. Interestingly, the pupae require parental care to maintain their health. If the secretion is not regularly removed, it can harm the developing ant. This discovery underscores the intricate social dynamics within ant colonies and the vital role that every member plays, even the seemingly inactive ones.

Similar to us humans who rely on language and cultural norms to build and maintain social bonds, insects have developed a more subtle yet equally effective system. Ants, like other social insects, communicate through a complex chemical language. A key element in this language is the chemical signature, a unique blend of compounds that coats an insect's body. This signature, genetically determined and specific to each colony, acts as a kind of identification badge. A newly hatched ant learns to recognize the scent of its nestmates, distinguishing them from intruders. Those who carry the correct chemical signature are welcomed, fed and protected. Conversely, those with a foreign scent are met with hostility or even aggression. This intricate chemical communication system allows these social insects to form highly organized and cooperative societies[1].

Ants, though small, are formidable creatures with a range of defence mechanisms. They often employ their powerful jaws to bite, but many species take it a step further. Armed with venomous stingers, they can inject potent toxins or spray irritating chemicals. Hailing from the rainforests of Central and South America, bullet ants (*paraponera clavata*) deliver the most painful insect sting known to humanity. Their venom, a potent neurotoxin, induces excruciating pain that can last for days. While rarely fatal, the experience is so intense that it has earned the top spot on the Schmidt Sting Pain Index[8], with a pain level of four. Entomologist Justin Schmidt who created this pain index describes the bullet ant sting as: 'Pure, intense, brilliant pain. Like walking over flaming charcoal with a three-inch nail embedded in your heel.' The next ant on this list with a pain level of 2.5 is the trap-jaw ant (*Odontomachus*), whose sting is described as: 'Instantaneous and excruciating. A rat trap snaps your index fingernail.'

Enduring the excruciating sting of bullet ants is a rite of passage for young boys of the Satere-Mawe tribe of the Amazon as part of their initiation into manhood. This extraordinary and painful ritual involves inserting their hands into a glove filled with hundreds of these insects, whose sting is among the most painful in the insect world. The boys must endure this ordeal for ten minutes, repeating the process multiple times until they can withstand the pain without flinching or crying[9].

Found in parts of Australia, jack jumper ants are known for their aggressive behaviour and ability to sting through clothing. Their venom can cause severe allergic reactions in some individuals, including life-threatening anaphylaxis. While fatalities are rare, it's crucial to seek immediate medical attention if stung[10].

Fire ants, native to South America, are notorious for their painful stings. Their venom, containing alkaloid toxins, causes burning sensations and itchy welts. Fire ants, belonging to the Solenopsis genus, are a group of over 200 species. Their common name is a fitting description, as their venom causes a burning sensation, often accompanied by itchy, red welts. These tiny insects pack a powerful punch, and their aggressive behaviour can make them a nuisance, especially in areas where they have become invasive. They pose a significant threat to ecosystems, pushing out native ants as well as humans. While most people experience mild discomfort, those with allergies may suffer severe reactions[11].

The impact of red fire ant infestations is far-reaching. These ants have established themselves in various regions, including the United States, Australia, and parts of Europe. Fire ants are the fifth most costly invasive species, causing damages of $6 billion each year. The red fire ant first made its way to the United States through the port of Mobile, Alabama, in the 1930s[1]. This small but formidable insect quickly spread across the southern states, causing widespread devastation. Farmers were forced to abandon their land as the ants swarmed, destroying crops and livestock.

In 2001, these invasive pests were first identified in the Brisbane area, Australia. Their rapid spread prompted the Australian government to classify them as a notifiable pest. A national cost-shared eradication program has been put into place requiring landowners to report any suspected sightings[12]. More recently, red fire ants were discovered in Europe for the first time. In late 2022, numerous colonies were found near a river estuary in Syracuse, Sicily[13]. Scientists expect that they will likely spread across Europe from Italy. In Europe, while previously detected in imported goods, their establishment in the wild has been a concern. The red fire ant's ability to thrive in warmer climates makes Europe increasingly vulnerable. Climate change is expected to further exacerbate the problem, creating suitable conditions for the species to establish itself in many European cities. This unexpected invasion has alarmed authorities and experts alike, as the potential consequences for local biodiversity and agriculture are severe[13].

While countries like Australia and New Zealand are investing heavily in eradication efforts, the challenge of controlling these invasive ants remains significant. The increasing global temperatures are further exacerbating the problem, as it creates more suitable habitats for these heat-loving insects. Even today, the red fire ant continues to wreak havoc, causing billions of dollars in damage to agriculture and infrastructure. As the red fire ant continues its global march, it is crucial for countries to implement effective prevention and control measures.

Detecting fire ants is crucial to prevent widespread infestations. It is possible to detect this ant due to its painful stings and the characteristic mounds of their nests. Recently, researchers at Lanzhou University have harnessed the power of AI to identify and locate fire ant nests with remarkable accuracy[14]. By feeding the AI system with images of fire ant nests from diverse environments, the researchers enabled the robot to recognize the distinctive characteristics of these nests. The robot, a Xiaomi CyberDog, was then deployed to survey nursery gardens, outperforming human surveyors in both speed and accuracy. This innovative approach not only reduces the risk of painful ant stings for humans but also significantly improves the efficiency of fire ant eradication efforts.

However, one region in India views fire ants not as pests but as potential life savers. The fire ant has been used as a unique remedy for malaria by the tribal communities of Bastar, a region plagued by this disease. Intrigued by this ancient wisdom, scientists from India decided to delve deeper. They collected fire ants from the Bastar forests and, using advanced techniques, isolated specific components of the venom known as peptides and alkaloids. Laboratory tests revealed that the peptide fraction of the fire ant venom demonstrated significant anti-malarial activity. When tested against *plasmodium falciparum*, the parasite responsible for the deadliest form of malaria, the peptide fraction effectively inhibited its growth. In contrast, the alkaloid fraction showed little to no impact. This research not only validates the traditional knowledge of the tribal communities but also opens new avenues for the development of novel anti-malarial drug[15].

The Argentine ant, a formidable species, is known for its remarkable adaptability and a knack for global domination. Its expansion in the late nineteenth and early twentieth centuries mirrors the rise of global trade itself. One notable instance of this invasion occurred in Porto, Portugal, following the 1894 Exhibition of the Islands and Colonies, a world fair showcasing displays from various countries. It is believed that the ants arrived on ornamental plants, which often carry soil and hidden hitchhikers[1].

The impact of the Argentine ant was so significant that it even caught the attention of world leaders. In 1927, Italian King Vittorio Emanuele III and Prime Minister Benito Mussolini enacted laws to combat the invasion, underscoring the severity of the problem. Italian writer Italo Calvino, inspired by the real-world struggles with the Argentine ant, penned a novella titled 'The Argentine Ant.'

This work of fiction captures the relentless nature of the invasion, portraying the ant as a symbol of enduring resilience and adaptability. Calvino's tale highlights the enduring legacy of this tiny but mighty insect, which continues to thrive in various parts of the world[1].

In twenty-first century India, yellow crazy ants have invaded villages in Tamil Nadu, and are causing a serious threat to the lives of animals. These invasive pests, notorious for their destructive behaviour, are wreaking havoc on local ecosystems and livelihoods. The ants, which don't bite or sting but spray formic acid, have been causing significant damage to livestock and crops. Cattle herders have been forced to abandon their settlements due to the intense infestation, while villagers report the deaths of various animals, including snakes and rabbits[16]. Experts are concerned about the potential ecological impact of these ants, as they have been known to displace native species and disrupt delicate ecosystems. Their aggressive behaviour and ability to thrive in diverse environments make them a formidable threat. While the immediate danger to humans may be limited to allergic reactions, the long-term consequences of this infestation could be severe for both the environment and the local communities.

The study of ants, myrmecology, has unveiled an astonishing world. These tiny insects exhibit behaviours that rival human ingenuity and complexity. From farming fungi to tending aphids, ants engage in intricate agricultural practices. They even possess advanced medical knowledge, performing surgeries and treating wounds with natural antibiotics. Perhaps most remarkably, ants enslave other ants, and engage in full-scale warfare, employing strategies and tactics that would be familiar to any military strategist.

Ants could be considered the pioneers of agriculture. They started farming fungi long before humans even thought about planting crops. A groundbreaking study published in the journal *Science* reveals that these tiny insects started cultivating fungi a whopping sixty-six million years ago[17]! Led by entomologist Ted Schultz, scientists at the Smithsonian's National Museum of Natural History traced the origins of ant agriculture to the aftermath of the asteroid impact that wiped out the dinosaurs. By analysing the DNA of hundreds of fungal and ant species, they uncovered a fascinating story of evolution and adaptation. While early ant farmers had a more rudimentary approach, it was during a period of global cooling, around forty million years ago, that they really stepped up their game. Leafcutter ants emerged as the pioneers of 'higher agriculture', harvesting fresh vegetation to feed their fungi. Today, these industrious insects are the most advanced farmers in the ant world, tending to their fungal gardens with meticulous care.

These fungal gardens are a marvel of nature, producing specialized structures called gongylidia that nourish the entire colony. Some leafcutter ant colonies can grow to millions of individuals, all relying on this symbiotic relationship for survival. By studying the evolution of ant agriculture, scientists hope to gain valuable insights into sustainable farming practices. After all, if ants can cultivate crops for millions of years, surely we humans can learn a thing or two from their ancient wisdom.

Scientists have discovered that ants aren't just industrious insects; they're also skilled surgeons! Researchers at the University of Würzburg have observed that *camponotus floridanus* ants can perform limb amputations on injured nest mates to increase their chances of survival[18]. When an ant suffers a severe leg injury, its colony members will meticulously bite and tug at the damaged limb until it cleanly separates from the body. This remarkable behaviour is driven by a complex decision-making process. The ants can accurately assess the severity of the injury, determining whether amputation is the best course of action. If the injury is deemed recoverable, they will proceed with the surgical procedure.

While this discovery highlights the sophisticated social behaviour of these insects, it also raises intriguing questions about their motivations. Are they driven by empathy, a sense of duty, or simply instinct? While we can't definitively know the answer, this research challenges our understanding of animal cognition and behaviour. It's clear that ants are far more complex creatures than we previously thought. Their ability to perform surgical procedures underscores the intricate social dynamics within their colonies and their capacity for collective problem-solving.

Matabele ants, one of the largest ant species on Earth, also have a remarkable ability to treat their wounds. These African ants often face life-threatening injuries during their hunts for termites, losing limbs in the process. But their resilience extends beyond just surviving these encounters. Scientists have discovered that Matabele ants have a sophisticated understanding of wound care. They can detect infections, particularly those caused by the harmful bacteria *pseudomonas aeruginosa*. When an ant is injured, its nest mates will often carry it back to the nest for treatment. Here, they meticulously clean the wound and apply a special saliva that contains potent antimicrobial compounds[19].

This saliva, a complex mixture of 112 components, is a natural pharmacy. Half of these components have known antimicrobial or wound-healing properties. The ants seem to be able to distinguish between infected and uninfected wounds, suggesting a high level of cognitive ability. By targeting the specific bacteria causing the infection, they can conserve energy by only producing the necessary antimicrobial compounds. This remarkable behaviour raises intriguing questions about the evolution of intelligence and self-medication in the animal kingdom. As antibiotic resistance becomes a growing global health concern, studying the natural antibiotics produced by these ants could lead to the development of new treatments for human infections.

Ant colonies, driven by instinct and survival, clash in epic battles that rival human conflicts in scale and intensity. When two colonies vie for the same resources or territory, a fierce confrontation ensues. These battles are not mere skirmishes; they are strategic engagements involving thousands of combatants. Like human armies, ant colonies deploy various tactics to gain an advantage. They may overwhelm their enemies with sheer numbers or employ specialized units to disrupt enemy lines. The ability to mobilize a larger force and sacrifice individual ants for the collective good is crucial to victory[20].

Unlike human warfare, ant battles are orchestrated without a central command. Instead, individual ants respond to pheromone signals and environmental cues, leading to emergent behaviour that benefits the colony as a whole. This decentralized approach allows ants to adapt quickly to changing circumstances and coordinate complex manoeuvres. One such strategy is the relentless offensive. Similar to the Chinese military strategist Sun Tzu's emphasis on rapidity, certain ant species, like army ants, adopt a relentless approach. They move in massive, synchronized formations, overwhelming their prey with sheer numbers and aggression. The African army ant, *dorylus nigricans*, is a prime example of this tactic. These ants form dense columns, sweeping across the landscape, devouring victims many times their size with their blade-like jaws[21].

The marauder ant colony employs a sophisticated strategy that maximizes efficiency and minimizes losses. The key to their success lies in their hierarchical structure and the strategic deployment of their workforce. At the forefront of the army, the tiny minor workers form a formidable barrier. These expendable soldiers, while individually weak, collectively present a powerful defence. Their sacrifice allows the larger, more valuable 'media and major' workers to strike decisive blows. This strategy mirrors ancient human warfare, where conscripted soldiers were often sacrificed to protect the elite fighting force. By targeting individual units and wearing down the enemy's strength, the marauder ants employ a tactic known as 'defeat in detail'. This approach allows them to overcome even larger and more powerful opponents.

American biologist Mark Moffet in an article in Scientific American notes that the synchronized, wave-like advances of army and marauder ants bear a striking resemblance to the military formations employed by human civilizations throughout history[21]. From the disciplined phalanxes of ancient Greece to the regimented lines of the American Civil War, these tactics have been used to maximize force and minimize individual risk. However, unlike human armies, which often have specific objectives and targets, ant raids are more opportunistic. They advance blindly, relying on chance encounters with prey or enemy colonies. This strategy, while effective, is inherently risky. It requires a constant supply of new recruits to replenish the losses incurred during each raid.

Marauder ants also engage in fierce territorial battles with their own kind. These intraspecific conflicts, often involving hundreds of combatants, are characterized by intense hand-to-hand combat. Minor workers, the expendable foot soldiers, form the frontline, grappling with their opponents in a deadly embrace. The goal is to incapacitate or kill the enemy, often at the cost of their own lives. The abundance of minor workers allows the colony to sustain significant losses without compromising its overall strength. In contrast, other ant species, such as the Formica wood ant and the Dorymyrmex bicolor ant, have evolved more sophisticated strategies. They employ long-range weapons, like chemical sprays and projectile stones, to inflict damage on their enemies from a safe distance[21].

Besides engaging in warfare, some ant species have evolved a more sinister strategy: slavery. Approximately fifty of the 12,000 known ant species are slave-makers. These ants, often closely related to their victims, target vulnerable colonies, particularly those in the process of relocating. They raid these colonies, stealing the pupae of their unsuspecting victims. When these pupae hatch, the young ants are integrated into the slave-maker colony, forced to work tirelessly for their captors. By raiding these colonies and stealing their pupae, they acquire a workforce of enslaved ants[22].

Once these enslaved ants emerge, they are forced to perform tasks like foraging, nest maintenance, and brood care. This practice, known as dulosis, can be obligatory or facultative. In obligatory dulosis, the slave-maker colony relies entirely on enslaved workers for its survival. Without them, the colony would perish. In facultative dulosis, slavery is more opportunistic, with the slave-maker colony occasionally raiding other nests to supplement its workforce.

Red wood ants are masters of manipulation, wielding their jaws with astonishing dexterity. These insects can rotate their mandibles in multiple directions, allowing them to capture prey with incredible precision or delicately handle their eggs. Inspired by this natural engineering marvel, researchers from the Leibniz Institute for the Analysis of Biodiversity Change have developed three innovative designs for endoscopic needle holders[23]. These bio-inspired tools mimic the ant's jaw movements, enabling surgeons to exert significantly more force during delicate procedures. This enhanced control and flexibility are crucial for navigating the confined spaces within the human body. By minimizing the risk of human error and improving precision, these ant-inspired tools could revolutionize minimally invasive surgery. While further clinical trials are essential, these findings offer a glimpse into the exciting potential of biomimicry to transform the field of medicine.

Ever thought ants could be medical marvels? These tiny creatures possess a remarkable ability that could revolutionize cancer detection. Ants, like many animals, are experts at detecting subtle changes in odours. They can pick up on specific volatile organic compounds (VOCs) emitted by our bodies, which can be altered by diseases like cancer. Researchers at the University Sorbonne Paris Nord in France have trained the humble silky ant, *formica fusca*, common across Europe, to sniff out breast cancer[24].

By training ants to associate the scent of cancerous cells with a sugar reward, scientists have effectively created tiny cancer detectives. In a fascinating experiment, researchers exposed ants to urine samples from mice with and without breast tumours. The trained ants showed a clear preference for the samples containing cancer-related VOCs, spending significantly more time investigating them. This innovative approach opens up exciting possibilities for early cancer detection, where ants could be used to screen urine or blood samples for signs of cancer.

Ants have long captured the human imagination, often serving as symbols of diligence, teamwork and foresight. From ancient proverbs to modern literature, these industrious insects have inspired and fascinated us. The Bible extols the virtues of ants, praising their tireless work ethic and cooperative spirit. Proverb 6:6–11 in the Book of Proverbs says, 'Go to the ant, you sluggard; consider its ways and be wise! It has no commander, no overseer or ruler, yet it stores its provisions in summer and gathers its food at harvest.' Aesop, the renowned Greek storyteller, also used ants to teach valuable lessons, as seen in his fable 'The Ant and the Grasshopper'.

Modern authors have explored deeper themes through the lens of ants. Robert Frost's poem 'Departmental' delves into the intricate social structure of ant colonies, drawing parallels to human society.

... Ants are a curious race;
One crossing with hurried tread
The body of one of their dead
Isn't given a moment's arrest—
Seems not even impressed ...

By observing the ants' methodical response to death, Frost underscores the often detached and routine nature of human existence. The poem highlights how the ants, as a collective, carry out their duties without emotion or individual thought. They efficiently dispose of the dead ant, a task that is part of their societal function. This robotic behaviour mirrors the way humans often approach life's challenges, particularly those that are unexpected or tragic.

Frost suggests that our modern, compartmentalized lives can lead to a certain degree of detachment and a loss of empathy. We become so focused on our individual tasks and roles that we may neglect the broader human experience. The ants, in their efficiency, serve as a cautionary tale, reminding us to pause and reflect on the deeper meaning of life.

British author T.H. White's fantasy novel *The Once and Future King* about the legend of King Arthur, offers a unique perspective on political systems through the eyes of a young boy, Wart, who transforms into various creatures. In one particular transformation, Wart becomes an ant, immersing himself in a society governed by strict collectivism. This ant colony, while seemingly efficient and harmonious, is revealed to be a totalitarian regime. The individual ant is subservient to the collective will, stripped of personal identity and autonomy. The colony's rigid social structure and relentless pursuit of productivity leave no room for individuality or dissent. Through this experience, Wart gains a firsthand understanding of the dangers of unchecked collectivism. This transformative experience shapes Wart's worldview and influences his future as King Arthur, enabling him to appreciate the value of individual liberty and the importance of a balanced society.

In ancient Greek mythology, ants play a role in divine intervention and a miraculous transformation of a kingdom. King Aeacus, ruler of the island of Aegina, faced a devastating plague that threatened to wipe out his entire kingdom. In desperation, he turned to the mighty Zeus, the king of the gods, pleading for a solution. Zeus, ever the compassionate deity, devised a unique plan. He gazed upon the sacred oak tree, teeming with countless ants, and a spark of inspiration ignited within him. With a divine touch, he transformed these industrious insects into a new race of warriors. In a flash, the ants morphed into strong, battle-ready humans. Their appearance was as sudden as it was awe-inspiring. These newly formed warriors were named Myrmidons, a name derived from the Greek word for 'ant'. The Myrmidons inherited the remarkable qualities of their former selves: unity, discipline, strength, and unwavering loyalty. They were a force to be reckoned with, renowned throughout the Greek world for their fearsome fighting prowess. Their story is a testament to the extraordinary power of the gods and the enduring legacy of the humble ant.

In the realm of Vedic astrology and Hindu mythology, the act of feeding ants holds profound spiritual significance. It is believed to be a potent ritual capable of attracting good fortune, fulfilling wishes, and mitigating negative planetary influences. Ants are considered sacred symbols of Lord Vishnu, one of the principal deities in Hinduism. Feeding them is seen as an act of devotion to the divine. The negative impact of Rahu, a shadow planet associated with obstacles and delays, can be alleviated by feeding ants. Conversely, Ketu, the planet of spiritual enlightenment and detachment, is believed to be pleased by this act. Feeding ants is thought to strengthen one's spiritual connection and accelerate spiritual growth[25].

A parable about ants from the Brahmavaivarta Purana offers a profound spiritual lesson, veiled in a seemingly mundane act[26]. It highlights the transience of earthly power and the eternal nature of the divine. According to the story, Indra, the king of the gods, becomes intoxicated with pride and arrogance. He goes on a building spree demanding more and more of Vishwakarma, the divine builder and architect. Exhausted, Vishwakarma appeals to Lord Brahma the creator, for help, who in turn seeks out Lord Vishnu. Vishnu, in the guise of Vamana, a humble Brahmin boy, starts narrating the chronicles of former Indras, much to Indra's horror. Just then, a line of ants enters the palace, and Vamana mockingly tells him that they are former Indras. This humbling realization shakes Indra to his core, forcing him to confront his own ego and acknowledge the higher power. The story ultimately teaches us the importance of humility and gratitude. Even the most powerful beings are subject to the laws of karma and the cycles of time.

Beliefs about ants in West Africa reveal a deep connection between humans and the natural world, particularly the often-overlooked realm of insects. Nitten Nair notes on the website, *Mythlok*, that in West African mythology, there are fairies, called Aziza, that live in the anthills with the ants. They pass on their wisdom of medicinal herbs and help travellers and hunters.

Author of fantasy books Jo-Anne Blanco writes on her blog about a similar notion of ant fairies in Cornwall, UK. Fairies known as Muryans, meaning 'ant', were considered to be benevolent and exceptionally beautiful. According to Cornwall mythology, Muryans wore ornate dresses made of velvet or embellished with ornaments. It is believed that ants are the souls of the fairies in a state of decay.

The idea of ants as fallen souls or fairies is a poignant one, suggesting a continuum between the human and the natural world. It highlights the belief in the spiritual significance of all living beings, even the smallest. The association with alchemy and magic adds another layer of intrigue to the mythology of ants. The concept of transformation and transmutation is a central theme in many ancient cultures, and the belief that ants can facilitate such processes underscores their perceived power and mystery.

Anecdotal observations associate the ant with the ability to predict rain, although there is no scientific evidence to prove this. It's true that ants possess highly sensitive antennae that can detect various environmental cues, including changes in temperature, humidity and chemical signals. It's plausible that they could use these sensory abilities to anticipate changes in weather patterns. However, more research is needed to fully understand the extent of their predictive capabilities[27].

While their ability to predict rain is questionable, there is no doubt about their abilities to survive the perils of flooding. Ants have evolved some truly remarkable strategies to adapt to floods. Some ant species can hold their breath for an astonishing eight to nine days when submerged in cool water! This incredible adaptation allows them to weather even the most severe floods. Mangrove ant soldiers use their large heads to physically block the nest entrance, keeping the rising waters at bay. Australian mangrove ants construct bell-shaped, watertight chambers that trap air bubbles. These ingenious structures serve as lifeboats during floods, providing a safe haven for the colony. Bamboo ants have a unique way of dealing with floods. They drink excess water and then collectively urinate outside the nest, reducing the water level inside. Some ant species have a dedicated flood response team. When a few ants detect rising waters, they trigger a mass evacuation, ensuring the safety of the entire colony. Ant species living in floodplains construct earthen levees around their nests within twenty-four hours of a major rain event to divert water and protect their homes from flooding[27].

The 2017 Texas floods brought devastation to the region, but amidst the chaos, a surprising sight emerged on social media: massive rafts of fire ants floating on the floodwaters. These resilient insects, feared for their painful stings, had adapted to the extreme conditions, forming extraordinary life-saving structures. Each raft, composed of tens of thousands of ants, is a marvel of engineering. The ants link together, using their waxy, water-resistant bodies to create a buoyant platform. At the heart of this living raft lies the queen, protected by her loyal subjects. As they drift along, the ants search for higher ground, a new place to establish their colony. The ants can float for weeks even if they don't find food. They sacrifice their young (in pupae form), feeding on them to survive. Once they get to dry land they will build a new nest and form a colony[28].

Ants are essential components of our planet's intricate ecosystem. Their disappearance would trigger a ripple effect with far-reaching consequences. They play a crucial role in soil aeration and nutrient cycling. Their absence would lead to compacted soil, hindering plant growth. Many ant species disperse seeds, contributing to plant diversity and forest regeneration. Ants are a vital food source for numerous animals, from birds to small mammals. Their disappearance would destabilize the food chain. Ants are natural predators of many agricultural pests, reducing the need for chemical pesticides.

These tiny creatures are the unsung heroes of our planet. They're the architects of the soil, tirelessly aerating it and recycling nutrients. Without them, our gardens and forests would struggle to thrive, their lifeblood choked by compacted earth. Ants are also master gardeners. Many species act as tiny farmers, cultivating and protecting fungi, while others meticulously disperse seeds, ensuring the survival of countless plant species. This intricate web of life, woven by ants, contributes to the breathtaking biodiversity that makes our planet so special. Ants are tireless hunters, keeping populations of harmful insects in check, reducing our reliance on harmful pesticides. They are a stark reminder of the interconnectedness of all life and the delicate balance that sustains us all.

There's plenty for us humans to learn from ants. Ant colonies provide a fascinating model for the study of complex social interactions, including division of labour, communication and decision-making. Altruism, cooperation and conflict resolution are not unique to humans; they are deeply ingrained in the social fabric of ant colonies. Although their march into our kitchens and pantries can be annoying, deep down we know that they are just following their instinct for survival. That is the right of every creature on earth after all, even one as tiny as the ant.

CHAPTER 12

THE BEE

AS the sun dappled above, casting playful shadows on the terrace of my apartment building, my school friends and I chased each other, squealing with joy and laughter. It was the summer holidays. The Mumbai heat allowed for only a few hours of playtime in the open terrace. We kids wanted to make every bit of it. However, our playtime was disturbed by an unwelcome guest—a few buzzing bees, whose hive was nestled in a cozy corner of the building. Our carefree play turned into cautious steps. Having heard painful stories of bee stings, we huddled together, hearts pounding with every buzz that echoed through the air. And soon we made a quick and stealthy escape from the terrace into the safety of the indoors.

Indeed, the fear of bees, apiphobia, is a common trope in various forms of media, often used to evoke fear, suspense, or even humour. In horror films, a swarm of angry bees can be a terrifying antagonist, chasing and attacking helpless victims. On the other hand, in romantic tales, a knight in shining armour might swoop in to rescue a damsel in distress from bees, showcasing their bravery and chivalry. In Kalidasa's play, when a bee hovers over Shakuntala, troubling her, the might king Dushyant arrives in a timely manner to save her, and falls in love with her. Similarly, in Bana's *Kadambari*, the hero enters to save the princess, who is pursued by a swarm of bees that are attracted to her parijata perfume, and cover her like a 'blue veil'.

Fortunately or unfortunately, my friends and I didn't have a knight in shining armour turning up at the terrace to rescue us. We were children of the twentieth century after all. Armed with hats and long-sleeved clothes, we ventured back into the terrace the next day to play. However, we still weren't bold enough to watch films such as *Killer Bees*, *The Swarm*, *The Savage Bees*, or *The Deadly Bees*, which depicted bees as dangerous creatures and killers, using them as a tool to create horror and fear.

Later, as a young woman with a strong interest in nature and the environment, I realized that while movies often portray a single, generic image of a bee, the reality is much more diverse. There are over 20,000 species of wild bees buzzing worldwide, each with unique characteristics and ecological roles[1]. In the United States and Canada alone, there are about 3,600 species. While honey bees, bumblebees, and stingless bees thrive in bustling colonies, over 90 per cent of bee species, including mason bees, carpenter bees, leafcutter bees and sweat bees, prefer a more solitary lifestyle. These bees prefer to live alone, nesting in cozy little spots like cracks in rocks, holes in trees, or even underground.

Apidae is the largest and most diverse family of bees, containing at least 5,700 species of bees. These include bumblebees, honeybees, stingless bees (also used for honey production), carpenter bees, orchid bees, cuckoo bees, and a number of other less widely known groups. In India, rock bees (*apis dorsata*) are the largest bees, constructing massive, single-comb nests that can reach up to 6 feet long and 3 feet deep. They prefer to build their nests in open areas, often under cliffs or tree branches. They are aggressive and cannot be domesticated, but they are highly productive, yielding around 36 kgs of honey per comb per year. They are known for their migratory behaviour, shifting their colonies in search of optimal foraging conditions[2].

Little bee (*apis florea*) are the smallest of the four *Apis* species found in India. They build small, single-comb nests, usually no larger than a palm, in various locations like tree branches, bushes or buildings. Their honey yield is relatively low, around half a kilogram per hive per year. Like the rock bee, they are prone to frequent relocation, making them difficult to domesticate[2].

The Indian hive bee (*apis cerana indica*) is the most commonly domesticated bee species in India. They build multiple parallel combs within their nests, and produce a moderate amount of honey, typically 6 to 8 kgs per colony per year. They are susceptible to swarming, when the colony splits into two or more, each raising a new queen; as well as absconding, a process in which all the bees leave the hive. Both swarming and absconding can impact honey production[2].

India is also home to two other fascinating species of stingless bees: Melipona and Trigona. These are much smaller than their honeybee cousins, but play a significant role in pollination, particularly for various food crops. They construct irregular combs made of wax and resins, in crevices, hollow tree trunks, or underground. While they can be domesticated, their honey yield is relatively low, around 100 gms per hive per year[2].

A beehive is like a tiny kingdom, with a queen bee at the helm. This royal bee is the only female in the hive who can lay eggs. When she's ready to mate, she takes a nuptial flight and mates with up to twenty male bees. She stores their sperms in her reproductive organ, and then spends the rest of her life, about two to five years, laying up to 2,000 eggs daily! If you have wondered about how the phrase 'busy as a bee' came about, now you know. The male bees, called drones, predictably have just one job. Like all males, their only interest is to fly out and find the queen. But this job comes with a consequence. Those who mate successfully, fall to the ground and die, as martyrs, sacrificing their life for their children. Most of the grunge work is left to the females in the hive. When these worker females are young, they clean up the hive and feed the baby bees. As they get older, they become foragers, flying out to collect flowers' sweet nectar and pollen. They're also the builders, creating beautiful honeycomb cells, and the guards, protecting the hive from intruders[3].

Worker bees are excellent communicators. One kind of communication is using pheromones or special scents. When there's danger, a particular pheromone is released, warning other bees of danger and getting them ready to sting. Only workers of twelve species of bees and wasps possess stingers. When they have to defend their colony, they release the barbed stinger that becomes lodged in the victim's skin. This proves fatal for the worker bee, as the removal of the stinger also tears away a portion of its abdomen. Honeybees, otherwise, are usually pretty chill. They only sting when they feel threatened. Wasps, hornets and carpenter bees, on the other hand, are more dangerous. They can sting multiple times, if provoked. So it's best to leave them alone. Stingless bees on the other hand, don't have stingers, but they defend their nests by biting intruders[4].

Worker bees have another fascinating way of communicating with each other. The 'waggle dance' isn't a literal dance, but a series of intricate movements that convey important information about the location of food sources. As a bee performs this dance, it vibrates its wings and moves its body in a figure-eight pattern. The intensity of the waggle, measured by the speed of the bee's abdomen movements, indicates the distance to the food source. Additionally, the angle of the bee's body relative to the sun provides a directional cue, pointing its nest mates towards the nectar-rich location, such as a field of flowers. It's a truly remarkable feat of biological engineering and a testament to the intelligence of these tiny creatures[5].

The queen bee, while being a busy mom, also sends out pheromones to communicate. But being the boss, the queen's pheromones tell the other bees what to do. These pheromones impart a distinctive scent to the hive, helping the bees recognize their queen and keep track of her health. When it's time to swarm, that is, when the queen wants to start a new bee colony, she signals her workers, takes half of them, and flies off to find a new home[4].

For centuries, our patriarchal ancestors were unaware that bee colonies were ruled by a female bee, the queen. Ancient thinkers like Aristotle, Varro, Pliny and Virgil described the hive using masculine terms like 'basileus', and 'hegemon', and the Latin terms 'rex', 'dux', and 'imperator', meaning 'king'. The Egyptians kings, the powerful pharaohs, used bees as symbols of royal power. This concept was reinforced by European monarchs who adopted the bee as a symbol of royal power. This long-held belief was challenged in the seventeenth century when Dutch biologist Jan Swammerdam discovered that the true ruler of the hive was a queen bee. This revelation caused quite a stir, as it overturned centuries of accepted wisdom[6].

While ancient civilizations may not have fully understood the gender dynamics of bee colonies, they were skilled beekeepers, harnessing the power of these industrious insects. American entomologist Gene Kritsky in his book, *The Tears of Re: Beekeeping in Ancient Egypt* offers fascinating insights into the ancient practice of beekeeping in Egypt. The solar temple of Pharaoh Nyuserre Ini, dating back to the twenty-fifth century BCE, provides tangible evidence of this ancient craft. The limestone blocks, etched with intricate scenes, depict a beekeeper kneeling before a row of horizontal hives. The beekeeper's actions, labelled with hieroglyphs, suggest a technique of 'calling' the ruling bee during swarming season. This practice, still used by modern Egyptian beekeepers, shows that the Egyptians understood bee behaviour thousands of years ago[7].

The interactions between humans and bees go back even further in time, 40,000 years ago. Journalist Holly Norton in a 2017 article in *The Guardian* indicates that the earliest record was found in a Spanish cave. A 40,000-year-old spear was found secured to the shaft with a sticky substance—beeswax. Ancient rock art, scattered across continents from southern Africa to Australia, paints a vivid picture of this ancient bond. Nomadic and semi-nomadic peoples, ever on the move, hunted wild honey. Their art, often depicting human figures reaching for hives, reveals a deep understanding of bee life cycles. Intriguingly, some Zimbabwean paintings don't just show honey and honeycomb. They depict the brood—the nursery of the hive where eggs are laid and grow into larvae. This knowledge would have been invaluable to these hunter-gatherers, helping them time their honey raids for maximum yield. And they didn't just take the honey; they also ate the brood, a rich source of protein and fat[8].

The earliest evidence of organized beekeeping, beyond simply collecting wild honey, comes from the ancient city of Tel Rehov in Israel. Around the tenth to ninth centuries BCE, this bustling city had a thriving beekeeping industry with about 100 hives. The excavated hives and those depicted in ancient Egyptian are cylindrical, horizontal hives made of clay or ceramic. In contrast, the Greeks used upright clay pots as hives. Although no lids have been found, experts suggest that ancient Greek beekeepers might have used movable combs, a technique similar to modern beekeeping. By using clay lids or wooden strips, they could manipulate the hives, showing a deep understanding of bee behaviour and hive management[8].

Medieval and early modern Europe had a distinctive style of beekeeping. They often kept bees in hollowed-out tree trunks or wall cavities, using wicker and mud baskets as hives. This method was popular across Europe, especially in England, Ireland and France. These beehives were usually found in gardens or near agricultural fields, such as vineyards. Beyond Europe, various cultures used natural materials for beekeeping. While honeybees are native to the Old World, the ancient Maya civilization in the Americas domesticated stingless bees. These bees were kept in hollowed-out logs sealed with stone discs, showcasing the diverse ways people have harnessed the power of bees throughout history[8].

Beekeeping today, also known as apiculture, was revolutionized by Lorenzo Langstroth, an American pastor, in 1851[9]. His groundbreaking invention, the Langstroth hive, patented in 1852, transformed beekeeping into a large-scale industry, and continues to be the standard today. The Langstroth hive is a modular design, consisting of wooden boxes stacked one upon the other. The key to its success lies in the concept of 'bee space', a precise distance between the frames within the hive. By maintaining this specific space, Langstroth ensured that bees could freely move about without building unwanted comb or hindering the beekeeper's ability to inspect and manage the hive.

A typical Langstroth hive includes a bottom board, brood chamber, and one or more honey supers. The honey supers are where bees store excess honey. The brood chamber is where the queen lays eggs and the colony raises its young. A queen excluder, a grid-like barrier, prevents the queen from entering the honey supers, ensuring the honey remains pure. The hive's exterior, often painted white, serves both aesthetic and functional purposes. The white colour helps to regulate the temperature inside the hive and makes it easier for bees to locate their home. Langstroth's ingenious design has allowed beekeepers to efficiently manage their colonies, harvest honey, and support the vital role of bees in pollination. His legacy continues to shape the future of beekeeping and the health of our planet.

Beekeeping is not just beneficial for the planet, it also has a positive impact on human mental health. A recent study published in the journal *Frontiers in Psychology* in 2024, revealed that beekeeping can significantly improve the psychological well-being of individuals[10]. Researchers examined a group of Irish farmers who participated in the 'Let It Bee' project, an initiative aimed at protecting biodiversity through sustainable agricultural practices. By introducing beekeeping into their routines, these farmers experienced a range of mental health benefits. Beekeepers took immense pride in their role as guardians of these vital pollinators. The shared passion for beekeeping fostered a sense of community, strengthening relationships with family and fellow beekeepers. Tending to bees provided a calming and meditative experience, allowing participants to connect with nature and reduce stress. Beekeepers felt a deep connection to the natural world and a desire to contribute to environmental conservation. The challenges and rewards of beekeeping helped participants develop new skills, such as patience, observation and problem-solving.

It turns out that bees, with brains a fraction of the size of ours, themselves have incredible problem-solving skills. In a fascinating experiment, German biologist and bee expert Lars Chittka unveiled the surprising intelligence of bumblebees[11]. These tiny creatures were tasked with a complex challenge: pulling a string to uncover a tasty reward of sugary water. The bees, eager for the sweet treat, quickly learned to manipulate the string. But the real surprise came when a second group of bees, who had observed their fellow bees, were introduced. They didn't need anyone to teach them; they just watched and copied. This shows that bees are not just mindless little workers; they're smart learners who can learn from each other. It's like they have their own little bee school, where they share tips and tricks.

Bees can count and even do simple math[12]. Scientists at the Australian National University designed a special maze to test the bees' numerical skills. The bees were presented with a pattern, a specific number of dots (S), at the entrance of a Y-shaped maze. When they entered the maze, they then had to choose between two paths, one with the same number of dots (S) and the other with a different number. The bees were rewarded with sugary water if they chose the path with the same number of dots they had encountered at the entrance. Remarkably, the bees could choose the right path up to four dots. However, they struggled with numbers larger than four. This ability to count is likely helpful for bees in navigating their environment. By counting landmarks, they can find their way back to their hive after foraging for food. The researchers believe that bees use two different memory systems: working memory to remember the number of symbols and long-term memory to apply rules for counting.

Building on this research, scientist wanted to check if bees can perform addition and subtraction. Scientists trained bees with colours, blue meant 'add one' and yellow meant 'subtract one'[13]. When presented with a certain number of shapes in either blue or yellow, the bees had to choose the correct path in a Y-shaped maze. If the shapes were blue, they had to choose the path with one more shape; if they were yellow, they had to choose the path with one less shape. Amazingly, the bees were quite successful at this task, correctly solving the problems 63 to 72 per cent of the time. This suggests that even tiny brains can perform complex cognitive tasks. This breakthrough could inspire new ways to develop artificial intelligence and machine learning.

Given the cognitive abilities that bees possess, it's intriguing to speculate whether they might also experience emotions. Scientists investigated whether bumblebees can consciously avoid pain based on the situation, as avoidance of pain is a complex behavior with both cognitive and emotional underpinnings. To test this, Lars Chittka and his team at Queen Mary University of London, presented bumblebees with a choice between two types of feeders: high-sugar, hot feeders, and low-sugar, cool feeders[14]. The bees, driven by their desire for the sugary reward, were willing to endure the discomfort of the hot feeders, a clear trade-off between pain and pleasure. Furthermore, the bees displayed remarkable memory and learning abilities. They could associate the colour of the heating pad with the temperature of the feeder, and avoided the hot ones when the sugar reward wasn't high enough. This suggests that bees can experience pain and make conscious decisions based on their perception of it. Although other scientists were not convinced that this is a sign of pain, this research challenges our conventional understanding of insect perceptions.

In fact, Stephen Buchmann, American pollination ecologist argues that bees are sentient beings, just like us. In his book, *What a Bee Knows: Exploring the Thoughts, Memories and Personalities of Bees*[15], he writes about research studies including his own, suggesting that bees have complex emotions, self-awareness and consciousness. He contends that these studies highlight the importance of considering the potential suffering of these creatures in various human activities, such as pest control in agriculture.

Playful behaviour is another sign of sentience and intelligence. Scientists have discovered that these busy little bees aren't just hardworking; they also know how to have fun. In a study conducted at Queen Mary University of London, researchers observed bumblebees rolling around colourful balls placed in their environment, for sheer enjoyment. While some bees used the balls as a means to reach a reward, others rolled the balls not because they have to, but just for fun. It's like they're having a bee-ball party! This behaviour was seen over multiple days, suggesting that the bees have feelings and can experience joy[16].

Honeybees can supposedly recognize human faces according to scientists at Cambridge University, led by visual scientist Adrian

Dyer. Inspired by bees' uncanny knack for differentiating between flowers, Dyer and his team wondered if their visual acumen could help them recognize human faces. To test this, they presented bees with a board displaying four different human faces and trained them to land on a specific face, for which they received a sugary reward[17]. Surprisingly, the bees not only learned to recognize the target face but also retained this memory for up to two days! We humans rely on a specialized brain part to recognize others, but this research suggests that these insects can do it without having complex brains like ours. While this idea is fascinating, it's likely that the way bees recognize faces is very different from how humans do. For bees, a face might simply be another complex pattern or a peculiar-looking flower. Nevertheless, this discovery highlights the incredible cognitive abilities of these tiny insects.

These super smart insects, with such cool abilities, may be the next big thing in human diagnostics. Bees have a sense of smell that's 100 times more powerful than ours. Scientists are harnessing this power to help us humans. They're training bees to sniff out dangerous chemicals, like those found in explosives, or even early signs of diseases like cancer and diabetes.

In 2013, Portuguese designer Susana Soares unveiled a bee-powered diagnostic device using the incredible olfactory abilities of bees to detect the subtle scent markers of diseases[18]. The device was a simple glass apparatus with two chambers, a small one housed within a larger one. Patients simply exhale into the smaller chamber. Trained bees are then introduced. If the bees detect the specific odour associated with the disease, they instinctively fly towards the breath in the smaller chamber, signalling a potential health issue. The training process for these tiny detectives is surprisingly quick. Within just ten minutes, bees can be conditioned to associate a particular odour with a sugary reward, achieving a 98 per cent accuracy rate. They even remember this association for life. Field tests of this innovative device have successfully identified a patient with diabetes, a finding that was subsequently confirmed by traditional medical tests.

While bee-powered health diagnostics is currently more of a scientific curiosity than a practical medical tool, they can actually provide clues about the health of our planet. Scientists at the UK Centre for Ecology & Hydrology are harnessing the power of bees to monitor climate and environmental changes[19]. As bees forage for nectar and pollen, they inadvertently collect a diverse range of plant material. By studying the pollen grains trapped in honey, the scientists can figure out what kinds of plants are growing in different areas. It's like a natural history book, written by bees!

This innovative approach, part of the National Honey Monitoring Scheme, involves collaborating with beekeepers across the UK. The honey samples collected from these hives serve as a natural archive, providing a long-term record of environmental conditions. This information allows researchers to track changes in plant diversity, abundance, and distribution over time. This bee-powered monitoring system offers a cost-effective and efficient way to assess environmental health.

Bees could also one day help us adapt to climate change and global warming. When temperatures soar, bees have a clever way to keep their colonies cool: they fan their wings! It's like a tiny air conditioning system, helping to regulate the temperature inside the hive. To understand this fascinating behaviour, researchers at the University of Wisconsin are studying individual bumblebees[20]. They've developed a system that tracks these bees as they navigate a simulated heatwave. By using advanced technology like deep learning, scientists can identify and analyse the bees' fanning behaviour in detail. By studying their responses to heat stress, we can develop strategies to protect these vital pollinators and ensure their survival in a warming world.

With all the hard work they do, it's natural that bees would buzz their way into our hearts and screens! From the sunny beaches of Disney's animated world to adorable adventures of Maya the Bee, a German book and TV show, these tiny creatures have captivated audiences of all ages. Bees also feature in mythology, spanning across cultures and centuries. In ancient Egypt, the sun god Re was believed to shed tears that transformed into bees. In Mayan mythology, the god Ah Muzen Cab and the one of the Maya Hero Twins, Xbalanque were associated with bees and beekeeping.

In the ancient lore of Africa, the bee, a symbol of wisdom, played a pivotal role in the genesis of humanity. At the dawn of time, when the world was submerged, the legendary hero Mantis emerged. Tasked with uncovering life's purpose, he sought guidance from the wise bee. To help the Mantis embark on his quest, the bee agreed to carry him across the turbulent waters. But as days turned into nights, the bee, weary and cold, struggled to maintain flight. Yet, the bee persevered, its wings carrying the weight of destiny. Finally, a glimmer of hope appeared: a magnificent white flower, half-opened, floated on the water's surface. The bee gently placed Mantis within its heart with a final act of selfless devotion, planted with him the seed of the first human, and succumbed to exhaustion. As the sun rose and its rays kissed the flower, a miracle unfolded. Mantis awoke, and from the seed left behind by the bee, the first bushman was born—a testament to the bee's wisdom and sacrifice[21].

In Greek mythology, a fascinating tale weaves its way through the lives of some of history's greatest minds. Legends tell of bees hovering around the mouths of infants destined for greatness, a divine sign of their future brilliance. One such infant was Sophocles, the renowned playwright. It is said that bees swarmed around his mouth as a newborn, as if drawn to the honeyed words he would one day weave into his plays[6]. Similarly, the poets Pindar and Plato were also believed to have been marked by this extraordinary visit. This mythical association between bees and poetic genius suggests a profound connection between nature and creativity. The industrious bee, gathering nectar from flowers, mirrors the poet, drawing inspiration from the world around them.

Hindu mythology also weaves bees into its stories. The goddess Parvati, when summoned to defeat the demon Arunasura, transformed into Bhramari Devi, the goddess of black bees. The bees, emerging from her body, played a crucial role in defeating the demon. In the Bhagavat Purana, Krishna is described as being surrounded by maidens and bees. The bees, drawn to his spiritual radiance, symbolize devotion and the sweetness of divine love. In the *Kumara Sambhava*, the harassment of goddesses like Uma and Saraswati by bees can be interpreted symbolically. It might represent the challenges and distractions that even divine beings face, or it could signify the transformative power of nature.

In ancient Tamil poetry, bees were symbols of love, their hum a romantic melody that stirred hearts. Spring, the season of love and desire, was their time to shine. Poets often associated the buzzing of bees with the passionate notes of flutes and the melodious songs of young maidens. This connection between bees and love runs deep. The bow of Kamadeva, the god of love, is decorated with flowers and bees, and the hum of these industrious creatures is likened to the twang of Kama's bow. They were seen as intoxicated with the nectar of the flowers, their drunken buzz a hazy, indistinct song of love's sweet madness.

Even today, Bollywood's lyricists take inspiration from bees to create romantic songs. From the legendary actress, Waheeda Rehman penning her love song in the film, *Sahib Bibi aur Ghulam*—'Bawra bada naadan hai', to the iconic yesteryear heroes Randhir Kapoor and Rajesh Khanna serenading their beloveds with '*bhanwre ki gunjan, hai mera dil*', and '*gun guna rahe bawre*', bees have always been a symbol of love and longing in Bollywood. Even the modern-day diva Kajol couldn't resist the charm of these buzzing insects, expressing her joy through a song about carefree, singing bees '*aawara bhawre jo hole hole gaaye*'. Perhaps, the familiar euphemism 'the birds and the bees' to explain the intricacies of reproduction owes its origins to this age-old association of bees with romance.

In fact, the world in a sense, owes its existence to bees. These busy insects play a crucial role in our ecosystem. Over 80 per cent of flowering plants rely on insect pollinators to reproduce. When a bee visits a flower to sip nectar or collect pollen, it unintentionally transfers pollen from one flower to another. This process, called pollination, is essential for the formation of fruits and seeds. Wild bees aren't just important for wildflowers; they're also vital for our food supply. Roughly three-quarters of crop species, which contribute to a third of global crop production, depend on pollinators[1]. So, the next time you enjoy a juicy apple or a bunch of berries, remember to thank the hardworking bees that helped bring it to your plate!

Beyond their ecological significance, wild bees have a substantial economic impact on agriculture. A 2020 study revealed that these tiny creatures contribute over $1.5 billion annually to the production of seven major crops, including apples and pumpkins[22]. In some cases, wild bees, particularly bumblebees, are even more effective pollinators than honeybees. Crops like tomatoes, blueberries and cranberries rely on the specific vibrational frequency of a bumblebee's buzz to release pollen.

While wild bees are essential to our ecosystem and economy, their populations are facing significant threats. A recent assessment of bumblebee species revealed that a third of them are in decline. Moreover, the number of bee species documented in a yearly survey from 2006 to 2015 has dropped by a quarter compared to earlier records. Climate change is taking a toll on our planet's vital pollinators, including honeybees. Rising temperatures are causing bumblebee nests to overheat, leading to the tragic loss of entire broods[23].

Additionally, extreme weather events, such as droughts and heavy rainfall, are disrupting the delicate balance of nature and limiting the availability of essential food resources, restricting the number of flying hours for bees, and hindering their ability to gather food. These climate-induced challenges are particularly harsh for managed bee colonies. Beekeepers are forced to supplement their hives with sugar water and pollen to keep their colonies alive. Some experienced beekeepers reported devastating losses of up to 70 per cent of their colonies during the winter of 2021–22[24].

The consequences of these declines are far-reaching. Crops like apples, blueberries and cherries in the US are already experiencing reduced yields due to insufficient pollination. As wild bee populations continue to dwindle, the future of our food supply and ecological balance hangs in the balance[1].

Fortunately, there are steps we can take to support these vital creatures. Urban pavements can serve as unexpected habitats for wild bees and wasps. Scientists in Berlin discovered that cobblestone streets can be a haven for wild bees and wasps[25]. These busy little insects find cozy nooks and crannies between the stones to build their homes. The best part? If these streets are near a park or garden, they're even more likely to be buzzing with insect life. The plants and flowers in these green spaces provide food and shelter for the insects, making the streets a perfect place to live. This research shows that even in our busy cities, we can create small havens for nature. By planting pollinator-friendly flowers, we can help bees thrive, and make our cities more beautiful and ensure the survival of these essential creatures, as well as our planet for future generations.

My home in Bengaluru is nestled among large trees, parks and beautiful home gardens adorned with crescendo of flowers. My own home is graced with a *thunbergia coccinea* vine. With its stunning orange-red tubular flowers cascading from the terrace, this creeper has become a magnet for bees. But unlike the little girl who made a run for the indoors, today, I stand proud and happy in the knowledge that my home is a tiny shelter providing food for these wonderful creatures.

CHAPTER 13

THE MOSQUITO

THE sound of firecrackers exacerbated the pain and discomfort that had been wrought by mosquitoes. It was my family's first Diwali after moving into our refurbished house. But fate or rather mosquitoes had other plans for me. I was diagnosed with dengue and due to my rapidly falling platelet counts, I was admitted in the ICU. I had to undergo platelet transfusion, but finding a donor during the festival season was proving to be difficult. But thankfully, in a couple of days, my extended family and friends rallied to donate their blood. After finding seven donors and undergoing seven rounds of platelet transfusion, my platelet levels rose up to normal. While recuperating at home, I wondered why mosquitoes even existed, considering they wreak havoc on us humans. Every year, mosquito-borne illnesses affect around 700 million people, and kill about one million[1]. While some pests have offered unexpected benefits to mankind, like cockroaches have inspired robotic designs and rats have been used for disease detection, we have not found any way to exploit mosquitoes for our benefit. Do these pesky insects then deserve to live alongside us and suck our blood?

After all, even in ancient times, mosquitoes were considered a source of annoyance and misery. Pliny the Younger, a first century CE Roman naturalist, famously lamented the loud noise these tiny creatures made. 'Who gave the mosquito so terrifying a voice, infinitely greater than it should be in comparison to the size of its body?'[2]. In 1727, when the French missionary Father Du Poisson travelled up the Mississippi River, he observed that, '… the greatest torture—without which everything else would have been only a recreation, but which passes all belief, and could never be imagined in France unless it had been experienced—is the mosquitoes, the cruel persecution of the mosquitoes. [...] This little creature has caused more swearing since the French came to Mississippi, than has been done before that time in all the rest of the world.'[3]

Henry David Thoreau (1817–1862), the American author and poet, took a more soft-hearted view about mosquitoes when he wrote in his book, *Walden*: 'Mornings bring back the heroic ages. I was as much affected by the faint hum of a mosquito making its invisible and unimaginable tour through my apartment at earliest dawn, when I was sitting with the door and windows open, as I could be by any trumpet that ever sang of fame. It was Homer's requiem; itself an Iliad and Odyssey in the air, singing its own wrath and wanderings. There was something cosmical about it; a standing advertisement, till forbidden, of the everlasting vigor and fertility of the world.'[2]

I suppose Thoreau can be forgiven for painting this romantic notion of mosquitoes. Being a nineteenth century American, he may not have been exposed to the dangers of mosquito-borne illnesses. My sentiments are more aligned with Pliny, the Younger, as would anyone else who has tried to sleep with a mosquito buzzing around his/her ear. As a light sleeper, the slightest buzz ruins my sleep. Thankfully, the twentieth century invention, the mosquito bat has become my loyal defender, ensuring a (somewhat) peaceful night's rest, especially during the monsoon season's nightly mosquito orchestra.

Unfortunately the ancient Egyptians, known for their pyramids and pharaohs, lacked this marvellous mosquito zapping machine. Instead, as Herodotus, a Greek historian, recounts, people living near the Nile River were forced to sleep on towers to escape the relentless attacks of mosquitoes. And it wasn't just humans who suffered. Ancient Mesopotamians claimed that even mighty lions, the kings of the jungle, would resort to desperate measures like drowning or self-mutilation to alleviate the torment inflicted by these tiny bloodsuckers[2].

Even our ancient Indian texts, particularly the Atharva Veda, were well versed in the knowledge of mosquitoes and their impact on human health. The Atharva Veda refers to the mosquito as 'makka' or 'maśaka' which was frequently used in Sanskrit classical literature. The text delves deep into the world of mosquitoes, describing their habitat, morphology, behaviour and seasonal patterns. It even categorizes mosquitoes based on their habitat, such as those found in mountainous regions, which were considered particularly dangerous. The Atharva Veda highlights the harmful effects of mosquito bites, including severe itching, swelling, and even life-threatening illnesses. It emphasizes the importance of sunlight as a natural disinfectant, capable of destroying harmful microorganisms, including mosquitoes[4].

While ancient Hindus referred to the mosquito as maśaka, Hispanic Americans referred to them as 'zancudos', for their long legs. In Europe, mosquitoes were more commonly known as 'gnats'. The word 'mosquito' originated in North America around 1583 from the Spanish or Portuguese word, musketas, meaning 'little fly'. The ancient Greek philosopher Aristotle acknowledged these blood-sucking creatures in his *Historia Animalium*, calling them 'empis', meaning 'gnat' or 'mosquito', and which also refers to a genus of dance flies in the Empididae family[5].

Mosquitoes belong to the family Culicidae, which includes over 3,500 species of mosquitoes worldwide. The mosquito is found in every continent except Antarctica. India has 404 species of this insect and over 12 per cent of the world's mosquito population[6]. Not all mosquito species are harmful. The three mosquito genera most notorious for transmitting deadly diseases are *Anopheles, Culex and Aedes. Anopheles* mosquitoes are the primary carrier of malaria, filariasis and encephalitis. *Culex* spreads viral encephalitis and filariasis in tropical and subtropical regions. *Aedes* mosquitoes spread serious diseases like yellow fever, dengue, Zika fever and encephalitis.

It's evident that mosquitoes are ancient creatures, and there are many stories about how they originated. One story comes from he Tlingit, a Pacific Northwest Tribe in the US. A long time ago, a fearsome giant terrorized the Tlingit people, feasting on their flesh and hearts. A brave man devised a plan to defeat the monster, pretending to be dead and luring the giant into a trap. With a swift strike, he killed the giant, but the creature's spirit vowed revenge, transforming into countless mosquitoes to continue its eternal feast.

Scientists have now found that mosquitoes date back 217 million years[7]. These blood-sucking insects emerged in South America on the supercontinent of Gondwana, long before it split into the continents we know today. Researchers at NC State University delved into the mosquito's evolutionary past, combining existing knowledge with cutting-edge genomic sequencing. Their findings reveal that the ability to feed on blood evolved early in mosquito history, even before some vertebrate groups like mammals and birds came along. It's believed that mosquitoes initially fed on amphibians, but as reptiles and birds emerged during the Jurassic period, they expanded their dietary repertoire.

As vertebrate animals evolved, so did mosquitoes. To adapt to the new food source, that is the blood of these vertebrate animals, they developed special mouthparts. This intricate system comprises six needle-like stylets that work together to pierce the skin and draw blood. These needles work together in a clever way. First, one set of needles cut through the skin, while others hold the skin open. Another needle, like a straw, sucks up the blood. To keep the blood flowing, the mosquito also injects saliva. This saliva prevents the blood from clotting, so the mosquito can easily drink its meal[8].

In 2013, scientists further uncovered the evolution of mosquitoes into blood-sucking insects. Buried deep within 130-million-year-old amber, they found the oldest known mosquito fossils[9]. These ancient insects, trapped in time during the Cretaceous period, were unearthed near the town of Hammana in Lebanon. To the astonishment of researchers, the male mosquitoes possessed elongated, piercing-sucking mouthparts, a feature typically associated with females. This discovery suggests that the earliest mosquitoes were all blood-feeders, regardless of their sex.

The evolution of flowering plants around the same time as the formation of Lebanese amber may have played a role in the loss of blood-sucking ability in male mosquitoes. As plant-based food sources became more abundant, scientists think that mosquitoes may have shifted their diet. These plant-based meals provide the energy they need for flight and essential nutrients for survival. We owe a debt of gratitude to plants; without them, we'd be plagued by mosquitoes of both sexes. It's a truly unsettling thought. Today, we know that all mosquitoes feed on nectar, fruit juices, plant sap and plant exudates, and only female mosquitoes suck blood.

The female mosquitoes bite as they need a blood meal to produce eggs. This blood meal provided the essential proteins needed for them to produce eggs. However, even without blood, female mosquitoes can survive and reproduce, albeit at a reduced rate. Interestingly, some mosquito species, like Toxorhynchites, can reproduce without ever taking a blood meal. On the other hand, disease-carrying mosquitoes, such as Anopheles and Aedes, rely on blood meals to complete their reproductive cycle. For these female mosquitoes, human blood is their first or second choice, followed by horse, cattle, smaller mammals and birds[10].

Considering that our blood is essential for mosquitoes to reproduce, it's no surprise that these tiny creatures have a knack for finding us, even in the darkest corners. While we've long known that they find us through the carbon dioxide we exhale, scientists have recently uncovered that they are also attracted by specific body odours.

This discovery was made by researchers in Zambia who set up a special tent where volunteers slept[11]. The air from these tents, filled with unique human scents, was pumped into a big room. Then, they unleashed hundreds of mosquitoes into this 'scent club', armed with tiny infrared cameras to spy on their every move. They found that some volunteers were like rockstars, attracting swarms of eager mosquitoes. Others, however, were like invisible ninjas, completely ignored by the biting horde.

It turns out that our bodies produce a fascinating cocktail of scents that either attract or repel these insects. For example, butyric acid, which gives some cheeses their pungent aroma, is like a mosquito magnet. On the other hand, eucalyptol, found in certain plants, seems to send mosquitoes running for the hills. This experiment explains why some people are always complaining of mosquito bites —they are simply more 'mosquito-licious' than others.

Mosquitoes are not just guided by our delicious scent! These tiny vampires have a secret weapon: infrared detection! Imagine mosquitoes equipped with tiny heat-seeking missiles. These insects can actually sense the heat we give off, making them even better at finding their next blood meal. Scientists at the University of Santa

Barbara discovered that mosquitoes have special sensors on their antennae called 'peg-in-pit' sensors[12]. These sensors are like super-sensitive thermometers, able to detect the heat we radiate. It's like they have built-in infrared goggles! To make things even worse (for us), mosquitoes use a special protein called TRPA1 to boost their heat-sensing powers. This protein amplifies their ability to detect the heat coming from warm-blooded creatures like us, from a distance of up to 2.5 feet!

Further, the attraction to human blood seems to be driven by a tango of hormones: neuropeptide F (NPF) and RYamide. By understanding this intricate role of hormones, scientists may be able to develop new strategies to control mosquito populations and prevent the spread of diseases like malaria and Zika. Scientists at the University of Georgia discovered that NPF, a gut hormone, surges when mosquitoes are in the mood for a blood meal[13]. This hormonal spike makes the mosquito more attracted to humans. After the mosquito feeds, the level of another hormone, RYamide, goes up. It suppresses NPF levels, making the mosquito less interested in feeding on blood. This hormonal interplay ensures that mosquitoes focus on egg-laying after a meal, rather than seeking out more blood.

Once the adult female mosquito has had its fill of blood, it can lay fifty to 200 eggs at a time. However, she mates just once in her entire life. This crucial event takes place in a mesmerizing aerial ballet, known as a mating swarm. As dusk falls, male mosquitoes gather in large numbers, forming these enchanting clouds. But what exactly triggers these mesmerizing mating swarms? While scientists have made significant strides in understanding mosquito behaviour, the specific factors that stimulate swarm formation remain somewhat mysterious. A recent study shed some light on this intriguing phenomenon. Researchers discovered that male mosquitoes release special pheromones, or scent signals, that attract individual females to the swarm. These alluring scents help to increase the chances of successful mating during the crucial dusk and dawn periods[14].

The sound of music too has a role in the mosquito dating game. Mosquitoes can harmonize their wingbeats to attract mates. Scientists have discovered that this musical ability plays a crucial role in their mating process, especially in the case of the malaria-carrying *anopheles gambiae* mosquito[15]. Different forms of *A. gambiae*, though physically similar, can be distinguished by subtle variations in their wingbeat frequencies. Males and females tune their wingbeats to harmonize, creating a unique duet that helps them identify suitable partners. This preference for harmonious mating is so strong that it may be driving the evolution of new mosquito species. By understanding the intricate details of mosquito mating behaviour, researchers can develop novel strategies to disrupt their breeding cycles.

Another recent study has revealed a surprising twist in the love lives of these insects. It turns out that hearing plays a crucial role in their mating rituals. Scientists from the University of California, Santa Barbara, focused on the *aedes aegypti* mosquito, a carrier of the dengue fever virus. It is known that male mosquitoes rely on their auditory senses to locate potential mates, but it was not clear if hearing is essential for mating. To test this, they used genetic technology to silence a specific gene, trpVa, which is essential for sound detection. When these genetically modified mosquitoes were introduced to females, they were completely oblivious to their presence. While normal male mosquitoes were quick to initiate courtship and mating, the hearing-impaired males did not try mating with females[16].

By understanding the sensory cues that drive mosquito mating, scientists can develop innovative strategies to disrupt their reproductive cycle and control the spread of deadly diseases.

One promising approach is the sterile insect technique (SIT)[17]. This method involves releasing large numbers of sterile male mosquitoes into the wild. When these sterile males mate with wild females, the resulting eggs don't hatch, leading to a decline in the mosquito population. However, a key challenge in SIT is ensuring that sterile males are as attractive to females as their wild counterparts. One strategy that scientists are considering is identifying and harnessing the power of pheromones released by males to enhance the allure of sterile males, making them more irresistible to females. With this knowledge, scientists can develop techniques to make sterile males more appealing, increasing their chances of mating with wild females. This, in turn, could lead to a significant reduction in disease transmission.

How exactly the disease is transmitted from mosquitoes to human has been of much interest to scientists and doctors. Although our ancient ancestors knew that mosquitoes caused ill-health, it was only in the last century or so that the mechanism of disease transmission was known. Ronald Ross, a British doctor, was the first to discover that malaria is transmitted by mosquitoes[18]. Born in the heart of India, Almora, in 1857, Ross dedicated his life to unravelling the mysteries of malaria. In the sweltering tropics, malaria was a scourge, causing fevers, chills, and often, death. Scientists had long suspected that a tiny parasite, lurking within the blood of infected individuals, was the culprit. However, the exact mode of transmission remained elusive.

Ross, stationed in India as a military medical officer, took up the challenge. After years of meticulous research, a breakthrough came in 1897. Ross discovered that a specific type of mosquito, after feeding on the blood of a malaria patient, harboured the parasite in its stomach. This crucial insight revealed the life cycle of the malaria parasite and provided the key to combating the disease. Ross's work extended beyond the laboratory. He developed mathematical models to predict the spread of malaria, a groundbreaking approach that laid the foundation for modern epidemiology. His discovery, that mosquitoes are the primary carriers of the deadly disease malaria, earned him the prestigious Nobel Prize in medicine in 1902.

Despite this discovery, for decades, malaria remained a silent killer, claiming hundreds of thousands of lives each year, mostly children. But in the early 2000s, a turning point arrived. Indoor spraying with a combination of long-lasting insecticides and bed nets treated with an insecticide called pyrethroid and indoor spraying helped to drastically reduce malaria cases and deaths[19]. However, the battle wasn't over. Mosquitoes, being resilient creatures, began developing resistance to the insecticides used in these nets. By 2020, the disease, once again, started to gain ground. In 2023, there were an estimated 263 million malaria cases and 5,97,000 malaria deaths in eighty-three countries[20].

Enter Dr Corine Ngufor, a UK based epidemiologist who turned her attention to a novel insecticide, chlorfenapyr[21]. Unlike traditional insecticides, chlorfenapyr works by blocking the mosquitoes' energy production. They are unable to fly and as a result, die. Her team tested chlorfenapyr treated nets in experimental huts—designed with one-way entry points for mosquitoes. Adult volunteers slept under the nets within these huts, and each morning, technicians collected the trapped mosquitoes. The researchers then recorded the number of mosquitoes that had entered the hut, the number that had died, and the number that had successfully fed on blood.

Dr Ngufor's innovative approach has yielded impressive results. Mosquito nets treated with a combination of the previously used pyrethroid along with chlorfenapyr, have proven to be highly effective in preventing malaria transmission. In randomized controlled trials conducted in Tanzania on 4,500 children, the pyrethroid-chlorfenapyr nets successfully reduced malarial infections by almost half[22]. In a significant step forward, in 2023, the World Health Organization

(WHO) officially recommended these nets as a powerful tool in the fight against malaria.

The *aedes aegypti* mosquito, a notorious carrier of dengue fever, has journeyed from its African origins to become a global menace. In the West African Sahel, *aedes aegypti* initially bred in human-stored water. Around 5,000 years ago, as the Sahara dried at the end of the African Humid Period, this mosquito evolved to specialize in biting humans, a consequence of breeding in close proximity during the region's intense dry seasons[23]. This human-specialist *Ae. aegypti* is believed to have travelled to the Americas via ships during the Atlantic Slave Trade about 500 years ago coinciding with the first recorded yellow fever outbreaks in the New World in the seventeenth century. Similarly, *Ae. aegypti*'s arrival in Asia and Oceania was followed by outbreaks of dengue, chikungunya, and later Zika, although yellow fever has not been observed in these regions.

The first epidemic of dengue was reported in the late 1700s and the virus it carries, was first identified in 1907 by P.M. Ashburn and Charles F. Craig, young officers of the US Army Medical Corps, when they were stationed in the Philippines[24]. Today, the WHO estimates that an astounding four billion people are currently at risk of dengue and related viruses. This number is projected to soar to five billion by 2050. Apart from the *aedes aegypti*, another species, *aedes albopictus* (Asian tiger mosquito) is also responsible for transmitting dengue. This adaptable species, with its dark body and striking white stripes, can thrive in a wider range of climates and urban environments. Its ability to breed in tiny amounts of standing water makes it a formidable threat[25].

Researchers have discovered that a specific protein in mosquito saliva, called sialokinin, is responsible for enhancing viral infection[26]. Sialokinin works by compromising the integrity of blood vessels, making it easier for the virus to enter the bloodstream. Interestingly, this protein is unique to Aedes mosquitoes and is absent in Anopheles mosquitoes, which are less efficient at transmitting many viruses. By understanding the role of sialokinin, scientists can develop new strategies to combat mosquito-borne diseases.

The saliva of the mosquito is also responsible for making some people susceptible to an irritating itch. Until recently scientists were puzzled why all humans do not have this allergic reaction. I have a friend who is never bothered by mosquito bites, while I'm always itching and uncomfortable, long after the mosquito has bitten. Recent research has revealed that our immune system plays a crucial role in this reaction[27]. Mosquito saliva contains various enzymes, including proteases. Our body's immune system, specifically a type of skin cell called GD3, responds to these proteases by producing a molecule called IL-3, which in turn, activates specific sensory neurons in the skin. These neurons are responsible for transmitting the sensation of itch to the brain. The severity of the itching sensation depends on how many of these GD3 cells a person has, and in turn how much IL3 is produced.

Lymphatic filariasis (LF) is another disease spread through the bite of infected mosquitoes. India accounts for 40 per cent of the global LF disease burden, and is the second most common mosquito-borne disease after malaria[18]. This painful and disfiguring disease usually starts in childhood with an infection that damages the lymphatic system (a system that is part of the immune system). This damage can lead to serious complications later in life, including swelling of limbs due to fluid buildup (lymphoedema), thickening of the skin and tissues (elephantiasis), and swelling of the scrotum. This debilitating condition is classified as a neglected tropical disease by the WHO. LF disproportionately affects impoverished communities. At the end of 2022, a staggering 794 million people lived in areas at risk of LF infection, spanning across continents like Asia, Africa, the western Pacific, and parts of the Americas[28].

Considering the life-threatening diseases wrought by mosquitoes, for centuries, humans have sought ways to ward off these pesky insects. In the mid-twentieth century, the need for effective insect repellents intensified during World War II. DEET, a synthetic compound, was developed to shield soldiers from disease-carrying mosquitoes. DEET repels mosquitoes by confusing their sensory system, making it difficult for them to find a host. DDT, on the other hand, which was used heavily in agriculture, is a powerful insecticide that directly killed mosquitoes[29]. However, its widespread use led to severe environmental damage, resulting in its ban in several countries. India, however, still uses DDT for vector control in a restricted way.

In India, tubes of Odomos cream were a must-have in every household. The oil of the citronella plant, a powerful mosquito repellent, is the key ingredient in Odomos and other popular products. Even today, its modern form like sprays and patches are the first point of repellents used in homes. Before the liquid dispellers such as All Out, my cousins and I used to lather ourselves with Odomos, especially when we came to Bengaluru during school vacations. It's like the mosquitoes knew that a fresh meal had arrived, and would take pleasure in biting us visitors.

In 2011, the World Mosquito Program (WMP), a non-profit organization, introduced a novel approach to combat mosquito-borne diseases: Wolbachia-modified mosquitoes[30]. These genetically modified insects, infected with the Wolbachia bacteria, disrupt the life cycle of disease-carrying mosquitoes. Male modified mosquitoes are released into the wild to mate with females. The resulting eggs, however, fail to hatch, thus reducing the mosquito population significantly. This innovative method has been successfully piloted in numerous cities across thirteen countries, including Australia and Brazil.

Brazil, in particular, has taken a bold step by launching a nationwide program to release billions of Wolbachia-modified mosquitoes annually. The country is building a factory that will mass-produce five billion mosquitoes a year. This ambitious initiative aims to protect millions of people from dengue fever and other mosquito-borne illnesses[31].

While many efforts are ongoing to control mosquitoes, and I myself have questioned the need for mosquito existence, one has to wonder about the consequences of eradicating mosquitoes (even though that may not ever happen). Mosquitoes do have an ecological role to play after all. As mosquitoes feed on the nectar of flowers, they transfer pollen from flower to flower, thus helping in pollination. Mosquitoes are an important part of the food web, by serving as a food source for fish, turtles, dragonflies, songbirds, bats and other wildlife. Though some ecologists such as Joe Conlon of the American Mosquito Control Association in Jacksonville, Florida, believe that if mosquitoes are eliminated, 'the ecosystems where they are active will hiccup and then get on with life. Something better or worse would take over.'[32]

It may seem counterintuitive, but preserving mosquitoes could actually benefit human health. By exposing us to low levels of disease, mosquitoes help to 'train' our immune systems, making us more resilient against future outbreaks. Madagascar's history with malaria serves as a cautionary tale. When the disease was nearly eradicated in the 1960s and 1970s, the population lost its natural immunity. As a result, subsequent outbreaks were more devastating[3].

Despite the havoc these insects bring upon us humans, mosquitoes are a source of inspiration for many artists and filmmakers. These insects inspired one of the earliest works of animation. *How a Mosquito Operates*, a 1912 animated short film by Winsor McCay, depicts a giant mosquito tormenting a sleeping man. The sci-fi horror film

Skeeter (1993) takes a fantastical approach to the mosquito menace. A small town is overrun by giant, bloodthirsty mutant mosquitoes, the result of a corporate disaster. It's a classic tale of nature's revenge, with a monstrous twist. A 2020 film, *Mosquito*, delves into the darker side of history. Set during World War I, it explores the impact of colonialism and war on the African continent, using the mosquito as a metaphor for the unseen dangers lurking in the shadows.

Perhaps it would be more judicious to eradicate the virus rather than the insect for the sake of the environment and public health. Ultimately, the question of our dominion over other species is a moral one. Author and professor of history Urmi Engineer Willoughby writes in the book *Mosquitopia: The Place of Pests in a Healthy World*[3]: 'Since humans accidently enabled the growth of mosquitoes, are they justified in their efforts to control these mosquitoes and even seek to eradicate them?' Vaccines that control the vector rather than the insect are a promising and safe way to prevent disease transmission. Vaccines for malaria have been approved recently in 2021 by the WHO, and dengue vaccines are still under trial in India. Until such a time that we have efficient and accessible vaccines, the mosquito zapping bat will continue to be my faithful companion at home. While George Michael sang of romantic caution with 'Once bitten, twice shy/I keep my distance ...', for me, the adage holds particularly true for mosquitoes.

ACKNOWLEDGEMENTS

WRITING a book is often a solitary journey. Bringing it to life requires an entire village. I'm grateful to all those who provided support, some silently in the background gently urging me on and checking on me from time to time, and those who actively worked to bring this vision to life. This book has been possible because of them all.

My husband, my unwavering pillar of support, who constantly inspires me to push my boundaries and strive for a better version of myself. Without him, this book—and indeed, all my writing—simply wouldn't be possible. My two sons for filling my life with joy, music, and meaning, and for allowing me to be my introvert self. My sister, my steadfast companion and support through thick and thin.

Kavitha Rao, who ushered me into the world of journalism and writing, and also provided invaluable feedback on this book. My online writing circle—Priti, Shruthi, Rohini, Madhumita, Kamala, Radhika and many others—for their feedback and constant encouragement while navigating the solitary world of writing. Prerna Gill, whose vision for this book was the driving force that truly motivated the author in me.

This work stands on the shoulders of the dedicated scientists who meticulously studied these incredible creatures, and the authors before me who so eloquently chronicled their lives. I have relied heavily on their foundational contributions.

And finally, my parents—their ideals, generosity and strength, have been the greatest inspiration, in shaping the person I am today. I'm especially grateful to my mother, Mayura, the bedrock of my life, for recognizing the writer in me and for her unconditional love and support.

REFERENCES

Chapter 1

1. Cohen, Rich. 2020. 'The Silurian hypothesis'. The Paris Review. https://www.theparisreview.org/blog/2020/01/23/the-silurian-hypothesis/#

2. Frembgen, JW. 1996. 'The Folklore of Geckos: Ethnographic data from South and West Asia'. Asian Folklore Studies. Volume 55, No. 1, pp 135-143.

3. Avril, Tom. 2022. 'This scientist is the lizard king, and he just found another one from the age of dinosaurs'. *Phys.org*.

4. Tri, Van Ngo et al. 2015. 'Gekko aaronbaueri, a new gecko (Squamata: Gekkonidae) from central Laos'. Zootaxa.

5. Stroud, J.T. et al. 2023. 'Fluctuating selection maintains distinct species phenotypes in an ecological community in the wild'. PNAS.

6. Amdekar, Madhura and Thaker, Maria. 2022. 'Colours of stress in male Indian rock agamas predict testosterone levels but not performance'. Hormones and Behavior.

7. Simões, T.R., et al. 2018. 'The origin of squamates revealed by a Middle Triassic lizard from the Italian Alps'. Nature. 557, pp 706-709.

8. Evans, Susan et al. 2010. 'The origin, early history and diversification of Lepidosauromorph Reptiles'. *New Aspects of*

Mesozoic Biodiversity, Lecture Notes in Earth Sciences. pp 27-44. Springer.

9.   Tałanda, M. et al. 2022. 'Synchrotron tomography of a stem lizard elucidates early squamate anatomy'. Nature. 611, pp 99-104.

10.   Hedges, S. and Thomas, Richard. 2000. 'At the lower size limit in Amniote Vertebrates: a new diminutive lizard from the West Indies'. Caribbean Journal of Science. 37.

11.   Banerjee, Neellohit. 'Meet the monitor lizards of India'. *Wildlife SOS*. 27 July, 2022.

12.   Mallik, Madhumay. 'Trailing the spiny-tailed lizard in Kachchh, Gujarat'. *Roundglass Sustain*. 6 November, 2024.

13.   Noble, G. K. and Kumpf, K. F. 1936. 'The functions of Jacobson's organ in lizards'. The Pedagogical Seminary and Journal of Genetic Psychology. 48, pp 371-382.

14.   Uetz, Peter et al. 2020. 'Gecko diversity: a history of global discovery'. Israel Journal of Ecology and Evolution. 66, pp 1-9.

15.   Cole, N. 2014. 'Hemidactylus frenatus'. Global Invasive Species Database. http://www.iucngisd.org/gisd/species.php?sc=1344

16.   Makoond, N. et al. 2024. 'Arresting failure propagation in buildings through collapse isolation'. Nature. 629, pp 592-596.

17.   Perfecto, Imma. 2023. 'Arthritis clues in how lizards build tails'. *Cosmos Magazine*.

18.   Coxworth, Ben. 2012. 'Leaping lizards inspire new robot design'. *New Atlas*.

19.   Jumle,V. and Badola, S. 2020. Traffic Post. Issue 34. https://wwfin.awsassets.panda.org/downloads/traffic_post__issue_34.pdf.

Chapter 2

1.   Rocio, Crespo et al. 2018. 'Galliformes and Columbiformes'. *Pathology of Wildlife and Zoo Animals*. Academic Press. pp 747-773.

2.   C.A. Stern and J.L. Dickinson. 2010. 'Pigeons'. *Encyclopaedia of Animal Behaviour*. Academic Press. pp 723-730.

3.   Johnston, Richard F. and Janiga, Marián. 1995. *Feral Pigeons*. Oxford Academic.

4.   Turner, Brandon M. et al. 2023. 'The pigeon as a machine: Complex category structures can be acquired by a simple associative model'. iScience. Vol 26, Issue 10.

5.   Smith, W. J. et al. 2022. 'Limited domestic introgression in a final refuge of the wild pigeon'. iScience. Vol 25, Issue 7.

6.   Walcott, Charles. 1996. 'Pigeon homing: observations, experiments and confusions'. Journal of Experimental Biology .199 (1), pp 21-27.

7.   Tepper, Yotam et al. 2017. 'Signs of soil fertigation in the desert: A pigeon tower structure near Byzantine Shivta, Israel'. Journal of Arid Environment. Vol 145.

8.   Grano, M. 2024. 'Peristeriones (Περιστεριώνες), the typical pigeon houses in Sifnos Island (Cyclades, Greece)'. Biodiversity Journal. 15 (2), pp 271-276.

9.   Sasaki, T. and Biro, D. 2017. 'Cumulative culture can emerge from collective intelligence in animal groups'. Nature Communications. Vol 8.

10.   Bieniek, Adam. 2016. 'Cher Ami: The pigeon that saved the lost battalion'. The U.S. World War I Centennial Commission. https://www.worldwar1centennial.org/index.php/communicate/press-media/wwi-centennial-news/1210-cher-ami-the-pigeon-that-saved-the-lost-battalion.html.

11.   Corera, G. 2018. *Operation Columba--The secret pigeon service: The untold story of world war II resistance in Europe*. William Morrow.

12.   'Indian pigeons lose out to e-mail'. *BBC*. 26 March, 2002.

13.   Degner, D. and Blechman, A. 2011. 'Cairos Fancy Fliers'. Aramco World.

14.   Blechman, A. 2007. *Pigeons: The Fascinating Saga of the World's Most Revered and Reviled Bird*. Grove press.

15.   Sridharan, V. 2018. 'Indian pigeon racing season reaches high point'. *Deutsch Welle*.

16.   Lozano, A.V. 2022. 'Pigeon racing and swan upping: Queen's love for animals extended beyond corgis'. *NBC News*.

17.   Patyal, H.C. 1990. 'Pigeon in the vedic mythology and ritual'. Annals of the Bhandarkar Oriental Research Institute. Vol. 71, No. 1/4, pp 310-317.

18.   'Immortal pigeons of Lord Shiva spotted in Amarnath India'. *News24 Online*. 20 September, 2023.

19.   Chaitanya, M. 'Pigeons a nuisance, shut Dadar kabutarkhana: MNS'. *Mumbai Mirror*. 9 June, 2017.

20.   Gangal, V. 'Mumbai's kabootar konnection'. *Mumbai Mirror*. 20 December, 2018.

21.   Finamore, E. 'Where did Trafalgar Square's pigeons come from ?' *Londonist*. 13 March, 2016.

22.   'The battle of Trafalgar Square's pigeons'. *Reuters*. 10 August, 2007.

23.   Khan, S. 2023. 'Feral pigeons and their relationship with humans: A dense assessment of totally urbanized bird species in 3 specific sites under LMRC Metro Stations at Lucknow city, Uttar Pradesh, India'. Journal of Emerging Technologies and Innovative Research. Vol 10, Issue 7.

24. Avery, M. 2014. *A Message from Martha: The Extinction of the Passenger Pigeon and Its Relevance Today*. Bloomsbury Nature Writing.

25. Ghai, R. 'Urban menace: The pigeon problem in Indian cities is human-caused; here is how'. *Down to Earth*. 20 June, 2023.

26. Haag-Wackernagel, D. 1995. 'Regulation of the street pigeon in Basel'. Wildlife Society Bulletin. Vol. 23, No. 2, pp. 256-260.

27. Legg, C. 'Your world is different from a pigeon's – but a new theory explains how we can still live in the same reality'. *The Conversation*. 24 July, 2024.

Chapter 3

1. Lihoreau, M. et al. 2012. 'The social biology of domiciliary cockroaches: colony structure, kin recognition and collective decisions'. Insectes Sociaux. 59, pp 445-452.

2. Prabakaran, S. and Senraj, M. 2018. 'A checklist of cockroaches (Insecta: Blattodea) from India'. Zoological Survey of India.

3. 'Smallest Cockroach'. Guinness World Records. https://www.guinnessworldrecords.com/world-records/106630-smallest-cockroach.

4. Xu, Liangwen et al. 2014. 'Burrowing energetics of the giant burrowing Cockroach *Macropanesthia rhinoceros*: An allometric study'. Journal of Insect Physiology. Vol 70, pp 81-87.

5. Clark, Debbie and Shanklin, Donna. 'Madagascar hissing cockroaches'. University of Kentucky College of Agriculture. https://entomology.ca.uky.edu/ef014.

6. *Megaloblatta longipennis* (MEGBLO)'. European and Mediterranean Plant Protection Organization database. https://gd.eppo.int/taxon/MEGBLO

7.   Wada-Katsumata, A. and Schal, C. 2019. 'Antennal grooming facilitates courtship performance in a group-living insect, the German cockroach *Blattella germanica*'. Scientific Reports.

8.   'The cockroach FAQ'. University of Massachusetts. https://www.bio.umass.edu/biology/kunkel/cockroach_faq.html.

9.   Halloy et al. 2007. 'Social integration of robots into groups of cockroaches to control self-organized choice'. Science. 318, pp 1155-1158.

10.   Bell, J. William et al. 2007. 'Cockroaches: ecology, behaviour, and natural history'. Johns Hopkins University Press.

11.   Nichols, Catherine. 2008. 'Animal Planet: The most extreme bugs'. Discovery Channel.

12.   Lin Edwards, L. 'Cockroaches control their breathing to save water'. *Phys.org.* 24 September, 2009.

13.   Choi, Chen. 'Fact or Fiction: Cockroach can live without the head'. *Scientific American.* 15 March, 2007

14.   Louis M. Roth. ESA Fellow. 1952. Entomological Society of America. https://www.entsoc.org/fellows/louis-m-roth-esa-fellow-1952.

15.   Evans, E. Howard. 1966. 'The intellectual and emotional world of the cockroach'. *Harper's Magazine.*

16.   'Hope, the Russian cockroach gives birth to first space babies'. *Sputnik International.* 23 October, 2007.

17.   Brown, S. Alan. 'Cockroach inspires robotic hand to get a grip'. *Phys.org.* 10 January, 2011.

18.   Kabutz, H. and Jayaram, K. 2023. 'Design of CLARI: A miniature modular origami passive shape-morphing robot'. Advanced Intelligent Systems. Vol 5.

19.   Isaac A. Adedara et al. 2022. 'Utility of cockroach as a model organism in the assessment of toxicological impacts of environmental pollutants'. Environmental Advances. Vol 8.

20. Botella, C. et al. 2010. 'Treating cockroach phobia with augmented reality'. Behaviour Therapy. 41(3), pp 401-413.

21. Chen, Stephen. 'A giant indoor farm in China is breeding 6 billion cockroaches a year. Here's why'. *South China Morning Post*. 19 April, 2018.

22. 'Cockroach cures'. *South China Morning Post*. 6 February, 2001.

23. Copeland, Marion. 2003. *Cockroach (Animal Series)*. Reaktion Books

24. 'How cockroaches could save lives'. *BBC News*. 3 November, 2015.

25. Clun, Rachel. 'Aussies, start your roaches: Story Bridge off to races for Australia Day'. *Brisbane Times*. 26 January, 2017.

26. 'Cockroach racing: athlete profiles'. Carnegie Museum of Natural History. https://carnegiemnh.org/cockroach-racing-athlete-profiles/.

27. 'Karratha's annual cockroach cup race puts roaches and stomachs to the test'. *ABC News*. 25 June, 2023.

28. Karnash, Chelsea. 'Romney comes out on top in presidential roach race'. *CBC News*. 20 August, 2012.

29. 'Kamala Harris roach wins annual Cockroach Derby; race has 84% correct prediction rate'. *Yahoo News*. 21 August, 2024.

30. Ian McEwan website. https://www.ianmcewan.com/books/cockroach.html.

31. Geist, E. William. 'About New York; The age-old battle against the cockroach'. *New York Times*. 17 April, 1985.

32. Twilley, Nicola. 'In defence of the cockroach'. *New Yorker*. 15 August, 2015.

33. Pippos, Andrew. 'Cockroach: object of disgust'. *Sydney Review of Books*. 21 June, 2018.

34.   Index to the Blattodea Culture Group Newsletter, volumes 1-14 (https://www.researchgate.net/publication/215676553_Index_to_the_Blattodea_Culture_Group_Newsletter). Bragg, P.E. 1997. *An Introduction to Rearing Cockroaches.* Ragge, D.R. 1965. *Grasshoppers, Crickets & Cockroaches of the British Isles.*

35.   Evans, Theo and Tang, Qian. 'A pest of our own making: revealing the true origins of the not-so-German cockroach'. *The Conversation.* 20 May, 2024.

36.   Bittel, Jason. 'Cockroach Reproduction Has Taken a Strange Turn'. *New York Times.* 27 May, 2022.

Chapter 4

1.   Lynd, Robert. 1922. *Solomon In all His Glory.*

2.   Summer-Smith, Denis. 2006. *On Sparrows and Man: A Love-Hate Relationship.*

3.   Mark, R. et al. 2018. 'Signatures of human-commensalism in the house sparrow genome'. Proceedings of the Royal Society B.

4.   Hanson, E.H. et al. 2020. 'The house sparrow in the service of basic and applied biology'. eLife.

5.   Martin, Lynn B. and Fitzgerald, Lisa. 2005. 'A taste for novelty in invading house sparrows, *Passer domesticus*'. Behavioral Ecology. Vol 16, Issue 4. pp 702-707

6.   Marshall, Peyton. 'The truth about sparrows'. *New York Times.* 14 May, 2014.

7.   'House sparrow guide: species facts, how to identify, and how to put up a nestbox for them'. *Discover Wildlife.* 20 March, 2020.

8.   Maruf, Sitara. 'The first experiments about the effects of high altitude; balloonists travel into the perils of the upper regions'. *LTA Science & Flight Magazine.* 18 January, 2016.

9.   Oza, Anil. 2023. 'This sparrow massively expands part of its brain in preparation for mating'. Nature.

10. Vágási, Csongor I. et al. 2021. 'Social groups with diverse personalities mitigate physiological stress in a songbird'. Proceedings of the Royal Society B.

11. Zanette, Liana et al. 2006. 'Food and predators affect egg production in song sparrows'. Ecology. Vol 87, No. 10. pp. 2459-2467.

12. Hultsch, Henrike and Todt, Dietmar. Editor(s): Peter Marler, Hans Slabbekoorn 2004. 'Learning to sing'. *Nature's Music*. Academic Press. pp 80-107.

13. Mennill, Daniel J. et al. 2018. 'Wild birds learn songs from experimental vocal tutors'. Current Biology. Vol 28, Issue 20, pp 3273-3278.

14. Luther, D. and Baptista, L. 2010. 'Urban noise and the cultural evolution of bird songs'. Proceedings of the Royal Society B. pp 469-473.

15. Soma, Masayo and Mori, Chihiro. 2015. 'The songbird as a percussionist: syntactic rules for non-vocal sound and song production in Java sparrows'. PLOS One.

16. Summers-Smith, J. Denis. 1988. *The Sparrows : A study of the genus Passer*. A & C Black Publishers Ltd.

17. 'Sparrow symbolism: Exploring the meanings and myths'. Bird Fact (online). 19 October, 2023. https://birdfact.com/articles/sparrow-symbolism.

18. 'Garuda and the sparrow (determination; God's grace)'. Iskcon Educational Services. (online). https://iskconeducationalservices.org/HoH/further-information-and-teaching-resources-secondary/values/sto-210-garuda-and-the-sparrow-determination-gods-grace/.

19. Mulroy, David. 2002. *The Complete Poetry of Cattalus.* University of Wisconsin Press.

20. Cowdery, William (ed.) 1990. *The Complete Mozart: A Guide to the Musical Works of Wolfgang Amadeus Mozart.* W.W. Norton

21. Barkham, Patrick. 'House sparrow population in Europe drops by 247M'. *The Guardian.* 16 November, 2021.

22. Sharma, Pratibha. and Binner, Manpreet. 2020. 'The decline of population of house sparrow in India'. International Journal of Agricultural Science. Vol 5, pp 1-4.

23. Murari, Krishan. 'Sparrows are coming back to Delhi finally. A new forest is now their safe haven'. *The Print.* 5 December, 2022.

24. Dunn, Rob. 'The story of the most common bird in the world'. *Smithsonian Magazine.* 2 March, 2012.

Chapter 5

1. D'souza, Pearl. '15 foot tall metallic squirrel from Bengaluru on way to Ayodhya'. *Times of India.* 11 Jan, 2024.

2. *Why The Chipmunk Has Black Stripes.* Whispering Books (online).

3. Sax, Boria. 2001. 'The mythical zoo: An encyclopaedia of animals in world myth, legend and literature'. ABC-CLIO.

4. Kelly, John. 'Meet Ratatoskr, mischievous messenger squirrel to the Viking gods'. *Washington Post.* 13 April, 2020.

5. Thorington R.W. and Ferrell K. E. 2006. *Squirrels: The Animal Answer Guide.* Johns Hopkins University Press.

6. Kay, Emily H. et al. 2008. 'Rodents'. Current Biology. Vol 18, Issue 10, pp 406 - 410

7. Thorington, R.W. 2012. *Squirrels of The World.* Johns Hopkins University Press.

8.   'All about flying squirrels'. Wildlife Conservation Society (online) 21 January, 2020.

9.   Sriramrajan, Visvajit. 'Logging poses a threat to the arboreal Travancore flying squirrel'. *Mongabay India.* 12 May, 2020.

10. Nair, Anirudh. 'Hop, skip and jump. The giant squirrels of India'. *Roundglass Sustain.* 20 January, 2021.

11. 'Why do squirrels have bushy tails'. *Nuts About Squirrels.* 9 November, 2012.

12. 'Squirrel breeding biology- gestation, birth & kitten development'. *Wildlife Online*, UK. https://www.wildlifeonline. me.uk/animals/article/squirrel-breeding-biology-gestation-birth-kitten-development

13. Bryce, Emma. 'Do squirrels remember where they buried their nuts'. *Scientific American.* 20 November, 2023.

14. Jacobs, Lucia F. and Liman, Emily R. 1991. 'Grey squirrels remember the locations of buried nuts'. Animal Behaviour. Vol 41, Issue 1, pp 103-110.

15. Rafferty, John. 'Is it true that squirrels forget where they bury about half of their food'. *Brittanica Encyclopaedia.* https:// www.britannica.com/story/is-it-true-that-squirrels-forget-where-they-bury-about-half-of-their-food#.

16. Jaclyn, R. et al. 2021. 'Bridging animal personality with space use and resource use in a free-ranging population of an asocial ground squirrel'. Animal Behaviour. Vol 180, pp 291-306.

17. Zarrelli, Natalie. 'When squirrels were one of America's most popular pets'. *Atlas Obscura.* 28 April, 2017.

18. Stein, Sadie. 'Alien squirrel.' *NY Mag.* 3 February, 2014.

19. Baillie, Katherine Unger. 'Penn researcher traces the history of the American urban squirrel'. *Penn Today.* 12 December, 2013.

20. 'Red squirrel'. *Wildlife Online. UK.* https://www.wildlifeonline. me.uk/animals/species/red-squirrel#

21.   Spieler, Marlena. 'Saving a squirrel by eating one'. *New York Times*. 6 January, 2009.

22.   Barkham, Patrick. 'Kill them, kill them, kill them': the volunteer army plotting to wipe out Britain's grey squirrels'. *The Guardian*. 2 June, 2017.

23.   Kelly, John. 'Benjamin Franklin's squirrel died in England in 1772 and was buried there'. *Washington Post*. 12 April, 2017.

24.   Kelly, John. 'Tommy Tucker, Washington's most famous squirrel'. *Washington Post*. 8 April, 2012.

25.   'Who run the world? Squirrels'. *Duke Today*. 5 Nov, 2020.

26.   Li, Lyric. and Timsit, Annabelle. 'A squad of drug-sniffing squirrels is training to join China's police'. *Washington Post*. 9 February, 2023.

27.   Hedgpeth, Dana. 'A rare white squirrel is spotted in a Virginia neighborhood'. *Washington Post*. 17 February, 2017.

28.   'UNT 101: UNT Trivia & History'. University of North Texas (online).   https://www.unt.edu/unt-101/2022/-unt-trivia-history.html.

29.   Roy, Esha. 'First-ever study has grim prognosis: Native squirrel could vanish from NE after 2050'. *Indian Express*. 4 December, 2020.

30.   Thampuran, A.Varma. 'Forest department envisages creating canopy bridges for squirrel conservation'. *On Manorama*. 22 January, 2024.

Chapter 6

1.   Ratner, Austin. 'In praise of the great rats in literature'. Literally. 8 July, 2021.

2.   D. J. Taylor. 'Orwell and the rats'. *Orwell Foundation*. https://www.orwellfoundation.com/the-orwell-foundation/orwell/articles/d-j-taylororwell-and-the-rats/

3.   Feldshuh, Hannah. 'Rats! How one vermin came to incur both reverence and contempt across different cultures'. *The Beijinger*. 5 February, 2020.

4.   Barnett, S. Anthony. 2002. *The story of rats: Their impact on us, and our impact on them*. Allen & Unwin.

5.   'Year of the rat'. *Smithsonian*. https://www.si.edu/spotlight/year-of-the-rat#.

6.   'Rat fact sheet'. *PBS*. May 21, 2021. https://www.pbs.org/wnet/nature/blog/rat-factsheet/.

7.   Shelar, Jyoti. 'Mumbai's great rat hunt and why it matters to you'. *Hindustan Times*, 23 November, 2021.

8.   'Mayor Adams anoints Kathleen Corradi as NYC's first-ever 'rat czar''. Nyc.gov, 12, April, 2023.

9.   Oladipo, Gloria. 'Shelter releases 1,000 feral cats on to Chicago streets to combat rat crisis'. *The Guardian*. 14 May, 2021.

10.   'Alberta's rat control program'. Alberta City website. https://www.alberta.ca/albertas-rat-control-program.

11.   Puckett, E.E. and Munshi-South, J. 2019. 'Brown rat demography reveals pre-commensal structure in eastern Asia before expansion into Southeast Asia'. Genome Research. pp 762-770.

12.   Harpak, A. et al. 2021.'Genetic adaptation in New York city rats'. Genome Biology and Evolution.

13.   Logan, C.A. 2005. 'The legacy of Adolf Meyer's comparative approach: Worcester rats and the strange birth of the animal model'. Integrative Physiological & Behavioral Science. Vol 40, pp 169-181.

14.   Garget, Jacqueline. 'Meet the ugly naked guys'. University of Cambridge. (online) https://www.cam.ac.uk/stories/weird-naked-mole-rats.

15.   Honda, Arata et al. 2017. 'Flexible adaptation of male germ cells from female iPSCs of endangered *Tokudaia osimensis*'. Scientific Advances.

16.   Graves J.A. 2004. 'The degenerate Y chromosome--can conversion save it?' Reproduction, Fertility and Development. Vol 16, pp 527-534.

17.   Foote, Allison L. and Crystal, Jonathon D. 2007. 'Metacognition in the rat'. Current Biology. Vol 17, Issue 6, pp 551-555.

18.   Chongxi, Lai. et al. 2023. 'Volitional activation of remote place representations with a hippocampal brain–machine interface'. Science.

19.   Bering, Jesse. 'Rats laugh, but not like humans'. *Scientific American*. 1 July, 2012.

20.   Gloveli, Natalie et al. 2023. 'Play and tickling responses map to the lateral columns of the rat periaqueductal gray'. Neuron. Vol 111, Issue 19.

21.   Yong, Ed. 'Empathic rats spring each other from jail'. *National Geographic*. 9 December, 2011.

22.   DeWeerdt, Sarah. 'Could rats and dogs detect disease better than the finest lab equipment?' Nature. 19 June, 2024.

23.   Hulme-Beaman, A. et al. 2021. 'The origins of the domesticate brown rat (*Rattus norvegicus*) and its pathways to domestication'. Animal Frontiers. 11(3), pp 78-86.

24.   American Fancy Rat and Mouse Association website. https://www.afrma.org/stdsrat.htm.

25.   Kumawat, M. Madan. 2016. 'Significance of Aran festival for rodent management by Adi Tribes of Arunachal Pradesh'. Journal of Global Communication. Vol. 9, No. 1, pp 15-21.

26. Tumuluru, Smitha. 'On a different route with rats in Bangalamedu'. *People's Archive of Rural India*, 25 July, 2020.

27. Parks, Shoshi. 'Gibnut: A royal rat that's fit for a queen'. *Atlas Obscura*. https://www.atlasobscura.com/foods/gibnut-belize-royal-rat.

28. Perkins, Olivera. 'Scabby the rat inflatable is more than a union prop'. *Signal Cleveland*, 24 January, 2024.

29. Sullivan, Robert. 2005. *Rats: Observations on the History and Habitat of the City's Most Unwanted Inhabitants.* Bloomsbury USA.

30. Berlinger, Joshua. 'Can humans and rats live together? Paris is trying to find out'. *CNN*. 10 June, 2023.

Chapter 7

1. Rozenbaum, Mia. 'Frogs in medical research'. Understanding Animal Research. 20 March, 2023.

2. 'Scientific background: Mature cells can be reprogrammed to become pluripotent'. The Nobel Prize. 2012.

3. 'Model organisms: The clawed frog'. Your Genome. Wellcome Sanger Institute.

4. S. Kriegman et al. 2020. 'A scalable pipeline for designing reconfigurable organisms'. PNAS. 117 (4), pp 1853-1859.

5. Chaudhuri, Zinnia Ray. 'Frogs have an abiding presence in Indian art and mythology. Then why don't we try to preserve them?' *Scroll.in*. 3 February, 2018.

6. Ghosh, Pria. 'Amphibians and culture III: restoring positive narratives in India and South Africa'. Synchronicity Earth. 6 June, 2023.

7. Shaji, K.A. 'How an underground lifestyle cost the Mahabali frog the tag of the official amphibian of Kerala'. *The South First*, 27 January, 2023.

8. Attia, Venice. 2018. 'Goddess Hekat (frog deity) in ancient Egypt.' https://www.researchgate.net/publication/325783835_Godess_Hekat_Frog_Diety_in_Ancient_Egypt

9. Feng, Yan-Jie et al. 2017. 'Phylogenomics reveals rapid, simultaneous diversification of three major clades of Gondwanan frogs at the Cretaceous–Paleogene boundary'. PNAS. 114 (29).

10. 'Frog fun facts'. American Museum of Natural History (website). https://www.amnh.org/exhibitions/frogs-a-chorus-of-colors/frog-fun-facts#.

11. Iuliis, De Gerardo. and Pulerà, Dino. 2011. *The Dissection of Vertebrates (Second Edition)*, Academic Press. pp 127-145.

12. Dinesh, K.P. et al. 2024. 'Checklist of fauna of India: Animalia: Chordata: Amphibia'. Version 1.0. Zoological Survey India .

13. Daniels, Ranjit. 2000. 'Project lifescape & amphibians'. Resonance Journal of Science Education.

14. Al-attar, Rasha and Storey, B. Kenneth. 2022. 'Lessons from nature: Leveraging the freeze-tolerant wood frog as a model to improve organ cryopreservation and biobanking'. Comparative Biochemistry and Physiology Part B: Biochemistry and Molecular Biology. Vol 261.

15. Arrigo, Elizabeth. 'Meet Australia's desert dwelling frogs'. *Australian Geographic*. 7 May, 2018.

16. Bittel, Jason. 'What makes glass frogs transparent? The secret is in their blood'. *National Geographic*. 23 December, 2022.

17. Bhat, S. Ananda et al. 2022. 'Behavioural context shapes vocal sequences in two anuran species with different repertoire sizes'. Animal Behaviour. Vol 184, pp 111-129.

18. Souza, F. Ubirata et al. 2024. 'Ultrasonic distress calls and associated defensive behaviors in neotropical frogs. acta ethologica. 27, pp 135–139.

19. Kimbrough, Liz. ' No croak. New silent species described from Tanzania's Sky Islan forests'. *Mongabay*. 9 February, 2023.

20. Baisas, Laura. 'The upside-down sex lives of Charles Darwin's frogs'. *Popular Science*. 30 July, 2024.

21. Quaglia, Sofia. 'Why do frogs keep trying to mate with the wrong things?' *Discover Magazine*. 7 November, 2023.

22. Posada, Claudia. 'An explosion of breeding frogs'. *BBC Earth*.

23. Dittrich, Carolin. and Rodel, Mark-Oliver. 2023. 'Drop dead! Female mate avoidance in an explosively breeding frog'. Royal Society Open Science.

24. 'The frog life cycle'. National Geographic Kids. https://www.natgeokids.com/uk/discover/science/nature/frog-life-cycle/

25. Sun, Jiefeng et al. 2023. 'Embedded shape morphing for morphologically adaptive robots'. Nature Communications. 14.

26. Brown, Mark. 'Frogs' legs may have been English delicacy 8,000 years before France'. *The Guardian*. 15 October, 2013.

27. Henley, John. 'Why we shouldn't eat frogs' legs'. *The Guardian*. 7 August, 2009.

28. Nuwer, Rachel. 'Europe's taste for frog legs obscures the 'extreme cruelty' of the trade'. *National Geographic*. 1 March, 2023.

29. Popova, Maria. 'Frida Kahlo on How Love Amplifies Beauty: Her Breathtaking Tribute to Diego Rivera'. The Marginalian. 22 January, 2016.

30. Morton, John. 2006. 'Tiddalik's Travels: The making and remaking of an aboriginal flood myth'. Advances in Ecological Research. Vol 39, pp 139-158.

31. Kimbrough, Liz. 'Frogs in the pot: Two in five amphibian species at risk amid climate crisis'. *Mongabay*. 5 October, 2023.

32. Gibbs, Anna. 'As fatal fungus takes its toll, can we save frog species on the brink?' *Yale Environment 360*. 21 February, 2023.

33. Kimbrough, Liz.. 'Haunting song pays tribute to Toughie, the frog whose extinction went unnoticed'. *Mongabay*, 10 April, 2024.

34. 'Frogman of India calls for ecosystem based conservation to save frogs'. *Times of India*. 26 November, 2024.

35. Padmanaban, Deepa. 'Why the dancing frog may no longer be able to shake a leg'. *Mongabay*. 13 April, 2023.

36. Kawanishi, Aya. 'The frogs of Borneo: more than just a race.' Asia Research News. 13 June, 2023.

37. Elton, Charlotte. 'India's weirdest frog and an 'ugly shark': These species aren't cuddly but they still need saving'. *Euronews*. 7 June, 2023.

38. Seshadri, K. S. et al. 2012. 'Anurans from wetlands of Puducherry, along the east coast of India'. Check List. 8(1): pp 23-26.

Chapter 8

1.   Frynta, Daniel et al. 2021. 'Emotions triggered by live arthropods shed light on spider phobia'. Scientific Reports. Vol 11.

2.   Shekhar, Laasya. 'From fear to fascination: more research and awareness to protect India's misunderstood spiders'. *Mongabay*. 5 July, 2024.

3.   'Tat Pada Vicāra – 3 Upādāna Kāraṇa'. Advaita Vision. 1 August, 2013.   https://www.advaita-vision.org/tat-pada-vicara-3-upadana-kara%E1%B9%87a/.

4.   Miate, Liana. 'Arachne.' World History Encyclopedia. 26 July, 2022.

5. Asante, Molefi Kete. 'Ananse.' Encyclopaedia Brittanica. https://www.britannica.com/topic/Ananse.

6. Orozco, José. ' "Spider-God" temple found in Peru'. *National Geographic.* 29 October, 2008.

7. Mammola, Stefano et al. 2017. 'Record breaking achievements by spiders and the scientists who study them.' PeerJ.

8. Briggs, Helen. ' "Extraordinary" fossil sheds light on origins of spiders'. *BBC.* 5 February, 2018.

9. Gamillo, Elizabeth. 'Scientists identify 50,000th spider species on earth—but thousands more are waiting to be discovered'. *Smithsonian Magazine.* 12 April, 2022.

10. 'Smallest spider'. Guinness World Records. https://www.guinnessworldrecords.com/world-records/smallest-spider

11. Williams, Leoma. '10 biggest spiders in the world: meet enormous arachnids as big as dinner plates'. *Discover Wildlife,* 24 October, 2024.

12. Kronestedt, Torbjorn. 2008. 'Carl Clerk and what became of his spiders'. European Arachnology. pp 105-107.

13. Atwal, Sanj. 2021. 'Scary spider records: bloodsuckers, bird-eaters and more'. Guinness World Records.

14. Pain, Stephanie. 'The ungentle joy of spider sex'. *Knowable Magazine.* 28 October, 2020.

15. 'Black widow spiders'. *National Geographic.* https://www.nationalgeographic.com/animals/invertebrates/facts/black-widow-spiders?

16. Blamires, Sean et al. 2017. 'Webs: Diversity, structure and function'. *Behaviour and Ecology of Spiders.* pp.137-164.

17. 'Buildings based on spider webs'. Find My Architect. https://www.find-my-architect.com/uk/en/actualite/buildings-based-on-spider-webs.

18. Fabricius, Daniela. 2016. 'Architecture before architecture: Frei Otto's deep history'. Journal of Architecture. Vol 21. Taylor & Francis

19. Soth, Amelia. 2018. 'The tangled history of weaving with spider silk.' JStor Daily.

20. 'Simon Peers and Nicholas Godley discuss golden spider silk'. Victoria and Albert Museum YouTube. 30 January, 2012. https://www.youtube.com/watch?v=-cx2YhqIP_M.

21. Saez, Natalie et al. 2010. 'Spider-venom peptides as therapeutics'. Toxins. Vol 2, pp 2851-2871.

22. Hadlington, Simon. 'Spider venom pesticide harmless to bees'. *Chemistry World*. 4 June, 2014.

23. Duggan, Nisharnthi M. et al. 2021. 'Total synthesis of the spider-venom peptide Hi1a'. Organic Letters. pp 8375-8379.

24. Klint, Julie K. 2015. 'Seven novel modulators of the analgesic target NaV1.7 uncovered using a high-throughput venom-based discovery approach'. British Journal of Pharmacology. Vol172, Issue10.

25. 'Venom as Medicine'. Cornell University Library. https://exhibits.library.cornell.edu/arachnophilia/feature/venom-as-medicine

26. 'ReachBot: The robot exploring moon and Mars caves like an insect'. *Interstellar News*. 21 June, 2024.

27. Kreslavsky, Mikhail and Head, James. 2024. '"Spiders" on the moon: Morphological evidence for geologically recent regolith drainage into subsurface voids.' The Planetary Science Journal.

28. Davis, K. Andrew and Vu, Christina. 2024. 'How to give a spider a heart attack: Evaluating cardiac stress reactions of *Trichonephila* and *Argiope* spiders'. Physiological Entomology, pp 1-10.

29. Mason, Betsy.. 'Spiders are much smarter than you think'. *Knowable magazine.* 28 October, 2021.

30. Andrew, Scottie. 'How jumping spiders became the new 'it' pets'. *CNN.* 25 March, 2023.

31. 'Beautiful ornamental tarantulas win global protections from pet trade'. Centre for Biological Diversity, Press Release. 26 August, 2019.

32. Nyffeler, M. and Birkhofer, K. 2017. 'An estimated 400–800 million tons of prey are annually killed by the global spider community'. The Science of Nature.

33. Singh, Sidharth. 'Arachnology, like spiders, languishes in the dark corners of Indian research'. *The Wire.* 8 March, 2021.

Chapter 9

1. Groves, C.P. 2005. 'Order primates'. *Mammal Species of the World: A Taxonomic and Geographic Reference*, 3rd Edition. Johns Hopkins University Press, Baltimore. pp 111-184.

2. DJangi, Parissa. 'The real history behind the legend of Sun Wukong, China's monkey king'. *National Geographic.* 29 August, 2024.

3. 'Dealing with the monkey king: Meditation techniques for people with unsettled monkey minds'. Buddha Weekly. https://buddhaweekly.com/meditation-techniques-for-people-with-unsettled-monkey-minds/#.

4. H. Braakhuis. 1987. 'Artificers of the days: Functions of the howler monkey gods among the Mayas'. Journal of the Humanities and Social Sciences of Southeast Asia. Vol 143.

5. Weisberger, Mindy. 'Are these ancient ruins in Honduras the legendary 'White City'?' *Live Wire.* 29 October, 2021.

6.   Donvito, Tina. 'How many types of monkeys are there in the world?' *Readers Digest*. 1 September, 2023.

7.   Kantha, S. Sachi. 2014. 'Subhuman primates in Shakespeare's oeuvre'. Current Science. 106(7), pp 1021-1024.

8.   Poe, Edgar Allen. 1841. *The Murders in the Rue Morgue.* Graham's Magazine.

9.   Rowan, Andrew. 2023. 'Monkey Business'. Well Being International.

10.   'History of the Polio Vaccine'. World Health Organisation. https://www.who.int/news-room/spotlight/history-of-vaccination/history-of-polio-vaccination#.

11.   Rensberger, Boyce. 'Export ban on monkeys poses threat to research'. *New York Times*. 23 January, 1978.

12.   Cooper E.B. et al. 2022. 'The rhesus macaque as a success story of the Anthropocene'. Elife.

13.   Muenstermann, Lacey. 'Meet Miss Baker—Huntsville's famous squirrel monkey who made space history'. Hville Blast. 6 May, 2024.

14.   Singh, Mewa. 2020. 'A history of primatology in India (In memory of Professor Sheo Dan Singh)'. Journal of Threatened Taxa. Volume12, pp 16715-16735.

15.   Karasu, Sylvia R. 'Traces of ourselves: The remarkable power of touch'. *Psychology Today*. 25 April, 2020.

16.   Smoulder, Adam. 2024. 'A neural basis of choking under pressure'. Neuron. Vol 112, Issue 20.

17.   J. Sliwa and W.A. Freiwald. 2017. 'A dedicated network for social interaction processing in the primate brain'. Science. 356, pp 745-749.

18.   Guy Oren et al. 2024. 'Vocal labeling of others by nonhuman primates'. Science. 385, pp 996-1003.

19. Liao, Z. et al. 2024. 'Reprogramming mechanism dissection and trophoblast replacement application in monkey somatic cell nuclear transfer'. Nature Communications.

20. Garber, A. Paul et al. 2024. 'Global wildlife trade and trafficking contribute to the world's nonhuman primate conservation crisis'. Frontiers in Conservation Science. Vol 5.

21. 'Miss Waldron's Red Colobus'. IUCN/SSC Primate Specialist Group. http://www.primate-sg.org/waldrons_red_colobus/.

22. Kulkarni, Chiranjeevi. 'Monkey encounters rise as city pushes its borders'. *Deccan Herald*. 16 August, 2023.

23. 'Karnataka HC takes up suo motu PIL over monkey deaths'. *Deccan Herald*, 31 July, 2021.

24. Mondal, Monika. 'Troops'. *Fiftytwo.in*. 23 July, 2023.

25. 'Rs 6 crore spent on feeding monkeys in sanctuary by Delhi govt'. *Economic Times*. 15 October, 2013

26. Joshi, Hridayesh. 'Monkey menace poses stiff challenge for Delhi government'. *Citizen Matters*. 23 October, 2019.

27. Singh, Para. 'Cut-outs of langur to scare off monkeys along G20 routes in Delhi'. *Hindustan Times*. 29 August, 2023.

28. Sengupta, Arjun. 'Why are langurs deployed to ward off monkeys'. *Indian Express*. 29 September, 2024.

Chapter 10

1. Jønsson, K.A. et al. 2012. 'Brains, tools, innovation and biogeography in crows and ravens'. BMC Evolutionary Biology.

2. Gadgil, Madhav. 2001. 'Project lifescape -crows'. Resonance Journal of Science Education.

3. Nahid, M. I. et al. 2019. 'Confirmation of house crows *Corvus splendens* laying immaculate blue eggs'. Bird Study. Vol 66, pp 141-144/

4.   'Do crows sing'. BirdNote. 24 August, 2023.

5.   Emery, Nathan J. and Clayton, Nicola S. 2004. 'The mentality of crows: convergent evolution of intelligence in corvids and apes'. Science. Vol 306, pp 1903-1907.

6.   Wascher, C.A.F. et al. 2012. 'You sound familiar: carrion crows can differentiate between the calls of known and unknown heterospecifics'. Animal Cognition. Vol 15, pp 1015-1019.

7.   Madrigal, Alexis C. 'Science can neither explain nor deny the awesomeness of this sledding crow'. *The Atlantic.* 13 January, 2012.

8.   Boffey, Daniel. 'Swedish firm deploys crows to pick up cigarette butts'. *The Guardian.* 1 February, 2022.

9.   The Crow Box website. https://www.thecrowbox.com/.

10.   Hunt, G. 1996. 'Manufacture and use of hook-tools by New Caledonian crows'. Nature. Vol 379, pp 249-251.

11.   Bayern A.M.P.V. et al. 2018. 'Compound tool construction by New Caledonian crows'. Scientific Reports. Vol 8.

12.   Liao, Diana A. et al. 2024. 'Crows "count" the number of self-generated vocalizations'. Science. Vol 384, pp 874-877.

13.   Johnston, Melissa. et al. 2023. 'Crows flexibly apply statistical inferences based on previous experience'. Current Biology. Vol 33, Issue 15.

14.   Swift K.N. et al. 2020. 'Brain activity underlying American crow processing of encounters with dead conspecifics'. Behavioural Brain Research. Volume 385.

15.   Swift K. N. and Marzluff J. M. 2015. 'Wild American crows gather around their dead to learn about danger'. Animal Behaviour. Vol 109, pp 187-197.

16.   'Why one should feed black crow as per Hindu shastras'. *Times of India.* 26 October, 2023.

17. Ferber, Michael. 1999. *A Dictionary of Literary Symbols*. Cambridge University Press.

18. 'When Do We Eat Crow'. Voice of America- Learning English Podcast. 12 August, 2017.

19. Oliver, Mary. 'Crows'. *New Yorker*. 25 September, 2000.

Chapter 11

1. Whitfield, John. 'Ant Geopolitics'. Aeon, 16 February, 2024.

2. Banks, Shannon. 'How many ants live on earth? At least 20 quadrillion, scientists say'. *Mongabay*. 12 December, 2022.

3. Ward, S. Philip. 2006. 'Ants.' Current Biology. Vol 16 No 5.

4. C. Jouault et al. 2024. 'The angiosperm terrestrial revolution buffered ants against extinction'. PNAS. Vol 121.

5. Britton, David. 'Ants: Family Formicidae'. Australian Museum. 26 November, 2018.

6. Carmona-Aldana et al. 2024. 'Phenomenon of reproductive plasticity in ants'. Current Opinion in Insect Science. Vol 63.

7. Snir, O. et al. 2022. 'The pupal moulting fluid has evolved social functions in ants'. Nature. Vol 612, pp 488-494.

8. 'The Schmidt sting pain index'. Natural History Museum, UK. https://www.nhm.ac.uk/discover/schmidt-pain-index-insect-stings.html

9. 'Initiation with ants'. National Geographic Channel. 21 December, 2007.

10. Brown, Simon G.A. et al. 2003. 'Prevalence, severity, and natural history of jack jumper ant venom allergy in Tasmania'. Journal of Allergy and Clinical Immunology. Vol 111, Issue 1, pp 187-192.

11. Srisong, Hathairat et al. 2016. 'Current advances in ant venom proteins causing hypersensitivity reactions in the Asia-Pacific region'. Molecular Immunology. Vol 69, pp 24-32.

12. 'Red imported fire ants'. Victoria State Government website. 23 October, 2024. https://agriculture.vic.gov.au/biosecurity/pest-insects-and-mites/priority-pest-insects and-mites/fire-ants

13. Barkham, Patrick. 'Red fire ant colonies found in Italy and could spread across Europe, says study'. *The Guardian*. 11 September, 2023.

14. Su, Xin et al. 2023. 'Use of artificial intelligence for automated detection and surveillance of red imported fire ants nests'. Preprint from *bioRxiv*.

15. Kumari, Jyoti et al. 2022. 'Studying the rationale of fire ant sting therapy usage by the tribal natives of Bastar revealed ant venom-derived peptides with promising anti-malarial activity'. Toxins. Vol 14.

16. Venkatesh, Prasanna and Kannan, Subagunam. 'Tamil Nadu: Yellow crazy ants cause chaos in India villages'. *BBC*. 18 August, 2022.

17. Schultz, Ted R. et al. 2024. 'The coevolution of fungus-ant agriculture'. Science. Vol 386, pp 105-110.

18. Frank, Erik T. et al. 2024. 'Wound-dependent leg amputations to combat infections in an ant society'. Current Biology. Vol 34, Issue 14, pp 3273-3278.

19. Frank, E.T. et al. 2023. 'Targeted treatment of injured nestmates with antimicrobial compounds in an ant society'. Nature Communications. Vol 14.

20. J Champer, Jackson and Schlenoff, Debra. 2024. 'Battles between ants (Hymenoptera: Formicidae): a review'. Journal of Insect Science. Vol 24, Issue 3.

21. Moffett, Mark. 'Battles among ants resemble human warfare'. *Scientific American.* 1 December, 2011.

22. Padmanaban, Deepa. 'When ant enslaves ant'. *Mint.* 9 April 2017.

23. B. Wipfler et al. 2024. 'Understanding the ant's unique biting system can improve surgical needle holders'. PNAS. Vol 121.

24. Piqueret, Baptiste. 2023. 'Ants act as olfactory bio-detectors of tumours in patient-derived xenograft mice'. Proceedings of the Royal Society B. 290.

25. 'The significance of feeding ants in astrology'. *Times of India.* 4 April, 2024.

26. Nadkarni, Vithal. 'The parable of ants'. *Economic Times.* 12 June, 2013.

27. Latty, Tanya. 'We've got apps and radars – but can ants predict rain?' *The Conversation.* 6 September, 2018.

28. 'Floating fire ants form rafts in Houston floodwaters'. *BBC.* 30 August, 2017.

Chapter 12:

1. Chrobak, Ula. 'The underappreciated benefits of wild bees'. *Knowable magazine.* 21 August, 2023.

2. 'Types of honey bees'. Tamil Nadu Agricultural University. Agritech Portal. https://agritech.tnau.ac.in/farm_enterprises/fe_api_typesofhoneybee.html

3. Hertzberg, Richie. 'With brains the size of sesame seeds, honeybees have to work together in different capacities to maintain a healthy nest'. *National Geographic,* 22 March, 2019.

4. Bortolotti, L. and Costa, C. 2014. 'Chemical communication in the honey bee society'. Neurobiology of Chemical Communication. CRC Press/Taylor & Francis.

5. Dong, Shihao et al. 2023. 'Social signal learning of the waggle dance in honey bees.' Science. Vol 379, pp 1015-1018.

6. Ferber, Michael. 1999. *A Dictionary of Literary Symbols*. Cambridge University Press.

7. Traynor, Kirsten. (2016). 'The tears of Re: Beekeeping in ancient Egypt.' American Entomologist. 62. pp 194-196.

8. Norton, Holly. 'Honey, I love You. Our 40,000 year relationship with the bumble bee'. *The Guardian*. 24 May, 2017.

9. 'How Lorenzo Langstroth's hive shaped beekeeping'. National Inventors Hall of Fame. 25 May, 2023.

10. Jolanta, Burke and Sean, Corrigan. 2024. 'Bee Well: a positive psychological impact of a pro-environmental intervention on beekeepers' and their families' wellbeing.' Frontiers in Psychology. Vol 15.

11. Buchmann, Stephen. 'Bees can learn, remember and make decisions. Here's a look at how they navigate the world'. *The Conversation*. 17 May, 2023.

12. Gross, Hans J. et al. 2009. 'Number-Based Visual Generalisation in the Honeybee'. PLoS ONE. 4(1).

13. Scarlett R. Howard et al. 2019. 'Numerical cognition in honeybees enables addition and subtraction'. Scientific Advances. Vol 5

14. Gibbons, Matilda et al. 2022. 'Motivational trade-offs and modulation of nociception in bumblebees'. PNAS. Vol 119(31).

15. Buchmann, Stephen. 2023. *What a bee knows: exploring the thoughts, memories, and personalities of bees*. Island Pr.

16. Hiruni S.G. Dona et al. 2022. 'Do bumble bees play?' Animal Behaviour. Vol 194, pp 239-251.

17. Dyer, Adrian G. et al. 2005. 'Honeybee (*Apis mellifera*) vision can discriminate between and recognise images of human

faces'. Journal of Experimental Biology. Vol 208 (24), pp 4709-4714.

18. Nguyen, Tuan C. 'Can bees be trained to sniff out cancer'. *Smithsonian Magazine*.13 December, 2013.

19. Stephens, Daisy and Cuthill, Jon. 'Laboratory using bees to track climate change'. *BBC*. 4 October, 2024.

20. Schubert, Charlotte. 'Scientists are using AI to study bee behavior, zebra movement, and insects on treadmills'. *Geekwire*. 17 January, 2024.

21. 'The First bushman/ San'. Gateway-Africa. https://www.gateway-africa.com/stories/The_First_Bushman_San.html

22. Reilly, J.R. et al. 2020. 'Crop production in the USA is frequently limited by a lack of pollinators.' Proceedings of the Royal Society B. Vol 287.

23. Kevan, Peter G. et al. 2024. 'Thermodynamics, thermal performance and climate change: temperature regimes for bumblebee (Bombus spp.) colonies as examples of superorganisms'. Frontiers in Bee Science. Vol 2.

24. Durant, Jennie L. 'Climate change is ratcheting up the pressure on bees'. UC Davis. 14 October, 2022.

25. Weber, C. et al. 2024. 'Urban pavements as a novel habitat for wild bees and other ground-nesting insects'. Urban Ecosystem. 27, pp 2453-2467.

Chapter 13

1. Qureshi, Adnan I. (Ed) 2018. 'Mosquito-borne diseases'. *Zika Virus Disease*. Academic Press, pp 27-45.

2. Mussulman, Joseph A. 'The mosquito in literature'. Lewis & Clark.

3.   Tamir, Dan and Hall, Marcus. (eds) 2021. *Mosquitopia: The place of pests in a healthy world*. Routledge Environmental Humanities.

4.   Yadav, Aditi et al. 2022. 'Contemporary and ancient review of mosquitoes - A review'. Journal of Ayurveda and Integrated Medical Sciences. Vol 7(8), pp 81-85.

5.   'Mosquito information'. Maryland Department of Agriculture. https://mda.maryland.gov/plants-pests/Pages/mosquito_information.aspx#:~:

6.   Tyagi, B.K. et al. 2015. 'A catalogue of Indian mosquitoes'. International Journal of Mosquito Research. Vol 2 (2), pp 50-97.

7.   Soghigian, J. et al. 2023. 'Phylogenomics reveals the history of host use in mosquitoes'. Nature Communications. 14.

8.   Quirós, Gabriela. 'Mosquitoes use 6 needles to suck your blood'. *NPR*. 7 June, 2016.

9.   Azar, Dany et al. 2023. 'The earliest fossil mosquito'. Current Biology. Vol 33, Issue 23, pp 5240-5246.

10.   Peach, D.A.H. and Gries, G. 2020. 'Mosquito phytophagy – sources exploited, ecological function, and evolutionary transition to haematophagy'. Entomologia Experimentalis et Applicata. Vol 168, pp 120-136.

11.   Giraldo, Diego et al. 2023. 'Human scent guides mosquito thermotaxis and host selection under naturalistic conditions'. Current Biology. Vol 33, Issue 12, pp 2367-2382.

12.   Chandel, A, et al. 2024. 'Thermal infrared directs host-seeking behaviour in *Aedes aegypti* mosquitoes'. Nature. Vol 633, pp 615-623.

13.   X. Dou et al. 2024. 'Reciprocal interactions between neuropeptide F and RYamide regulate host attraction in the mosquito *Aedes aegypti*'. PNAS.

14. Mozūraitis, R. et al. 2020. 'Male swarming aggregation pheromones increase female attraction and mating success among multiple African malaria vector mosquito species'. Nature Ecology and Evolution. Vol 4, pp 1395-1401.

15. Pennetier, Cédric et al. 2010. 'Singing on the wing" as a mechanism for species recognition in the malarial mosquito *Anopheles gambiae*'. Current Biology. Vol 20, Issue 2, pp 131-136.

16. Y. Wang, et al. 2024. 'Deafness due to loss of a TRPV channel eliminates mating behavior in *Aedes aegypti* males'. PNAS.121 (47).

17. Alphey, L. et al. 2010. 'Sterile-insect methods for control of mosquito-borne diseases: an analysis'. Vector Borne Zoonotic Diseases. pp 295-311.

18. Naik, B. Reddya et al. 2023. 'Mosquito-borne diseases in India over the past 50 years and their global public health implications: A systematic review'. Journal of the American Mosquito Control Association. 39 (4), pp 258-277.

19. Pryce J. et al. 2022. 'Indoor residual spraying for preventing malaria in communities using insecticide-treated nets'. Cochrane Database of Systematic Reviews. 1(1).

20. 'Malaria fact sheet'. WHO. 11 December, 2024. https://www.who.int/news-room/fact-sheets/detail/malaria

21. Gardy, Jennifer. 'The researcher versus the mosquitoes'. Gates Foundation Blog, 19 August, 2024.

22. Mosha, Jacklin F. et al. 2022. 'Effectiveness and cost-effectiveness against malaria of three types of dual-active-ingredient long-lasting insecticidal nets (LLINs) compared with pyrethroid-only LLINs in Tanzania: a four-arm, cluster-randomised trial'. The Lancet. Vol 399, Issue 10331, pp 1227-1241.

23.   Rose, Noah H. et al. 2023. 'Dating the origin and spread of specialization on human hosts in *Aedes aegypti* mosquitoes'. Elife.

24.   Ashburn P.M. and Craig C.F. 'Experimental investigations regarding the etiology of dengue'. The Journal of Infectious Diseases. Vol 189, Issue 9, pp 1744-1783.

25.   Lay, Kat et al. 'Dengue fever: with a record 12.4m cases in 2024 so far, what is driving the world's largest outbreak?' *The Guardian*, 23 October, 2024.

26.   Lefteri, D.A. et al. 2022. 'Mosquito saliva enhances virus infection through sialokinin-dependent vascular leakage'. PNAS. 119 (24).

27.   Flayer, C.H. et al. 2024. 'A γδ T cell–IL-3 axis controls allergic responses through sensory neurons'. Nature. 634, pp 440-446.

28.   Johnson, Sarah. 'Growth the size of a melon: a scrotum-swelling disease threatening thousands'. *The Guardian*. 25 October, 2024.

29.   Boswell, Evelyn. 'Ward off mosquitoes with DEET and treated clothes'. Montana State University News. 14 April, 2004.

30.   Walker, T. et al., 2011. 'The *w*Mel *Wolbachia* strain blocks dengue and invades caged *Aedes aegypti* populations'. Nature. 476, pp 450-453.

31.   Padmanaban, Deepa. 'Can mass-produced mosquitoes slow dengue's spread?' *Harvard Public Health Magazine*. 15 August, 2023.

32.   Fang, J. 2010. 'Ecology: A world without mosquitoes'. Nature. 466, pp 432-434.

ABOUT THE AUTHOR

Deepa Padmanaban is a Bengaluru-based writer and journalist. Her work has appeared in *The Guardian*, BBC, *Scientific American*, *Discover magazine*, *Mint*, *The Hindu* and various other publications.

HarperCollins *Publishers* India

At HarperCollins India, we believe in telling the best stories and finding the widest readership for our books in every format possible. We started publishing in 1992; a great deal has changed since then, but what has remained constant is the passion with which our authors write their books, the love with which readers receive them, and the sheer joy and excitement that we as publishers feel in being a part of the publishing process.

Over the years, we've had the pleasure of publishing some of the finest writing from the subcontinent and around the world, including several award-winning titles and some of the biggest bestsellers in India's publishing history. But nothing has meant more to us than the fact that millions of people have read the books we published, and that somewhere, a book of ours might have made a difference.

As we look to the future, we go back to that one word—a word which has been a driving force for us all these years.

Read.

 Harper Collins

 4th

 HARPER **FICTION**

 HARPER **NON-FICTION**

 HARPER BUSINESS

 HCCB HARPERCOLLINS CHILDREN'S BOOKS

 HARPER DESIGN

 Harper Sport

 HARPER **PERENNIAL**

 HARPER VANTAGE

 हार्पर हिन्दी

 **B**OOKTOPUS